Rooted and Radiant

A volume in
Contemporary Perspectives on Leadership Learning
Kathy L. Guthrie, *Series Editor*

Contemporary Perspectives on Leadership Learning

Kathy L. Guthrie, *Series Editor*

Introduction to Research in Leadership (2023)
  David M. Rosch, Lori E. Kniffin, and Kathy L. Guthrie

Engaging Black Men in College Through Leadership Learning (2023)
  Cameron C. Beatty and Jesse R. Ford

Navigating Complexities in Leadership: Moving Toward Critical Hope (2022)
  Kathy L. Guthrie and Kerry L. Priest

Operationalizing Culturally Relevant Leadership Learning (2021)
  Cameron C. Beatty and Kathy L. Guthrie

Shifting the Mindset: Socially Just Leadership Education (2021)
  Kathy L. Guthrie and Vivechkanand S. Chunoo

Engaging in the Leadership Process: Identity, Capacity, and Efficacy for College Students (2021)
  Kathy L. Guthrie, Cameron C. Beatty, and Erica R. Wiborg

Transforming Learning: Instructional and Assessment Strategies for Leadership Education (2020)
  Kathy L. Guthrie and Daniel M. Jenkins

Thinking to Transform: Reflection in Leadership Learning (2019)
  Jillian M. Volpe White, Kathy L. Guthrie, and Maritza Torres

Thinking to Transform Companion Manual: Facilitating Reflection in Leadership Learning (2019)
  Jillian M. Volpe White, Kathy L. Guthrie, and Maritza Torres

Changing the Narrative: Socially Just Leadership Education (2018)
  Kathy L. Guthrie and Vivechkanand S. Chunoo

The Role of Leadership Educators: Transforming Learning (2018)
  Kathy L. Guthrie and Daniel M. Jenkins

Rooted and Radiant

Women's Narratives of Leadership

edited by

Trisha Teig
University of Denver

Brittany Devies
University of Maryland, College Park

Rebecca "Becka" Shetty
The University of Texas at Arlington

INFORMATION AGE PUBLISHING, INC.
Charlotte, NC • www.infoagepub.com

Library of Congress Cataloging-in-Publication Data

A CIP record for this book is available from the Library of Congress
http://www.loc.gov

ISBN: 979-8-88730-456-4 (Paperback)
       979-8-88730-457-1 (Hardcover)
       979-8-88730-458-8 (E-Book)

Cover art by Sam Searfoss

Copyright © 2024 Information Age Publishing Inc.

All rights reserved. No part of this publication may be reproduced, stored in a retrieval system, or transmitted, in any form or by any means, electronic, mechanical, photocopying, microfilming, recording or otherwise, without written permission from the publisher.

Printed in the United States of America

Dedication

*To the Colorado Women's College Leadership Scholars:
Your stories are why we started this project and why we will continue
to promote and share women's narratives of leadership.*

*To our narrative authors: May you know the power of your voice
and your stories change the world.*

*To all who read this book: We invite you to the adventure of exploring women's
understandings of leadership and for you to share your own.*

*To the women who have been silenced, belittled, shamed, and shunned
when you have led before: We hope these stories show you that your leadership
is needed, valued, celebrated, and encouraged—we believe in you.*

CONTENTS

Foreword xi
Kathy L. Guthrie

Preface—Better Together: Channeling Our Collective Power
and Purpose xv
Brittany Devies, Rebecca Shetty, and Trisha Teig

Acknowledgments xxi
Trisha Teig, Brittany Devies, and Rebecca Shetty

PART I

APPROACHING THE NARRATIVES

1 Setting the Stage: Leadership Contexts 3
   Rebecca Shetty, Brittany Devies, Michele Tyson, and Shenhaye Ferguson

2 Centering Higher Education Environments for Women's
   Leadership Learning 19
   *Michele Tyson, Shenhaye Ferguson, Rebecca Shetty, Brittany Devies,
   and Valeria Gomez*

3 The Meaning to Our Methods 41
   Trisha Teig and Maritza Torres

PART II

EXPLORING THE NARRATIVES—CONTEXT

4 "Me! I am Leadership!" Evolutions and Disruptions by Black, Indigenous, and Women of Color 59
   Sharrell Hassell-Goodman, Aoi Yamanaka, Kristen Pender, and Neda Kikhia

5 "Until We Couldn't Fly": Bitches, Scars, Breath 79
   Trisha Teig

6 "They Made Me Who I Am": How Family Shapes Leadership Identity Development for Women of Color 93
   Lauren Contreras

7 Mirror, Mirror on the Wall: College Women Leaders Reflect on Their Role Models 113
   Simone A. F. Gause

EXPLORING THE NARRATIVES—GROWTH

8 Am I Doing It Right? College Women Leaders and Their Experiences With Imposter Syndrome 131
   Adrian L. Bitton

9 Blooming Where We Are Planted: Growth in Leadership Development 147
   Brittany Devies

10 What Leadership *Isn't*: Conceptualizing Leadership Through Reflection 161
   Rebecca Shetty

EXPLORING THE NARRATIVES—ENACTMENT

11 Leadership Looks Like . . . Me 179
   Julie Henriquez Aldana and Lauren Contreras

12 Navigating Shifting Tides: The Development of Feminist Leadership Identities 195
   Julie E. Owen and Adrian L. Bitton

13 Taking Up Your Leadership: Women's Courage, Strength, and Persistence in Enacting Leadership 209
    Paige Haber-Curran

14 The Transformational Power of Feminist Women's Leadership Education 223
    Sasha Taner

PART III
WEAVING AND APPLYING THE NARRATIVES

15 We Are the Sun 239
    Trisha Teig, Rebecca Shetty, and Brittany Devies

About the Editors 259

About the Contributors 261

FOREWORD

When I heard of the idea for this book, I sat back in my chair and smiled. I was excited knowing what happens when brilliant, enthusiastic, and engaged people get together—it can be pure magic. That is what I feel happened with this book. Trisha, Brittany, and Becka are not only individuals passionate about gender issues and leadership, but they are focused on collectively moving leadership learning forward. Being able to witness the evolution of this book from a dream Trisha had started formulating during her doctoral studies to her reaching out to Brittany and Becka to developing a collective team with diverse authors to seeing the final manuscript was an honor.

Trisha's passion for exploring issues of gender in leadership was evident the moment she began her doctoral journey at Florida State University. She took initiative and created a gender and leadership undergraduate course, in which Brittany then taught for several years after Trisha moved to a faculty role at another university. Simultaneously, Becka was finishing up her dissertation and, being an experienced leadership educator, was engaged in these conversations for years. I provide this background because this book did not just happen. It came from almost a decade of listening, thinking, and activating ideas of several people, individually and collectively. I had the opportunity to observe and participate in research gathered from the undergraduate gender and leadership course at Florida State. I have seen the depth of learning that has occurred in one short semester. When I assisted in analyzing early findings from this study, it revealed the need for more conversation about women's leadership experiences. I am glad this book does just that.

Focusing on women's narratives of their leadership experiences and essentially disrupting the dominant patriarchal frame for understanding leadership is what grabbed and held my attention. This book amplifies authors' voices from various racial, socioeconomic, religious, and sexual identities, but as seen in the narratives, their womanhood connected them through shared experiences. These shared experiences were centered around fighting the common notion of leadership that only centers masculinity. Sharing these narratives makes advances in embracing the complexity in which leadership is experienced by women. The wise individuals who shared their stories allowed me to personally feel validated, to learn from their experiences, and motivate me to continue the conversation about changing the continued misrepresentation of leadership for women.

The book title, *Rooted and Radiant: Women's Narratives of Leadership*, is layered in beautiful complexity and gives the reader a hint of what is to come. I was especially drawn to "rooted and radiant" as concepts in relation to women's leadership. According to Merriam-Webster (n.d.b), *rooted* means "an underlying support" and "the essential core." When looking at these two definitions for the word rooted, I see how both are important for the context of this book. In honoring the women who have come before us and fought despite endless obstacles, rooted means standing with the underlying support of those who have been fighting gender inequality while being rooted in the essential core of the collective. According to Merriam-Webster (n.d.a), *radiant* means "vividly bright and shining," which describes the stories shared in this book. While situated in critical hope, there are women glowing in leadership. One of the women who shared her story in this book, Skye (see Chapter 11), said this:

> Many nights grew long, and spirits flew low.
> And I came to understand my purpose through feeling purposeless.
> Rationalizing the irrational until the sun comes up.
> And on that day, hope and leadership radiated all around me.
> You showed me I wasn't alone. That I didn't have to lead singularly.
> You taught me how to ask for help and admit when I could no
>   longer pay the wages of the world.
> My definition of leadership expanded and grew.
> Cultivating a passion of hoping for a better future.

This passage, as many others in this book, stopped me in my tracks. I think of the women before me, those who I am lucky to currently learn from and who lift me up daily, and how young women are motivated to work towards a better future. This book offers future generations, and those who are raising daughters (like I am) stories to connect with and learn from in our journey to dismantle harmful perspectives (and practices) of leadership. If you have any people you love in your life who identify as a woman, this read is a must. Read, reflect, and act on making positive change for those women in your life and our world.

— **Kathy L. Guthrie**

REFERENCES

Merriam-Webster. (n.d.a). Radiant. In *Merriam-Webster.com dictionary*. https://www.merriam-webster.com/dictionary/radiant

Merriam-Webster. (n.d.b). Rooted. In *Merriam-Webster.com dictionary*. https://www.merriam-webster.com/dictionary/rooted

PREFACE

BETTER TOGETHER

Channeling Our Collective Power and Purpose

On a cold afternoon in early December, I (Trisha) found myself telling her the idea, half-formed and hesitant, yet hopeful. It was your average zoom meeting. A recorded interview with my colleague and friend, Julie Owen, as a favor for the gender and leadership course I was teaching. After we'd wrapped up, the usual chit chat ensued. That's when it happened, the ideas spilled out of me. This concept had been swirling around in my head for the past 2 years—to share the stories of women from the leadership program I directed. The women in the program are wonderful, brilliant, and think about leadership in unique ways that need to be out in the world. It was a simple concept: Gather narratives and share them out in some fashion—an article, a blog, a book? I didn't know; besides, I said, "I can do it later." Julie—in her enthusiastic and supportive way—said, "What are you waiting for?" She encouraged me to start the process by exploring the idea with friends and colleagues who were leadership educators focused on gender equity. Emboldened by Julie's advice, I sent out cold emails! Some of the women I contacted I knew, some I knew of but had never really met, and some I did not know at all! At that first meeting, I was a mix of elated and terrified. To my wonder, almost everyone I invited decided to join the project and even

> the people who did not jump on board were excited about the idea. I realized, after that push from a mentor/friend, I was not alone in wanting to share and learn from stories of women and leadership.

In the Spring of 2021, a group of 12 women met to discuss and dissect, improve and improvise, collaborate and coordinate. As the group contemplated possible research opportunities, we kept coming back to gathering and sharing stories of women as examples of how the dominant narrative of leadership (hierarchical, masculine, Western and White-centric) was not true for so many women's experiences. We recognized the capturing and sharing of these narratives could be a purposeful act to disrupt persistent hegemonic perspectives of leadership that seem to persist no matter how much we insist they are no longer *true*.

From these beginnings, we concluded: the purpose of this book is to capture and explore women's narratives of leadership across time, space, and generations. From these collaborative beginnings, the team accelerated and expanded. We identified six research sites to collect narratives, implemented a pilot collection and analysis of narratives, submitted, and were accepted for a book proposal, and began the process of collecting data—all in spring, summer, and fall of 2021 (see Chapter 3 on methods for greater detail on our research design and process). We committed to a deeper collaboration than many edited works. We gathered a collective of 18 coauthors, researchers, and friends to undertake the adventure, meeting quarterly to touch base, to check-in with each other and the project, and to hold true to our purpose by discussing our own stories. We embraced the messiness this type of process required, including the effort to weave ideas and content across chapters and across the entire work. While each chapter in the book can stand alone, they are better understood in their collective as a collaborative understanding of leadership through the power of narratives.

We hope by sharing and analyzing these stories we can make strides in disrupting a single understanding of leadership and instead embrace the complex, unique, and crucial ways leadership in multiplicity can be articulated through women's voices. We believe this book stands on the shoulders of our (often silenced or ignored) foremothers who spoke and practiced leadership in the margins and against all odds. We believe this book serves as a bellwether for needed change in understanding leadership from an alternative and pluralistic view. We believe this book offers future generations the tools to use narratives as sources of truth-telling for dismantling harmful practices and perspectives of leadership. As poet and scholar Audre Lorde (1984) emphasized, we are stronger when we embrace and learn from our differences and in that strength, we can lead change.

POSITIONALITY

When our initial group gathered to discuss the possibility of this book coming to fruition, we immediately and easily recognized that the group was predominately White women. This is not entirely surprising given the larger landscape and demographics of leadership educators in higher education, student affairs, and academia; a truth we grapple with and one that we hope changes. We knew we needed more diverse voices and perspectives in our group and to honestly acknowledge the identities of the authors in this text. We understand the privileges many of our authors and editors possess influence the ways we experience life and that our leadership experiences may or may not match the experiences of the narrative authors throughout this book. We do not take this lightly.

We want to immediately recognize that our editorial team (Trisha, Brittany, and Becka) all identify as White, cisgender, straight women. All three of us also have educational privilege. At the time of writing this, two of our editors have doctoral degrees and the third will be defending her dissertation in the coming months. This access to information, diversity of thought, and other academic colleagues certainly informs how we approach this work. Our privilege carries responsibility to put in the work, to remain self-aware and to explore our biases and ways that we personally perpetuate systems of oppression. We must combat our socialized ways of thinking that demean, disparage, or lead to harming those who do not identify as we do. We approach this work humbly with deep gratitude for the chapter and narrative authors who identify as Women of Color or with other historically oppressed identities. We are grateful they would share their voice and relate to one another in ways that we cannot.

Our chapter authors include early career and mid- to senior-level professionals in higher education serving as student affairs practitioners, faculty, aspiring faculty, doctoral students and candidates, researchers, and advocates. We have 18 authors; 10 identify as Women of Color (Black or African-American, Japanese, Latinx, Middle Eastern, and multiracial) and 8 identify as White. We have one author whose Jewish identity is particularly salient to them. A couple of our authors identify as queer. For our authors who have historically excluded and oppressed identities, their experiences with marginalization anchor their desire for building solidarity, shedding light on injustice, and working to create a more just society for other women.

While our authors have varying racial, socioeconomic, religious, and sexual identities, our womanhood certainly brought us all together. Our womanhood unites us through shared experiences of combatting notions of leadership that center men and masculinity. We are proud to be women uplifting other women and sharing the stories of the next generation. At the same time, we recognize and affirm that not all women have the same experiences and shared identities as the identity "woman" does not and never will create a monolithic community. Further, we find strength in our differences and recognize by discussing inequities and distinctions across difference, we can come to a better shared understanding in our efforts for societal change (Lorde, 1984). Each contributor to this book holds distinct identities in race, class, religion, sexuality, and a host of other ways that inform their understanding and existence in the world. These identities directly informed our varied and intrepidly creative outcomes to responding to a shared prompt.

For those of us who have many privileges related to race, religion, socioeconomic status, education, and more, we approach this work with humility, honor, and awe at the courage of both our chapter and narrative authors who chose to disclose raw and vulnerable moments related to their leadership journeys. We also approach this text as a way to center the narratives of women in their authentic form so that their words are seen, heard, and felt. For those of us with privilege, our goal was to decenter ourselves as much as possible to allow the narrative authors' voices to emerge as the creators of knowledge and the trail blazers forging new ways to conceptualize leadership. We hope to honor our narrative authors by amplifying their already powerful voices.

We are proud that our 39 narrative authors are a radically diverse group of women. We asked these authors to self-identify and share with us any identities they felt were salient to them or relevant to this work. Because of this, we do not have the same demographic information or same social identity information for all 39 authors. However, we can share what they did provide that demonstrates the identities most important to them as they considered their leadership experiences and journey.

We have tremendous racial and ethnic diversity with women self-identifying as Black/African-American, Asian American (Indian, Japanese-American, Chinese-American, Vietnamese, South Asian, Filipino, Nepalese, Bangladeshi), Middle Eastern (Afghani-American, Arab-American), Latina/x (Cuban, Salvadoran, Columbian, Bolivian, Mexican), Native American, and White. We also have 12 narrative authors who identify as bi/multiracial/ethnic; some of these women also identify with the previous list of racial and ethnic identities and expanded on their mixed heritage rather than just providing "biracial" as their only identifier. While most narrative authors are traditionally college-aged, we have several narratives of women out of college as well as nontraditional students. Sexual orientation varies amongst the collective group with six narrative authors who shared their LGBTQ+ identities with us. While almost all of our narrative others identify as cisgender, we do have one genderqueer narrative author. We recognize the lack of genderqueer and transgender individuals is a limitation of this research and book. We have narrative authors that identify as being from lower socioeconomic backgrounds, as first-generation college students (11), as undocumented (2), as first, 1.5, and second-generation Americans (7), as neurodiverse, as living with visible and invisible disabilities, and as having various religious backgrounds (though, if mentioned, Islam, Christianity, and Catholicism are more prevalent). The intersectional identities of these women shape everything about their narratives and create the soul of this book.

Our narrative and chapter authors were asked to describe the ways in which their gender and other identities informed an experience of leadership. Our positionality as women leaders is central to this work. We write raw, unfiltered words filled with beauty, pain, and longing. Our identities are intricately woven into our narratives, and our identities cannot be separated from our experiences with leadership. Our narrative authors, experiencing marginalization for their womanhood and other identities, weave a new perspective of leadership that pushes, tears against, and rages against current, dominant narratives of leadership. Through this work, we honor you: Pam, Mia, Isabel, Camiya (Chapter 4), Prasamsha, Maddie, Ariana, Amna (Chapter 5), Bianca, Kat, Negin, Sophia (Chapter 6), Faith, Ameena, Emma, Anahi (Chapter 7), Katherine, Stephanie, Nicollette (Chapter 8), Jessie, Kat, Deya, Mollie (Chapter 9), Skye, Mio, Alea (Chapter 10), Imani, Melanie, Sam (Chapter 11), Andrea, Renuka, Jocelyn (Chapter 12), Jasmin, JoAnne, Cathy (Chapter 13), Lien, Hadiya, Sadia, Laila, and Acela (Chapter 14).

—**Brittany Devies**
Rebecca Shetty
Trisha Teig

REFERENCE

Lorde, A. (1984). *Sister, outsider*. The Crossing Press.

ACKNOWLEDGMENTS

This book was a collective, communal process. First and foremost, to our research/author team, this book would be nothing without you all. To our chapter authors, Adrian, Aoi, Julie H., Julie O., Kristen, Lauren, Maritza, Michele, Neda, Paige, Sasha, Sharrell, Shenhaye, Simone, and Valeria: Thank you for saying yes to this journey and giving your time and energy to sharing these narratives so beautifully. To our narrative authors, Acela, Alea, Ameena, Anahi, Andrea, Anna, Ariana, Bianca, Camiya, Cathy, Deya, Emma, Faith, Hadiya, Imani, Isabel, Jasmin, Jessie, JoAnne, Jocelyn, Kat, Katherine, Laila, Lien, Maddie, Melanie, Mia, Mio, Mollie, Negin, Nicollette, Pam, Prasamsha, Renuka, Sadia, Sam, Skye, Sophia, and Stephanie: Thank you for trusting us with your words, your experiences, and your voices. This book would not exist without your beautiful contributions.

To Kathy Guthrie—the Contemporary Perspectives in Leadership Learning series editor, our friend, and mentor—thank you for believing in and championing this process and project since its very inception. To Sam, thank you for creating a stunning piece of art for the cover of this book. Sam is also one of the brilliant narrative authors in this book (you can see her narrative in Chapter 12). Thank you also to narrative authors Imani, Prasamsha, and Kat for contributing illustrations highlighted in the book. To Crystal and Ileya, our inquisitive, thought-provoking critical readers. Thank you for your expertise and insights, thoughtful critique and helpful pushes to mold the stories (Crystal) and aesthetics (Ileya) towards a more powerful collective work.

Trisha needs to first give gratitude to the Colorado Women's College Leadership Scholars for being astoundingly amazing humans who consistently make me smile, think, laugh, and want to work with you to make the world a better place. Thank you next to Julie Owen—who asked the question—"Why not now?" And to Kathy Guthrie, who gives me encouragement and sees the possibilities in my hopes and ideas. I next cannot begin to say enough thank yous to the authors and editors of this work. I remember being uncertain but hopeful when I asked a small bunch of brilliant women to come together and I could not have dreamed it would become something so beautiful. Thank you to our narrative authors for your vulnerability and thoughtful engagement. Thank you to our chapter authors for going with the flow, being willing to trust the process, and questioning, pushing, and co-creating to make the book a better work for everyone. I also wholeheartedly want to express my deep appreciation for Brittany and Becka—who raised their hands when in an early ideation meeting, I asked if anyone was interested in the coediting process. I didn't quite know what I was asking of them at the time but I am so grateful I had such wonderful partners throughout the journey. Brittany—you are the APA queen (remind me to ship you my tiara) and I love your drive, structure, and fearless ability to take on any challenge; Becka—your organization, enthusiasm, and ability to make ideas on a page into a beautiful, dynamic, and compelling story made you irreplaceable. Finally, thank you to my most important loves (both human and furry). To my wonderful family who is always excited by my next adventures; to my ever-curious friends, who ask questions that drive me to expand my perspectives. To my animal companions, Sophie, Sampson, and Dale; y'all gave me licks, purrs, and unconditional love and lap sits while writing this book! And I have to end with a funny story: While sharing how I was grappling with the final elements of gender theory in Chapter 16, Luke, my always supportive partner, took my hand, smiled, and said, "I want to have conversations like these for the rest of our lives, will you marry me?" And then brought out a beautiful amethyst, diamond, and gold ring. This book has been so powerful in my world, it even was present during my engagement! I am grateful for a partner who is always interested in my geeky theory, wants to support me in whatever I undertake, and will be my reader, my listener, and my biggest fan.

Brittany would like to thank her family for being so incredibly supportive in this process, including a winter break spent in the depths of editing this book. Your support is what got me here and what encourages me to keep going. To Ryan, you championed me through every step the last 2 years—you celebrated every win and supported every setback. Thank you will never be enough. To Kathy Guthrie, thank you for being my mentor, friend, champion, and partner in this work; I am so thankful to do this work alongside you. To Trisha, who created the gender and leadership course I have been so fortunate to teach, it has been an honor to follow in your footsteps and care for this curriculum the last 3 years. Even more so, I cannot thank you enough for championing my scholarly voice and efficacy well beyond your time at FSU; it has been an absolute gift to do this project alongside you. Becka, I am so thankful for you in every sense of the word. You have been such a wonderful friend, mentor, and champion to me in this season of my life. To my gender and leadership teaching assistants, Joey and Grant, who supported this course with me in the data collection and writing processes, thank you for your constant support and being thought partners for me in this work. And finally to the chapter authors and narrative authors in this book, you all are my why. This book is just the start of our work and I am constantly inspired by every single one of you.

Becka would like to thank Trisha for inviting me to this project, for believing in my ability to contribute, and for treating me as an equal when imposter syndrome threatened to wreck my psyche. Thank you, Trisha, for believing so deeply in women and their stories and for allowing me to journey through this project alongside you. Thank you to Brittany for being a steady rock throughout this process, a constant encouragement, and a true friend. To our chapter authors who trusted me and our editorial team to share women's stories and to create this book together, I am humbled and honored to have worked with you. To our narrative authors, you are the future of leadership, you are powerful, you are able, and I am so proud to know you will be change agents in a broken world. To Anil, Aria, Rohan, and Rani, every professional thing I do is for you—to better the world we live in and to show you how powerful women are. May you grow to fight against injustice and for the rights of the marginalized. Thank you for giving me the time and space to create this work. Thank you to Anil, my love and my partner, for championing every dream I have and for supporting me in every endeavor. To the innumerable mentors and friends who have shaped me as a leader and leadership educator, the list is vast, and I thank each one of you from the depths of my heart.

—**Trisha Teig**
Brittany Devies
Rebecca Shetty

PART I

APPROACHING THE NARRATIVES

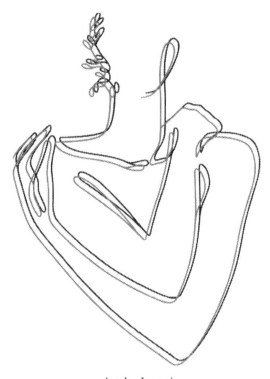

Art by Imani

Sometimes leadership isn't about how we lead others, rather the strongest leaders are those developed through leading our own personal narratives.
—Jasmin, Chapter 13, p. 214

CHAPTER 1

SETTING THE STAGE

Leadership Contexts

Rebecca Shetty
Brittany Devies
Michele Tyson
Shenhaye Ferguson

I (Brittany) still remember the day I learned I would be teaching a gender and leadership course the following semester. I spent the summer before I taught the course trying to learn everything I could about college student gender and leadership development. I knew the importance of this course and wanted to ensure I was prepared. I remember my disappointment when my conversations with my students confirmed what I expected to be true: there is very little scholarship around gender and leadership development in college students, including for college women. There was women's studies literature that did not speak to the leadership process and leadership literature that was written primarily by and for men. This lack of literature on this population and phenomenon led me to keep searching and trying to find community to do this work with. Much of that community seeking led to my work co-creating this book. This book includes the profound lived experiences of students who had taken the gender and leadership course I

> teach alongside many other women who engaged brilliantly in the leadership process. It is a full circle moment to me that their voices are the center of the book they have continued to ask for.

Throughout this book, each scholar seeks to elevate the voices of other women. As you read, you will find the narratives of women in the throes of leadership development, exploring how the concept of leadership emerged in their lives and how leadership intersects with their key social identities including their gender. These narratives are one piece in the larger landscape of leadership literature that has long forgotten the stories of women with numerous, intersecting identities (Ayman & Korabik, 2010; Christo Baker et al., 2012; Davis & Maldonado, 2015; Hall et al., 2007; Parker, 2005). The purpose of this book is to shed further light on the stories of women in leadership and to provide considerations and recommendations for the future of women in leadership. This chapter will provide general context for our focus on women, critical approaches to leadership education, and leadership as a socialized process.

First, we discuss how women have been situated within leadership education, particularly in a higher education context. Next, we outline key concepts and definitions related to our work and leadership scholarship, broadly. Chapter authors may reference this context, history, and key concepts as they explore the narratives of our participants within individual chapters. We then situate this book within the existing scholarship on critical perspectives in leadership education. Many scholars continue to take a critical lens to the role, function, and implementation of leadership education, a lens we also hope to utilize through the findings in this book. Finally, we discuss the role socialization plays in how leadership is defined, experienced, and taught. Our hope is that by reading this chapter, you will understand the gap in research related to women and leadership and the necessity for continued inquiry in this area.

WHY WOMEN AND LEADERSHIP?

Over decades, institutions of higher education have become places for leadership learning and development (Gallagher et al., 2014; Kodama & Dugan, 2013). In addition, the number of student leadership development programs found within colleges and universities has expanded dramatically in the last 2 decades (Guthrie et al., 2018). The trending discourse centers on employability as the primary benefits of this leadership learning, as demonstrated in individual program mission statements. What is often missing is the growing understanding of leadership development as a process of collaboration for the purpose of advancing social responsibility and social justice. Bell (2007) describes social justice as "both a goal and a process. The goal of social justice is full and equitable participation of people from all social identity group in a society that is mutually shaped to meet their needs" (p. 3). Bell continues to write that the ultimate goal of social justice is a world in which "all members are physically and psychologically safe and secure, recognized, and treated with respect" (p. 3). Leadership and social justice are inexplicably intertwined, a notion argued by Guthrie and Chunoo (2018) in their text *Changing the Narrative: Socially Just Leadership Education.* To paraphrase Vernon Wall in their Foreword, you can't have leadership without social justice, and you can't have social justice without leadership. If scholars and educators are to progress the field of leadership and leadership education, a social justice lens must be incorporated into leadership research and leadership learning.

This book seeks to elevate the voices of women from a myriad of backgrounds and identities to better understand the experiences of diverse women related to leadership. We want to acknowledge that much of the extant literature related to leadership centers the experiences of White men and White women and often excludes those with historically excluded and marginalized identities (Ayman & Korabik, 2010; Christo-Baker et al., 2012; Parker, 2005). The narratives of Women of Color are often excluded in conversations around leadership; these women often face discrimination and other challenges when seeking leadership experiences. This book attempts to decenter privileged identities in pursuit of more justice-oriented perspectives related to leadership, leadership identity, and leadership development.

The exposure and vulnerability in the narratives of this book continue to demonstrate the need for liberation and liberatory practices in the fields of leadership and leadership education. As aforementioned, the socialization of what it means to be or not to be a leader influences how we are received and perceived as leaders. When considering the experiences of women in the workplace, sexism permeates, as leadership is often thought of as more masculine and male-dominated (Christo Baker et al., 2012; Davis & Maldonado, 2015), automatically setting up women for more difficulty. Women of color in leadership are often compared to White and/or male counterparts while also working doubly hard to advocate for their peers with shared identities (Sanchez-Hucles & Sanchez, 2007). Gender non-confirming, non-binary, and trans individuals are not perceived as authentic leaders (Jourian, 2014). Lesbian, gay, bi, and queer individuals face heteronormative expectations for leader performance (Renn, 2007). The intersection of social justice and leadership is of particular concern because the societal standards related to leadership are marred by historical notions of leadership rooted in oppression and marginalization.

To continue to combat socialized notions of leadership, the leadership development process itself must include reflective practices aimed at exploring personal identities and considering how to work among diverse teams (Volpe White et al., 2019). Gender identity, specifically, has the potential to greatly influence how an individual comes to understand leadership, approaches leadership opportunities, or integrates "leader" into their existing persona or identity. Two studies on women's leader identity development indicate that college women leaders, specifically, have a difficult time naming themselves as leaders given the discrimination faced by their gender and other intersecting identities (McKenzie, 2015, 2018; Shetty, 2020). In addition, the participants of these studies indicated they had seen leadership as dominated by men, often wealthy, White, straight, cisgender men. Women need tremendous support, affirmation, and mentoring to overcome imposter syndrome and to process microaggressions that are consistently faced as women leaders. Many themes in these studies are also reflected in the narratives in this book. This book aims to contribute further to research on women in leadership and to press against oppressive systems with difficult questions on how to improve our world for a generation of rising women leaders.

DEFINITIONS AND GROUNDING ASSUMPTIONS

This book operates from the assumption that leadership and gender are both socially constructed concepts (Billsberry, 2009; Dugan, 2017; Guthrie et al., 2021; Guthrie et al., 2013; Haber-Curran & Tillapaugh, 2018; Owen, 2020; Volpe White et al., 2019; West & Zimmerman, 1987). This means our lived experiences help construct and shape how we understand and define leadership and gender. While clarified definitions do not constitute the only approaches to understanding these words, to ground the work in this text, the following definitions help contextualize how our team understands leadership and gender as phenomena.

Leader and Leadership

Kellerman (2012) discovered the existence of more than 1,500 definitions and 40 models of leadership. Guthrie and Jenkins (2018) noted, "The language of leader and leadership directly influences who is identified as a leader, the development of leadership capacity (potential) in students, and the ability to reach students from all backgrounds" (p. 6). We acknowledge that it would be antithetical to the purpose of this book to provide a singular definition of leadership considering the vast number of possible options and with the knowledge that leadership is a socially constructed process. How chapter authors and contributors understand leadership may differ, and each difference informs individual approaches to conceptualizing and analyzing leadership growth. These differences are important and essential as we consider how intersecting identities shape the landscape of leadership. However, at the most basic level, and for the purposes of this book, we operate from the understanding that *leader* is an individual person and *leadership* is a process (Bertrand Jones et al., 2016; Komives et al., 2006; Rost, 1993). Both leader and leadership are heavily dependent on context and culture, thus the social construction of the phenomenon (Fairhurst & Grant, 2010). This basic understanding helps situate the women's narratives within the book.

Gender

Gender identity can be defined as "a person's internal, deeply held sense of their gender," which differs from sex which can be understood as "the classification of a person as male or female" (Owen, 2020, p. 22). Sex and gender are terms that are often conflated and restricted on a male/female and man/women binary (Owen, 2020). It is critical to understand that one's sex identity is not synonymous with one's gender identity. Additionally, it is important to note that one's gender identity does not operate in a silo, but rather intersects with one's race, ability, sexual orientation, religion, biological sex, social class, and more (Crenshaw, 1991; Richardson & Loubier, 2008).

In addition to using definitions and language that provide a shared understanding, this book is grounded in several assumptions about gender and leadership, many informed by the assumptions laid out by Dr. Julie Owen (2020) and many others formed throughout our collective writing process. These assumptions include:

- Leadership is not defined or restricted by a position. Leadership is a collective process that is socially constructed based on the social, cultural, and environmental context (Billsberry, 2009; Dugan, 2017; Guthrie et al., 2021; Guthrie et al., 2013; Volpe White et al., 2019).
- Gender is also socially constructed (Butler, 2004; Haber-Curran & Tillapaugh, 2018; Owen, 2020; West & Zimmerman, 1987), and "woman" was an identity that chapter authors and narrative contributors self-identified with to opt into this project.
- As a socially constructed idea, understandings and experiences of leadership are affected by our social identities (race/ethnicity,

gender, class, religion, etc.) and their intersections (Dugan, 2017; Ospina & Foldy, 2009; Owen, 2020).
- This book is shaped and formed by the voices of the narrative contributors and authors. Our own voices, identities, and lived experiences have shaped this book into what it is today.

We also want to note some purposeful decisions made throughout the book for the sake of consistency and in alignment with the value-orientation of this work. First, we describe the writers in this book in two contexts—*chapter authors* and *narrative authors*. The chapter authors served as researchers, weavers, and writers within the project. The narrative authors contributed narratives describing their experiences with leadership, and some also participated in feedback within the research process. In each chapter, the chapter and narrative authors have a written narrative included in grey boxes. Finally, we did not edit any of the narrative authors' words after their final submission. This was an intentional choice to ensure we stayed true to their words in their entirety. Therefore, any discrepancies in grammar or mechanics are embraced as the authenticity of the narrative authors' voices and serve as an example of pushing against any expectation of perfection in our knowledge creation.

CONTEXTS OF CRITICAL LEADERSHIP EDUCATION

Given the scope of this book, we will not be discussing the history and context of leadership education as a whole. Instead, we will turn our attention to the specific way the landscape of leadership education has changed to include critical theories, perspectives, and pedagogies. This is particularly important context for our discussion regarding how women have been engaged or excluded in leadership education over time, particularly at institutions of higher education. In this section, we explore the changes and adaptations in the approach to leadership education that are relevant to this book and to our explicit emphasis on women.

New attention has been given to critical perspectives in leadership and leadership education with an emphasis on understanding how varying identities influence and contribute to leadership development, behaviors, and practices (Dugan, 2017). Critical perspectives aim to study the lived experiences of people and to examine systems that bestow privilege or enforce oppression for varying groups of people based on social identities (Dugan, 2017; Tapia-Fuselier & Irwin, 2019). For years, models like servant leadership, the social change model, relational leadership model, the student leadership challenge, as well as historical leadership theories did not explicitly consider the identities of individuals involved in the leadership process. These models and theories do not mention the important role social identities play when considering how an individual develops their leadership identity or enacts leadership practices. In addition, some of these theories are implicitly Eurocentric or White-centric in their approach, lacking the necessary inclusive perspectives to engage all leaders (Dugan, 2017; Tapia-Fuselier & Irwin, 2019; Teig & Dilworth, 2022).

In an attempt to decenter privileged identities in leadership, scholars have begun to examine the impact of critical theories in leadership education and the incorporation of socially just approaches in institutions of higher learning (Beatty et al., 2020; Dugan, 2017; Guthrie & Chunoo, 2018, 2021). Dugan (2017) suggested adopting a critical lens for engaging in interpretation of leadership theory, but also as a tool to deconstruct leadership. Other researchers point to ways in which privilege and oppression are present in leadership (Beatty & Manning-Ouellette, 2018; Beatty & Tillapaugh, 2017; Dugan, 2017; Dugan & Leonette, 2021) and address the need to adopt critical frameworks to account for the complexities of social identities and to increase equitable outcomes in leadership learning (Beatty et al., 2020). Scholars are working to interrupt inequitable and exclusionary legacies and current practices in leadership (Honig & Honsa, 2020; Liu, 2020).

At the time this book is being written, there are numerous models and pedagogies for leadership education taking into account the role of criticality. We offer a brief review of a few of these approaches below.

Integrated Model of Critical Leadership Development

Dugan and Humbles (2018) developed the integrated model of critical leadership development to give educators a resource when approaching leadership education through a critical lens. Taking a "critical" lens to leadership education and development stems from critical social theories and requires looking intentionally at leadership processes in the ways they do (and/or do not) address societal inequities (Agger, 2013; Brookfield, 2005; Dugan, 2017; Dugan & Humbles, 2018; Levinson et al., 2011). Critical leadership development interrogates "how taken-for-granted assumptions, power, and inequity influence how leader roles and leadership processes are understood, experienced, and enacted" (Dugan & Humbles, 2018, p. 11; Dugan, 2017). The integrated model of critical leadership development includes examination of the three following areas related to leadership: knowledge, ideology/hegemony, and social location (Dugan, 2017; Dugan & Humbles, 2018). These three meta-themes are operationalized in the model alongside leadership theory, leadership development, and critical perspectives (Dugan & Humbles, 2018). Dugan and Humbles (2018) noted, "The integrated model offers a means to conceptualize how these three elements (i.e., leadership theory, leadership development, critical perspectives) interact and, more importantly, how educators can intervene to accelerate and maximize leadership education" (p. 12).

Deconstructing and Reconstructing Leadership Theories

In his 2017 work, *Leadership Theory: Cultivating Critical Perspectives*, Dugan revisited and evaluated a myriad of broadly used leadership theories. Dugan wrote on the importance of critically examining these widely used theories and models in an attempt to center justice as an essential aspect of the leadership process. Because most leadership theories do not intentionally consider social identities of those involved in the leadership process, existing theories and models may inherently enforce oppressive thinking or behaviors. The goal of reconstructing existing models and theories suggests the theories themselves are not to be thrown out altogether but developed anew so as to integrate identities, understanding of privilege, power, and oppression, and to improve upon existing ways of thinking about the leadership process.

Culturally Relevant Leadership Learning Model

The culturally relevant leadership learning (CRLL) model was created by Bertrand Jones et al. (2016) as a tool for leadership educators to create learning spaces that accounted for the contextual elements of the educational setting and to understand the ways individuals and systems can enhance equity and inclusion and work to interrupt systemic oppression in organizations. Guthrie et al. (2017) stated, "CRLL recognizes the power inherent in leadership, with special focus on the use of language, and power to influence students' identity, capacity, and efficacy through institutional culture and climate" (p. 62). This model moves beyond the individual and demands an integration of systemic dynamics (Owen et al., 2017); it (see Figure 1.1) encompasses eight core elements that capture the development of leaders and the leadership process (Beatty & Guthrie, 2021; Bertrand Jones et al., 2016). The internal pieces focus on the leader (individual) and the leadership process (Beatty & Guthrie, 2021; Bertrand Jones et al., 2016). As leaders engage in the leadership process, they are developing their leadership identity, capacity, and efficacy (Beatty & Guthrie, 2021; Bertrand Jones et al., 2016).

Leadership identity is the "ever-evolving self-portrait" of one's identification as a leader (Bertrand Jones et al., 2016, p. 13). Leadership capacity is

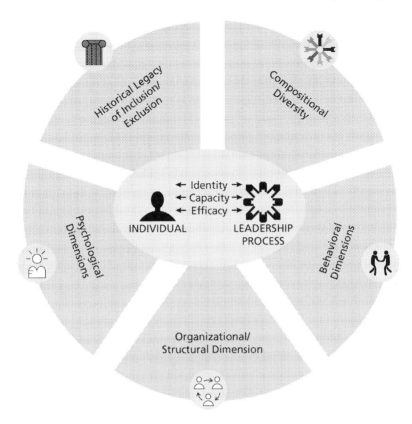

Figure 1.1 Culturally relevant leadership learning model. *Source:* Reprinted with permission from Beatty & Guthrie, 2021.

the "integration of students' knowledge, attitudes, and skills that collectively reflect their overall ability to behave effectively in the leadership process" (Bertrand Jones et al., 2016, p. 14; Dugan, 2011). Leadership efficacy is "our belief in our ability to effectively engage in the process of leadership using our knowledge, skills, values, and attitudes we have learned" (Guthrie et al., 2021, pp. 11–12).

There are five external dimensions that capture the context in which the leadership learning occurs: historical legacy of inclusion/exclusion, compositional diversity, behavioral dimension, organizational/structural dimension, and psychological dimension (Beatty & Guthrie, 2021; Bertrand Jones et al., 2016; Hurtado et al., 1998; Milem et al., 2005). Unlike other theories or models that seem to explore the leadership process in a vacuum, void of cultural and contextual influences, the CRLL model emphasizes the need to address these external dimensions that radically influence how an individual may experience leadership or may be impacted by the leadership process. The CRLL model assumes a critical perspective that benefits the learner as they unpack their own identities in relation to leadership and considers how systems, both oppressive and liberating, influence our leadership experiences.

Theory to Practice

Emerging research and literature acknowledge the shortcomings of past models and theories and encourage scholars, practitioners, and educators to reconsider how we teach leadership and to whom (Beatty & Guthrie, 2021; Bertrand Jones et al., 2016; Dugan, 2017; Guthrie & Chunoo, 2018, 2021; Owen, 2020). The chapter authors within this book approached their analyses of the narratives with a critical lens, understanding the necessity of including intersectional identities in the story of what it means to be a leader. While we are not addressing the history of leadership education, it is important to note where this text lands in the timeline and landscape of existing literature. We hope to position ourselves within the new wave of leadership education and research by affirming and emphasizing the necessity of taking a critical approach to leadership education through inclusive practices.

While we emphasize women in this book, we hope it is made obvious how intersectionality also plays a role in leadership learning and that we honor and respect the additional, salient identities our women participants also hold. When we think of both leaders and leadership as concepts that are socially constructed, we can deconstruct and rebuild the concept of leadership identity and leadership development. The next section further discusses the role of socialization in the leadership process and important considerations as context for this book.

SOCIALIZATION AND LEADERSHIP

Throughout history, society has placed value on particular skills and experiences depending on how people were socialized to think about leaders and leadership. We have often been socialized to think of leaders based on position and power (Sinclair, 2008). Often, White, cisgender, wealthy men have been considered those with the most leadership power and prowess (Fine, 2016; Ladkin & Patrick, 2022; Sinclair, 2008). This teaching perpetuates a certain lens in how the role of leader and leadership is perceived and considered. As aforementioned, more recent leadership theories and models have been designed to disrupt the thinking that inherently developed as a result of this dominant socialization. However, it is helpful to understand how socialization plays a role in leader identity and leadership processes.

The Cycle of Socialization

One model that helps us conceptualize gender socialization is the cycle of socialization, which displays the complexities of how people are socialized through systems and how many forces contribute to socialization (Harro, 2013). Harro's (2013) model shows how socialization is "pervasive, consistent, circular, self-perpetuating, and often invisible or unconscious and unnamed" (Owen, 2020, p. 71). Socialization is not a one-time incident, but rather a culmination of events, experiences, and messages throughout someone's life (Adams & Zuniga, 2016). This model moves from the beginning of one's life through first socializations, institutional and cultural socializations, enforcements, results, and directions for change (Harro, 2013). Owen (2020) noted the cycle of socialization helps understand negative impacts on college women's gender socializations, like effortless perfection, imposter syndrome, internalized oppression, microaggressions, social pressure, stress, and anxiety.

Throughout this text, the women's narratives and their conceptualizations of leadership are driven by the contexts, cultures, and backgrounds they come from; this includes the socialization they have received throughout their lives about what it means to be a leader. In many cases, we see the narrative authors realizing their notions and socialized understanding of leadership are not accurate, correct, or how they want to view leadership as they move into their futures. The breaking down of socialized barriers allows our narrative authors to break free from outdated philosophies and to soar into more liberating views of leadership.

CONCLUDING THOUGHTS

The landscape of leadership is wide and vast. Across the country there are academic curriculum, co-curricular experiences, research and scholarship, and professional associations dedicated to the field of leadership. However, as we have seen from the previous section, women have often been excluded from intentional consideration in the field of leadership education and development. The participants who contributed to this book are representative of women living in the murky waters of leadership education and its lack of emphasis on women's stories and narratives. These women benefit from the professionalization of leadership education as a field and discipline, but also live in a landscape where women still need and deserve more attention. This book aims to contribute to the narrative and research on women in leadership education by highlighting and amplifying the voices of women. In light of what we know about the discrimination of women in leadership across industries and disciplines, let us now, in Chapter 2, discuss how leadership education on college campuses has included or excluded women in the past and currently.

REFERENCES

Adams, M., & Zuniga, X. (2016). Getting started: Core concepts for social justice education. In M. Adams, & L. A. Bell (Eds.), *Teaching for diversity and social justice* (3rd ed., pp. 95–130). Routledge.

Agger, B. (2013). *Critical social theories* (3rd ed.). Oxford University Press.

Ayman, R., & Korabik, K. (2010). Leadership: Why gender and culture matter. *American Psychologist, 65*(3), 157–170. https://doi.org/10.1037/a0018806

Beatty, C. C., & Guthrie, K. L. (2021). *Operationalizing the culturally relevant leadership learning*. Information Age Publishing.

Beatty, C. C., Irwin, L., Owen, J. E., Tapia-Fuselier, N., Guthrie, K. L., Cohen-Derr, E., Hassell-Goodman, S., Rocco, M. L., & Yamanaka, A. (2020). A call for centering social identities: Priority 1 of the National Leadership Education Research Agenda 2020–2025. *Journal of Leadership Studies, 14*(3), 39–44. https://doi.org/10.1002/jls.21719

Beatty, C. C., & Manning-Ouellette, A. (2018). The role of liberatory pedagogy in socially just leadership education. In K. L. Guthrie & V. S. Chunoo (Eds.), *Changing the narrative: Socially just leadership education* (pp. 229–243). Information Age Publishing.

Beatty, C. C., & Tillapaugh, D. (2017). Masculinity, leadership, and liberatory pedagogy: Supporting men through leadership development and education. *New Directions for Student Leadership, 2017*(154), 47–58. https://doi.org/10.1002/yd.20239

Bell, L. A. (2007). Theoretical foundations for social justice education. In M. Adams, L. A. Bell, & P. Griffin (Eds.), *Teaching for diversity and social justice* (pp. 1–14). Routledge.

Bertrand Jones, T., Guthrie, K. L., & Osteen, L. (2016). Critical domains of culturally relevant leadership learning: A call to transform leadership programs. *New Directions for Student Leadership, 2016*(152), 9–21. https://doi.org/10.1002/yd.20205

Billsberry, J. (2009). The social construction of leadership education. *Journal of Leadership Education, 8*(2), 1–9. https://doi.org/10.12806/v8/i2/ab1

Brookfield, S. D. (2005). *The power of critical theory: Liberating adult learning and teaching*. Open University Press.

Butler, J. (2004). *Undoing gender*. Routledge.

Christo-Baker, E. A., Roberts, C., & Rogalin, C. L. (2012). Spirituality as a vehicle for passing through the stained glass ceiling: Perspectives on African American women's leadership in US organizations. *The Journal of Pan African Studies* 5(2), 5–26. http://www.jpanafrican.org/docs/vol5no2/5.2Spirituality.pdf

Crenshaw, K. (1991). Mapping the margins: Intersectionality, identity politics, and violence against women of color. *Stanford Law Review, 43*(6), 1241–1299. https://doi.org/10.2307/1229039

Davis, D. R., & Maldonado, C. (2015). Shattering the glass ceiling: The leadership development of African American women in higher education. *Advancing Women in Leadership, 35*, 48–64. https://doi.org/10.21423/awlj-v35.a125

Dugan, J. P. (2011). Research on college student leadership. In S. R. Komives, J. P. Dugan, J. E. Owen, C. Slack, W. Wagner, & Associates (Eds.), *The handbook for student leadership development* (2nd ed., pp. 59–85). Jossey-Bass.

Dugan, J. P. (2017). *Leadership theory: Cultivating critical perspectives*. Jossey-Bass.

Dugan, J. P., & Humbles, A. D. (2018). A paradigm shift in leadership education: Integrating critical perspectives into leadership development. *New Directions for Student Leadership, 2018*(159), 9–26. https://doi.org/10.1002/yd.20294

Dugan, J. P., & Leonette, H. (2021). The complicit omission: Leadership development's radical silence on equity. *Journal of College Student Development, 62*(3), 379–382. https://doi.org/10.1353/csd.2021.0030

Fairhurst, G. T., & Grant, D. (2010). The social construction of leadership: A sailing guide. *Management Communication Quarterly, 24*(2), 171–210. https://doi.org/10.1177/0893318909359697

Fine, L. E. (2016). Judith Butler and leadership: Reimagining intelligibility, social change, and leadership discourse. *Journal of Leadership Studies, 10*(2), 69–81. https://doi.org/10.1002/jls.21466

Gallagher, M. L., Marshall, J. C., Pories, M. L., & Daughety, M. (2014). Factors effecting undergraduate leadership behaviors. *Journal of Leadership Education, 13*(1), 46–56. https://doi.org/10.12806/V13/I1/R4

Guthrie, K. L., Beatty, C. C., & Wiborg, E. R. (2021). *Engaging in the leadership process: Identity, capacity, and efficacy for college students*. Information Age Publishing.

Guthrie, K. L., Bertrand Jones, T., Osteen, L., & Hu, S. (2013). Cultivating leader identity and capacity in students from diverse backgrounds. *ASHE Higher Education Report, 39*(4). Wiley. https://doi.org/10.1002/aehe.v39.4

Guthrie, K. L., Bertrand Jones, T., & Osteen, L. (2017). The teaching, learning, and being of leadership: Exploring context and practice of the culturally relevant leadership learning model. *Journal of Leadership Studies, 11*(3), 61–67. https://doi.org/10.1002/jls.21547

Guthrie, K. L., & Chunoo, V. S. (Eds.). (2018). *Changing the narrative: Socially just leadership education*. Information Age Publishing.

Guthrie, K. L., & Chunoo, V. S. (Eds.). (2021). *Shifting the mindset: Socially just leadership education*. Information Age Publishing.

Guthrie, K. L., & Jenkins, D. M. (2018). *The role of leadership educators: Transforming learning*. Information Age Publishing.

Guthrie, K. L., Teig, T., & Hu, P. (2018). *Academic leadership programs in the United States*. Leadership Learning Research Center, Florida State University.

Haber-Curran, P., & Tillapaugh, D. (2018). Beyond the binary: Advancing socially just leadership through the lens of gender. In K. L. Guthrie, & V. S. Chunoo

(Eds.), *Changing the narrative: Socially just leadership education* (pp. 77–92). Information Age Publishing.

Hall, R. L., Garrett-Akinsanya, B., & Hucles, M. (2007). Voices of Black feminist leaders: Making spaces for ourselves. In J. L. Chin, B. Lott, J. K. Rice, & J. Sanchez-Hucles (Eds.), *Women and leadership: Transforming visions and diverse voices* (pp. 281–296). Blackwell Publishing.

Harro, B. (2013). The cycle of socialization. In M. Adams, W. J. Blumfield, C. R. Castaneda, H. W. Hackman, M. L. Peters, & X. Zuniga (Eds.), *Readings for diversity and social justice* (3rd ed., pp. 45–52). Routledge.

Honig, M. I., & Honsa, A. (2020). Systems-focused equity leadership learning: Shifting practice through practice. *Journal of Research on Leadership Education*, *15*(3), 192–209. https://doi.org/10.1177/1942775120936303

Hurtado, S., Milem, J. F., Clayton-Pedersen, A. R., & Allen, W. R. (1998). Enhancing campus climates for racial/ethnic diversity: Educational policy and practice. *The Review of Higher Education 21*(3), 279–302. https://doi.org/10.1353/rhe.1998.0003

Jourian, T. J. (2014). Trans* forming authentic leadership: A conceptual framework. *Journal of Critical Thought and Praxis*, *2*(2), 113–115. https://doi.org/10.31274/jctp-180810-78

Kellerman, B. (2012). *The end of leadership*. Harper Business.

Kodama, C. M., & Dugan, J. P. (2013). Leveraging leadership efficacy for college students: Disaggregating data to examine unique predictors by race. *Equity & Excellence in Education*, *46*(2), 184–201. https://doi.org/10.1080/10665684.2013.780646

Komives, S. R., Longerbeam, S. D., Owen, J. E., Mainella, F. C., & Osteen, L. (2006). A leadership identity model: Applications from a grounded theory. *Journal of College Student Development*, *47*(4), 401–418. https://doi.org/10.1353/csd.2006.0048

Ladkin, D., & Patrick, C. B. (2022). Whiteness in leadership theorizing: A critical analysis of race in Bass' transformation a leadership theory. *Leadership*, *18*(2), 205–223. https://doi.org/10.1177/17427150211066442

Levinson, B. A. U., Gross, J. P. K., Hanks, C., Heimer Dadds, J., Kumasi, K. D., Link, J., & Metro-Roland, D. (2011). *Beyond critique: Exploring critical social theories and education*. Paradigm.

Liu, H. (2020). *Redeeming leadership: An anti-racist, feminist intervention*. Policy Press.

McKenzie, B. L. (2015). *Leadership identity development in traditional-aged female undergraduate college students: A grounded theory* [Unpublished doctoral dissertation], Kent State University. http://rave.ohiolink.edu/etdc/view?acc_num=kent1428585168

McKenzie, B. L. (2018). Am I a leader? Female students' leadership identity development. *Journal of Leadership Education*, *17*(2), 1–18. https://doi.org/10.12806/V17/I2/R1

Milem, J. F., Chang, M. J., & Antonio, A. L. (2005). *Making diversity work on campus: A research-based perspective*. Association of American Colleges and Universities.

Opsina, S., & Foldy, E. (2009). A critical review of race and ethnicity in the leadership literature: Surfacing context, power and the collective dimensions of leadership. *The Leadership Quarterly, 20*(6), 876–896. https://doi.org/10.1016/j.leaqua.2009.09.005

Owen, J. E. (2020). *We are the leaders we've been waiting for: Women and leadership development in college*. Stylus.

Owen, J. E., Hassell-Goodman, S., & Yamanaka, A. (2017). Culturally-relevant leadership learning: Identity, capacity, and efficacy. *Journal of Leadership Studies, 11*(3), 48–54. https://doi.org/10.1002/jls.21545

Parker, P. S. (2005). *Race, gender, and leadership: Re-envisioning organizational leadership from the perspectives of African American women executives*. Lawrence Erlbaum Associates.

Renn, K. A. (2007). LGBT student leaders and queer activists: Identities of lesbian, gay, bisexual, transgender, and queer identified college student leaders and activists. *Journal of College Student Development, 48*(3), 311–330. https://doi.org/10.1353/csd.2007.0029

Richardson, A., & Loubier, C. (2008). Intersectionality and leadership. *International Journal of Leadership Studies, 3*(2), 142–161. https://www.regent.edu/acad/global/publications/ijls/new/vol3iss2/IJLS_V3Is2_Richardson_Loubier.pdf

Rost, J. C. (1993). *Leadership for the twenty-first century*. Praeger.

Sanchez-Hucles, J., & Sanchez, P. (2007). From margin to center: The voices of diverse feminist leaders. In J. L. Chin, B. Lott, J. K. Rice, & J. Sanchez-Hucles (Eds.), *Women and leadership: Transforming visions and diverse voices* (pp. 209–227). Blackwell Publishing.

Shetty, R. L. (2020). *The leader identity development of Black women in college: A grounded theory* [Unpublished doctoral dissertation]. University of Georgia.

Sinclair, A. (2008). *Leadership for the disillusioned: Moving beyond myths and heroes to leadership that liberates*. Allen & Unwin.

Tapia-Fuselier, N., & Irwin, L. (2019). Strengths so white: Interrogating strengthsquest education through a critical whiteness lens. *Journal of Critical Scholarship on Higher Education and Student Affairs, 5*(1), 30–44. https://ecommons.luc.edu/cgi/viewcontent.cgi?article=1113&context=jcshesa

Teig, T., & Dilworth, D. (2022). Part II: Reimagining leadership education in student affairs through a critical lens. *ACPA Developments, 19*(1). https://developments.myacpa.org/private7J9pRkXzLq/16/part-ii-reimagining-leadership-education-in-student-affairs-through-a-critical-lens-teig-dilworth/1609/

Volpe White, J. M., Guthrie, K. L., & Torres, M. (2019). *Thinking to transform: Reflection in leadership learning*. Information Age Publishing.

West, C., & Zimmerman, D. H. (1987). Doing gender. *Gender and Society, 1*(2), 125–151. https://doi.org/10.1177/0891243287001002002

CHAPTER 2

CENTERING HIGHER EDUCATION ENVIRONMENTS FOR WOMEN'S LEADERSHIP LEARNING

Michele Tyson
Shenhaye Ferguson
Rebecca Shetty
Brittany Devies
Valeria Gomez

I (Michele) once took a job that literally changed my life. The work I did and the people I engaged with challenged everything I thought I knew about higher education, changed the way that I thought about leadership, and influenced my orientation to my own leadership learning. This job was at a women's college. It was here where I began to understand that leadership is not taught, rather it is shaped. The students I worked with were unique in every way, and therefore described as "non" or "post-traditional." The population was diverse in terms of race, ethnicity, and socioeconomic backgrounds. There was some diversity in academic ability as well as gender identity. These individuals had a plethora of responsibilities outside of school

> that included full-time work, full time caretaking responsibilities, and often deep-seeded roles in their communities. What made the group most unique however was the age of the students, averaging in the mid-thirties. The life experiences of the students were indicators that these women were already leading before they ever even walked in the door of the educational space. It was not that these individuals needed to learn how to be a leader. It was that they needed the supportive environment to learn about and make sense of their life experiences to see themselves as leaders. For me, being a part of that values-based learning environment—where women were allowed to be themselves in every way—changed my life as a student affairs professional and later as an academic, forever. My most significant lesson in leadership was watching the organic connections that these women made with and among each other and how they used the knowledge that came from those connections to lead in new and different ways. They inspired me in so many ways, but most importantly, they inspired me to learn more—to better understand the world I live in and the people within it. They inspired me to be better and do more, which I truly believe is the power and purpose of education.

As unpacking the facets of leadership continues to evolve, the definition of leadership has broadened and the understanding of who is and can become a leader has diversified. While prior work has been done to identify the who, what, where, why, when, and how questions of leadership broadly, this chapter focuses on the who and the how. Who are the emerging leaders and how are they learning and developing leadership skills? To answer this question, we need to challenge our thinking to reimagine learning environments that will redefine leadership and leadership learning in the 21st century. We must understand how leaders have been identified and trained in the past, and then we need to broaden those perspectives.

In recent years, the study of leadership has shifted away from a focus on the individual person and their individual aspirations of leadership. The study of leadership has shifted to a greater acknowledgment of the experiences and skills an individual already has and how those funds of knowledge contribute to the process of leadership learning and development. This chapter will explore (a) women's access to educational environments, (b) how those environments influence their concept of leadership development, (c) the increasingly diverse social identities of women-identifying leadership learners, (d) the strategies incorporated into leadership teaching and learning practices, and (e) how women and leadership development programs are represented across the United States.

BUILDING CAPACITY FOR WOMEN'S LEADERSHIP LEARNING

There has been an increasing emergence of leadership studies programs in higher education since the 1970s, with a significant jump in the new millennium. This increase can be found in both academic and cocurricular leadership programs (Guthrie et al., 2018; Komives et al., 2005). Recent research notes over 1,500 academic leadership programs in the United States (Guthrie et al., 2018). While many of these programs are offered at the graduate level, undergraduate leadership development programs have also increased, particularly in the past 20 years. The curricular programs generally result in a certification or an academic minor as evidence of having completed the required coursework and demonstration of specific leadership competencies. While undergraduate leadership programs are widespread across higher education institutions, women and leadership programs centering women are more dispersed and less frequently found. In an independent, comprehensive search, we identified fewer than 40 programs for "women's leadership" or "women and leadership" in higher education institutions in the United States. These findings will be further addressed later in the chapter.

As emerging concepts of leadership development spread across higher education curriculum, the conversation has expanded to include critical perspectives on leadership access for marginalized identity groups (Beatty & Guthrie, 2021; Dugan, 2017). Programs specifically dedicated to women have emerged, seemingly as a result of broader conversation and research acknowledging the barriers that women face in accessing positions of leadership. Research has focused on how women lead, women's access and barriers to leadership roles, biases faced by women in those roles, and the limitations of gender and leadership. While these topics expanded the broader understanding of experiences, styles, and expectations of women leaders, research about leadership development remained narrow and continued to marginalize a significant number of women. The sheer variety and scope of this research illuminates both the gaps in understanding the leadership development process of entire communities of women and negates the unique challenges of historically marginalized groups, particularly Women of Color, in relationship to the concept of leader or leadership. Additionally, much of the existing scholarship addresses gender identity as a binary of man/woman or male/female by offering comparative studies for analysis of differences but offers very little in uncovering leadership learning and development for those that do not identify on that binary.

The concept of leadership has historical and current associations with particular privileged social identities (including male, masculine, cisgender, straight, White, high socioeconomic status, etc.). The leadership identity development of those that identify as women remains understudied, yet increasingly more relevant. Unfortunately, much of the current scholarship on leadership does not yet use methodology rooted in social constructivist or postmodern understandings of identity fluidity in response to systemic gender power and oppression. The limitations presented by the lack of research in this area point to a need to further explore the role of identity, as gender and race and ethnicity intersect, as well as the intersections of other social identities. The impact of these intersections on leadership potential is endless, as demonstrated throughout this book.

Leadership development programs found at colleges and universities have the opportunity to fill these gaps and address the shortcomings, particularly in how an individual learns to understand themselves as a leader. The quality of educational programming depends on meeting students where they are and teaching to the increasingly diverse demographic of today's women. Foundations of this work can be traced back to the learning environment of women's colleges. The next section will explore this historical foundation and legacy.

WOMEN'S LEADERSHIP LEARNING AND THE TRADITION OF WOMEN'S COLLEGES

The mission of women's colleges in the United States changed as the philosophical purpose for educating women evolved (and continues to do so). The purpose of educating women in the early 19th century was supported by the need for women to be raising good sons as they became men. This philosophy, known as "republican motherhood," centered on the belief that in order for women to raise these good men, they must be educated in good citizenship themselves (Palmieri, 1987). Therefore, the first generation of women's colleges and formalized women's education focused on the value of women being educated for the good of society. This belief system existed through the 1920s. However, it is critically important to note that this education was designed and intended for wealthy White women, exclusively. Some institutions, such as Mount Holyoke, were founded with the distinct purpose of serving the working-class or women from a lower socioeconomic class (Marthers, 2013), but were not open for Black women until much later.

A teacher-shortage in the mid-1800s led to additional demand for women's education, and institutions specifically designed for women began to emerge (Hartwarth et al., 1997). The curriculum at these institutions focused on liberal arts and civic education and were framed around providing this education while protecting the existing ideas surrounding White women's femininity and women's proper place in society (Cohen & Kisker,

2010). The need to produce grammar-school teachers was also a factor in the creation of institutions for Black women, as the first institutions open to Black women were normal schools (Bell-Scott, 1984), which later became known as teacher's colleges. Many of the schools open to Black women were established through missionary work, and character education was a pillar of the educational experience (Bell-Scott, 1984). By the early 1900s, many existing colleges and universities, as well as newly formed institutions, were becoming co-educational and admitted both Black and White women, which had an impact on enrollment at women's colleges. However, the compositional gender diversity at these co-educational institutions did not necessarily equate to an equal education in terms of rigor and academic quality (Cohen & Kisker, 2010). Women were rarely represented in the faculties of these institutions, funding was rarely provided for women's programming, and campus climates were competitive, often not welcoming to women students (DiPrete & Buchmann, 2013). Debate about whether Black and White women should learn together or separately (segregation) persisted into the 20th century, as did the ongoing debate about whether women should be exposed to the same curriculum as men (Bell-Scott, 1984). Black women were more likely to attend co-educational institutions, rather than women's colleges, which had to do with the push and focus on vocational training for Black communities in general.

This change to higher education broadly led to the second generation of women's education, which existed from 1930 to 1960. Around the time of WWII, women comprised 55% of all college students (Miller-Bernal & Poulson, 2006), but when men returned from war and could benefit from Servicemen's Readjustment Act (the GI Bill), the number of men dramatically increased and women's enrollment fell to 30% as more White women chose marriage and parenting over education (Miller-Bernal & Poulson, 2006). Most educational opportunities continued to be for White women. At that time, the purpose of an education was for women to learn to be good wives. Most often, there were no specific career goals for these women and very little desire to use knowledge as a mechanism for social reform (Palmieri, 1987), though it was believed that holding a college degree elevated one's social standing. For years, women's colleges were nimble in responding to the needs of White women as the demand for education evolved and increased. The educational opportunities made available for Black women looked drastically different. Fewer than 500 Black women had attended the Seven Sisters, the female equivalent of the once predominantly male Ivy League schools prior to 1960 (Perkins, 1997). These individuals were often daughters of educated parents.

By the 1970s Black and White women were integrated in most educational environments. Many institutions responded to the demands of women that wanted formal education after marriage and childbearing (such as Vassar and Barnard colleges), while others recognized that women needed a curriculum to prepare them for emerging jobs and careers that were suddenly opening up to women and aspired to prepare the working woman for success (Marthers, 2013). Marthers (2013) described this time as "I can do anything you can do feminism" (p. 6), where women fought for equal opportunity in the workplace and in educational spaces. The purpose and value of women's colleges grew increasingly more critical for equitable women's education in the third generation, roughly from the 1960s to 2000. In 1990, women's college students had higher graduation rates and increased satisfaction over women attending co-ed institutions (Smith, 1990), which was indicative of the learning environments that existed in these single-gendered spaces.

The most recent generation of women's colleges likely marks the end of the "women's college." Since the 1990s, these institutions have both appealed to and responded to the needs of different populations—expanding to reach historically minoritized and underrepresented women as well as the nontraditional, working, part-time student. Even with this expansion in the type of women served, there have been no new women's colleges founded in decades and many existing institutions have been forced to close (Kim & Alvarez, 1995). Those still in existence at the turn of the 21st century struggled to maintain enrollment and made plans to merge with other institutions, to transform into co-educational institutions, or to close entirely. On occasion, individual programs within these women's colleges survived upon the mergers and were embedded into the co-educational institution. Thirty-eight women's colleges remain in 2022 (Women's College Coalition, 2023).

Through each of these generations of women's education at women's colleges, it was the value-centered learning, the positive effect on self-confidence (Kim & Alvarez, 1995; Miller-Bernal & Poulson, 2006), the positive effect on academic ability (Kim & Alvarez, 1995), the focus on critical thinking (Women's College Coalition, 2023), and the attention and respect for diverse values and beliefs that empowered students to become leaders. The single-gendered learning environment is a powerful place for leadership training (Miller-Bernal & Poulson, 2006). Women's colleges are not solely colleges for women but are gendered organizations with constant tension surrounding the changes of the notion of what it means to be a woman (Nanney & Brunsma, 2017). Historically, as more women attended co-educational institutions, they found ways to claim space for themselves, and it was often through these spaces (i.e., clubs and resource centers) that they were able to adapt to the institution (Horowitz, 1993).

Because of these benefits, some coeducational institutions have recognized the value of such curricular and co-curricular spaces and have moved toward hosting programs that are exclusively for women-identifying students, often within their preexisting coeducational institutional model

(Nanney & Brunsma, 2017). While the historical role of women's colleges no longer seems necessary, the value and benefit of gender-specific educational environments cannot be ignored. Research has demonstrated that in a coeducational learning environment, women were less likely to be called upon by their instructors when prepared to speak, faculty members were less likely to know women students' names, professors interrupted female students disproportionality more often, and women were given less time and attention than male students (Miller-Bernal & Poulson, 2006). All of this contributes to a chilly academic climate in which women are made to feel that they do not belong. In addition, campus-wide issues of sexual assault, sexual harassment, and lack of representation on key student leadership committees have added to this chilly climate, exacerbating the feelings of being unsafe and disrespected.

It is important to note that women-identifying students continue to comprise more than 50% of the population attending colleges (DiPrete & Buchmann, 2013). While the number of student leadership development programs found within colleges and universities has expanded in recent decades, there is certainly room to grow. Providing the space and the environment for modern, inclusive leadership learning will help facilitate a more effective leadership development process for women, particularly Women of Color attending predominately White institutions (PWI). The value of gender-specific educational environments, whether women's college or women's spaces at coed institutions, have remained consistent through generational changes and continue to remain necessary for women's leadership development.

Understanding the tradition of the women's college and related experiences for students is critical in considering the possibilities for the future of leadership development. What role could a modern women's college or women's program play in leadership development for women-identifying students? What responsibility do colleges and universities have to provide single-gendered leadership programs to Women of Color at PWIs? How could institutions focus on supporting women's leadership development as mentioned above? What would be the impact on women, and their self-understanding as a leader, if intersecting identities and life experiences were centered in the curriculum? These are just a few of the many possibilities for leadership learning in the current educational environment.

PRESENT: TODAY'S WOMEN STUDENTS

Today's women have varied and diverse experiences on college campuses in the United States. These women's social identities impact the ways in which they experience college life, the lens through which they make sense of the academic curriculum, the ways they learn about leadership, and how they develop their self-image as a leader. The demographic of college women in the 21st century is racially and ethnically diverse. These women are often low-income students and do not always identify according to the gender binary. These women may be older than the typical college student and are more likely than ever before to be first-generation college students, while often also first-generation United States citizens or immigrants (Soares, 2013; Tyson 2021). College campuses were not designed for these students, and the adjustments they must make in these environments can be significant. More likely than not, the institutions in which women are enrolling are PWIs, where the student aggregate may not look like them (Strange & Banning, 2015), and where the services available may not support their needs (Baber, 2019; Tyson, 2019). Women of color at PWIs have experienced negative racial climates (Arao & Clemens, 2013; Solorzano et al., 2000; Wright-Mair, 2019; Yosso et al., 2009), microaggressions based on gender and race/ethnicity (Corbin et al., 2018; Domingue, 2015; Esposito, 2011; Leath & Chavous, 2018; Vaccaro & Camba-Kelsay, 2016), and the feelings of both invisibility and tokenism in their learning environments, such as classrooms and residence halls (Leath & Chavous, 2018; Linder, 2011; Vaccaro & Camba-Kelsay, 2016).

To combat these negative experiences on campus, many People of Color in general, and women more specifically, have found there is significant value in finding a space on campus that validates their many identities and creates opportunities to build networks of support that go beyond the institution's offerings at large. These spaces may look different on each campus, but often take the form of cultural centers or affinity groups that are co-curricular by nature. The curricular opportunities to support these efforts exist in the form of ethnic studies programs, for example. Students report needing these spaces to cope with the gendered and racialized macroaggressions, racism, and sexism that shape the way they experience campus climate and culture (Castellanos, 2016; Flores & Garcia, 2009; Lewis et al., 2013). Delgado-Guerrero et al. (2014) and Greyerbiehl and Mitchell (2014) point to Black and Latina sororities as examples of co-curricular spaces that create this sense of place by providing the social support for this intersectionality. These spaces provide benefits such as validation of cultural and social identities, a sense of belonging at the institution, and an opportunity to foster a sense of pride in their culture (Castellanos, 2016; Flores & Garcia, 2009; Vaccaro & Camba-Kelsay, 2016). In addition, leadership development opportunities are a direct result of the impact of these kinds of spaces.

The classroom can be another place to create this inclusive and validating experience for students. Vaccaro and Camba-Kelsay (2016) found Women of Color enrolled in a course centering their experiences allowed them to feel less isolated on campus because they were able to connect with other Women of Color on campus. The women felt excited to come to this class because it provided them a "getaway from White normalcy and the discomfort other classes caused them to experience" (p. 56). Educators should see it as an opportunity to offer these spaces to students through leadership development programming in the classroom or through broader programs that connect the curricular and co-curricular.

History of College-Level Women's Leadership Programs in the United States

Women's leadership development at the college level has been a historical focus since the inception of women's higher education. However, programs focused exclusively on women and leadership development are a newer trend in higher education following the growth of collegiate leadership programs across the United States beginning in the 1990s (Watkins, 2020). While historical programs may have existed, the team for this book explored current programs focused on women and leadership across the United States. From this exploration, we found 36 programs meeting our parameters. The following summarizes the results of this research and gives context for the current status of women and leadership programs in higher education today.

Methodology

In order to locate leadership programs available to women on college campuses, we implemented a Boolean search method used for searching terms on Google. Google was the primary search engine utilized because the majority of the data was found on institutional websites best accessed through Google. The search terms included:

"women and leadership groups"
"women colleges with leadership programs"
"women colleges with leadership programs for People of Color"
"leadership programs in college"
"leadership programs only women"
"leadership programs in underserved communities"
"historically Black colleges and universities with leadership programs"

Additionally, women's college websites were explored to see if a women and leadership program existed. We recognize and acknowledge there are a plethora of co-curricular leadership programs with a similar mission and values as the ones included in our findings, but for the purpose of this research, we have chosen only to include programs with an academic requirement or component. Although these search terms were able to capture various programs around the country, we understand that we may have missed programs that did not arise from our search criterion.

When compiling data, we identified and classified four different types of leadership programs: minor curricular, minor co-curricular, certificate curricular, certificate co-curricular. Minor curricular programs are programs where students earn a minor in leadership, and the program has specific class and curriculum requirements. Minor co-curricular programs also have specific class and curriculum requirements, but also include co-curricular activities and excursions including retreats, networking events, mentoring, and other community building activities outside of the classroom. Certificate curricular programs have some course requirements, some require university offered courses, and some require nonaccredited courses provided by the leadership program where they earn a certificate upon completion. Certificate co-curricular is the same as certificate curricular programs but also includes activities outside of the traditional classroom learning setting. The research does not include co-curricular only programs.

Women and Leadership Programs Overview

Of the programs we reviewed, the oldest college-level women's leadership program still in existence was founded in 2000 at American University entitled: Women, Policy, and Political Leadership. Most of the institutions with leadership programs for women are within private universities and colleges with a small class size. These institutions usually have a student population between 1,000 and 2,000 students. Three of the programs are at women's colleges and another three are located as legacies of historical women's colleges that are no longer functioning as institutions.

The mission statements of the programs differ, but most programs provide opportunities to learn skills that support students' futures in leadership. They emphasize the importance of developing leadership, analytical, and critical thinking skills, and enable women to cultivate relationships through networking and offer mentoring with like-minded individuals. There is a focus on creativity, integrity, service, and inclusivity while building a supportive and encouraging environment. Students in these programs foster deeper understanding of their roles and contributions to society simultaneous to learning to communicate a vision on high performing teams.

From the sample of programs we researched, there were echoing intentions for educated women to maximize their potential through transformation by augmenting the skills that make a powerful leader in a female-led, feminist environment. For example, the mission of The Bonner Leader Program at Mary Baldwin University is to transform the lives of students and members through service and leadership (Mary Baldwin University, n.d.). Rutgers Institute for Women's Leadership hopes to use storytelling, conversations, and media to inspire social action (Institute for Women's Leadership at Rutgers University, n.d.). The Women in Leadership Certificate at Antioch University is committed to the development of knowledge and skills to support future leaders (Antioch, n.d.). There are many similar messages on the landing pages of these programs where there is an evident collective vision for a more diverse, female future. The majority of programs are interdisciplinary in nature; students learn about the interconnections between gender, sexuality, class, race, and worldwide issues using gender and sexuality as critical elements of inquiry into leadership. Thirteen programs have a focus on social justice and advocacy. Many programs explore ideas of gender, sexuality, and leadership as social constructs and analyze their impact on culture and themselves. There are eight programs that have some overlap with gender studies.

The programs have a wide range of class size but on average range from 10 to 30 students in a program. Some of the programs also offer scholarships to their students, ranging in amounts from $1,500 to $6,000 per year. One program only offers scholarship to alumnae of the program once they graduate with their bachelor's degree to help fund graduate or law school. There is one program which requires a paid fee of $3,000 by the student in order to participate, but there are scholarship options available.

Programs focused on women and leadership in the United States also offer a diverse array of program requirements and credit hours. The leadership programs requiring a minor have higher credit hour course requirements than those of the certificate programs, ranging from 8 to 24 credit hours. As aforementioned, the "minor co-curricular" programs have requirements for co-curricular activities outside of class, one program even requires military cadet training. Another program offers research opportunities with grants upon approval. One program has community service requirements of 1,000 hours per year. Leadership certificate programs' curriculum requirements are slightly less demanding, ranging between 4 and 12 credits for certificate completion, and the "certificate co-curricular" programs also usually require workshop attendance outside of class. Figure 2.1 shows data for the breakdown of the women and leadership programs by academic type.

We also explored where in the country these programs are being offered and separated them into four regions: west, midwest, south, and northeast, based on the region designation of the United States Census (Census Bureau, 2021). As shown in Figure 2.2, the vast majority of the 36 programs are centered on the east coast, with a proliferation in New England.

As we connect the need for women-focused leadership development in the higher education landscape, it is important to consider where programs are succeeding. Table 2.1 and Table 2.2 shares a breakdown of the programs identified by school, type, and location.

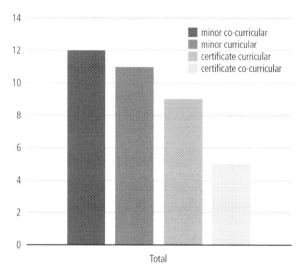

Figure 2.1 Women and leadership programs in the United States by academic type.

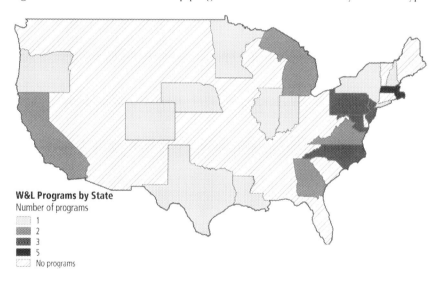

Figure 2.2 Map of women and leadership programs across the United States by state.

TABLE 2.1 Programs Reviewed	
Key:	
Minor curricular	MC
Minor co-curricular	MCC
Certificate curricular	CC
Certificate co-curricular	CCC

Centering Higher Education Environments for Women's Leadership Learning • 31

TABLE 2.2 Women and Leadership Programs in the United States

	Program Name	Program Type	University	Location (city, state)	Region
1	Catalyst Leaders Program	MC	Agnes Scott College*	Decatur, GA	S
2	Rutgers Institute for Women's Leadership	MC	Rutgers University**	Brunswick, NJ	NE
3	Virginia Women's Institute for Leadership (VWIL)	MC	Mary Baldwin University**	Staunton, VA	S
4	We Empower Learners & Leaders (WELL) Program	MC	Baypath University*	Longmeadow, MA	NE
5	Women's Leadership Academy	MC	Alfred University	Alfred, NY	NE
6	Adele's Circle of Women	MCC	University of Maryland	College Park, MD	S
7	Baldwin Scholars	MCC	Duke University	Durham, NC	S
8	Bonner Leaders	MCC	Notre Dame of Maryland University**	Baltimore, MD	S
9	Colorado Women's College** Leadership Scholars Program	MCC	University of Denver	Denver, CO	W
10	Gannon Scholars	MCC	Loyola University Chicago	Chicago, IL	MW
11	INSPIRE	MCC	University of Texas at Austin	Austin, TX	S
12	Laspa Center for Leadership	MCC	Scripps College*	Claremont, CA	W
13	Newcomb Scholars Program**	MCC	Tulane University	New Orleans, LA	S
14	Sophie Lanneau Women's Leadership Development Program	MCC	Meredith College*	Raleigh, NC	S
15	Then National Bonner Leader Program	MCC	College of Saint Benedict* & Saint John's University	St. Joseph, MN	MW
16	Women In Learning and Leadership (WILL)	MCC	University of Michigan	Ann Arbor, MI	MW
17	Women, Policy & Political Leadership Undergraduate certificate	MCC	American University	Washington, DC	NE
18	Ascending Leadership Certificate Program (ALC)	CC	Bryn Mawr College*	Mawr, PA	NE

(*continued*)

TABLE 2.2 Women and Leadership Programs in the United States

	Program Name	Program Type	University	Location (city, state)	Region
19	Batten Leadership Institute	CC	Hollins University*	Roanoke, VA	S
20	Certificate in Women in Leadership	CC	Franklin Pierce University	Rindge, NH	NE
21	Undergraduate Certificate Program in Women's Leadership	CC	Portland State University	Portland, OR	W
22	Undergraduate Leadership Certificate	CC	Cedar Crest College	Allentown, PA	NE
23	Women BUILD (Business Undergraduates in Leadership Development)	CC	Rutgers's Business School, Rutgers's University**	Brunswick, NJ	NE
24	Women in Leadership Certificate	CC	Antioch University (Santa Barbara)	Culver City, CA	W
25	Women's Leadership Certificate Program	CC	Brenau University*	Gainesville, GA	S
26	Women's Leadership Collective	CC	Towson University	Towson, MD	S
27	Women's Leadership Initiative (WLI)	CC	Pennsylvania State University	State College, PA	NE
28	CWEL Scholar's Program	CCC	Babson College	Babson Park, MA	NE
29	Global Women's Leadership Institute	CCC	St. Mary's College	Notre Dame, IN	S
30	Leaders in Training	CCC	Salem College*	Winston-Salem, NC	S
31	Leadership Leap Program	CCC	College of Saint Mary*	Omaha, NE	MW
32	Serenbetz Institute for Women's leadership, Social Responsibility & Global Awareness	CCC	Cottey College*	Nevada, MI	MW
33	Strategic Leadership for Women Certificate	CCC	Simmons University*	Boston, MA	NE
34	Student Involvement Studio workshops	CCC	Mount Holyoke College*	South Hadley, MA	NE
35	Women in Learning & Leadership (WILL)	CCC	The College of New Jersey	Ewing, NJ	NE
36	Women's Leadership Program	CCC	Bentley University	Waltham, MA	NE

* Indicates a current Women's College
** Indicates an historic Women's College

FUTURE: DIRECTIONS FOR LEADERSHIP LEARNING

As leadership development programs grow to meet the needs of emergent women leaders, the curriculum and pedagogy must expand. In many ways, it already has. One of the greatest shifts has been through a change in focus from leadership teaching to leadership learning. It is not simply about the content taught in leadership courses, but more about how leadership can be learned, the social responsibility that comes with positions of leadership, and the application of how learning about leaders and leadership can be applied in the real world to address societal problems. This line of thinking about leadership learning also allows students to see how their skills and their passions can be applied to problems right now while they are still in school as well as problems that will come up in the future, after they have completed their degrees or certifications.

THE NEXT LEVEL OF LEADERSHIP LEARNING

The next steps institutions take to offer opportunities for leadership development will be crucial to the effectiveness of such programming for the women students of today. We must consider where we go from here. We must identify the most effective aspects of how women learn about leadership, and more importantly, how they come to understand themselves as leaders. We must inquire not only about the role of gender and the effects of single-gendered learning environments in the development of leaders on college campuses but also about the impacts of learning environments for Women of Color. What are the specific aspects of women's leadership development that speak to Students of Color? The interactions of gender with race and ethnicity reflect many paths toward leadership that have not yet been thoroughly explored. It will be critical for these students to be in learning environments that embrace the wisdom of their life experiences and that they be given the opportunity to identify how those experiences have contributed to their own informal leadership development and personal growth.

Leadership learning has traditionally focused on the growth of the individual, as we have been socialized to think of leadership as an individual process of development for the benefit of the individual. Future leadership learning, specifically for Women of Color must focus on shared and collaborative learning with more of a focus on the growth of a group of people as they explore aspects of leadership together. Centering concepts such as emotional intelligence and reflexivity, and positioning those into current social, political, and economic contexts, will challenge those initial socializations.

CONCLUSION

Higher education institutions have a responsibility to create learning environments where women develop new skills in leadership and to assist them in maximizing the skills they already possessed upon entering college. These programs need to be embedded in institutions to ensure they are sustainable and not a singular attempt or a superficial and performative approach. To truly provide identity-focused leadership learning opportunities, we need to understand who the emerging leaders are and how they develop by reimagining the environments in which they learn. We must acknowledge and seek the stories of the growing diversity of women-identifying students and the increasing number of Women of Color who will need opportunities to explore their life experiences and honor the leadership skills those experiences have already created. This book is a further attempt to contribute to the leadership literature exposing and shedding light on women's stories, the future leaders of our society.

REFERENCES

Agnes Scott College. (n.d.). *Gué Pardue Hudson center for leadership and service*. Retrieved October 20, 2022, from https://www.agnesscott.edu/center-for-leadership-and-service/index.html

Alfred University. (n.d.). *Womens leadership center: Alfred university*. Retrieved October 21, 2022, from https://www.alfred.edu/student-life/leadership-diversity/womens-leadership-center.cfm

American University. (n.d.). *Women & politics institute*. Retrieved October 21, 2022, from https://www.american.edu/spa/wpi/

Antioch University. (n.d.). *Women in leadership 'Antioch university.'* Retrieved October 21, 2022, from https://www.antioch.edu/academics/leadership-management/certificates/women-in-leadership-certificate/

Arao, B., & Clemens, K. (2013). From safe spaces to brave spaces: A new way to frame dialogue around diversity and social justice. In L. Landreman (Ed.), *The art of effective facilitation: Reflections from social justice educators* (pp. 135–150). Stylus Publishing.

Baber, L. (2019). Understanding the needs of various diverse populations. In C. Akens, R. Wright-Mair, & J. Martin Stevenson (Eds.), *College students and their environments: Understanding the role student affairs educators play in shaping campus environments* (pp. 112–131). Charles C. Thomas Publisher.

Babson College. (n.d.). *CWEL scholars*. Retrieved October 21, 2022, from https://www.babson.edu/womens-leadership-institute/campus-programs/undergraduate-programs/cwel-scholars/

Baypath University. (n.d.). *Well program—Leadership development*. Retrieved October 20, 2022, from https://www.baypath.edu/academics/we-empower-learners-and-leaders/the-american-women-s-college-well-program/

Beatty, C. C., & Guthrie, K. L. (2021). *Operationalizing culturally relevant leadership learning*. Information Age Publishing.

Bell-Scott, P. (1984). Black women's higher education: Our legacy. *SAGE: A Scholarly Journal on Black Women, 1*(1), 8–11.

Bentley University. (n.d.). *Women's leadership program*. Retrieved October 21, 2022, from https://www.bentley.edu/university-life/diversity-equity-inclusion/womens-leadership-program

Brenau University. (n.d.). *Women's leadership certificate program*. Retrieved October 21, 2022, from https://www.brenau.edu/fineartshumanities/humanities-department/wlcp/

Bryn Mawr College. (n.d.). *Nonprofit executive leadership institute*. Retrieved October 21, 2022, from https://www.brynmawr.edu/socialwork/affiliated-centers-programs/nonprofit-executive-leadership-institute

Castellanos, M. (2016). Sustaining Latina student organizations. *Journal of Hispanic Higher Education, 15*(3), 240–259. https://doi.org/10.1177/1538192715592926

Cedar Crest College. (n.d.). *Undergraduate leadership certificate*. Retrieved October 21, 2022, from https://www.cedarcrest.edu/academics/business/leadership.shtm

Census Bureau. (2021). *Census regions and divisions of the United States*. https://www2.census.gov/geo/pdfs/maps-data/maps/reference/us_regdiv.pdf

Cohen, A. M., & Kisker, C. B. (2010). *The shaping of American higher education* (2nd ed.). Jossey-Bass.

College of Saint Benedict & Saint John's University. (n.d.). *Bonner leader program*. Retrieved October 21, 2022, from https://www.csbsju.edu/xpd/students/experience-based-programs/bonner-leader

College of Saint Mary. (n.d.). *Leadership*. Retrieved October 21, 2022, from https://www.csm.edu/student-life/get-involved/leadership

Corbin, N. A., Smith, W. A., & Garcia, J. R. (2018). Trapped between justified anger and being the strong black woman: Black college women coping with racial battle fatigue at historically and predominantly white institutions. *International Journal of Qualitative Studies in Education, 31*(7), 626–643. https://doi.org/10.1080/09518398.2018.1468045

Cottey College. (n.d.). *Serenbetz institute*. Retrieved October 21, 2022, from https://cottey.edu/serenbetz-institute/

Delgado-Guerrero, M., Cherniack, M. A., & Gloria, A. M. (2014). Family away from home: Factors influencing undergraduate women of color's decisions to join a cultural-specific sorority. *Journal of Diversity in Higher Education, 7*(1), 45–57. https://doi.org/10.1037/a0036070

DiPrete, T. A., & Buchmann, C. (2013). *The rise of women: The growing gender gap in education and what it means for American schools*. Russell Sage Foundation.

Domingue, A. D. (2015). "Our leaders are just we ourself": Black women college student leaders' experiences with oppression and sources of nourishment on a predominantly White college campus. *Equity & Excellence in Education, 48*(3), 454–472. https://doi.org/10.1080/10665684.2015.1056713

Dugan, J. P. (2017). *Leadership theory: Cultivating critical perspectives*. Jossey-Bass.

Duke University. (n.d.). *Baldwin scholars*. Retrieved October 21, 2022, from https://baldwinscholars.duke.edu/

Esposito, J. (2011). Negotiating the gaze and learning the hidden curriculum: A critical race analysis of the embodiment of female students of color at a predominantly White institution. *Journal for Critical Education Policy Studies, 9*(2), 143–164. https://eric.ed.gov/?id=EJ960609

Flores, J., & Garcia, S. (2009). Latina "testimonios": A reflexive, critical analysis of a "Latina space" at a predominantly white campus. *Race, Ethnicity and Education, 12*(2), 155–172. https://doi.org/10.1080/13613320902995434

Franklin Pierce University. (n.d.). *Women in leadership.* Retrieved October 21, 2022, from https://www.franklinpierce.edu/academics/programs/women-leadership.html

Greyerbiehl, L., & Mitchell, D. (2014). An intersectional social capital analysis of the influence of historically Black sororities on African American women's college experiences at a predominantly White institution. *Journal of Diversity in Higher Education, 7*(4), 282–294. https://doi.org/10.1037/a0037605

Guthrie, K. L., Teig, T., & Hu, P. (2018). *Academic leadership programs in the United States.* Leadership Learning Research Center, Florida State University.

Hartwarth, I., Maline, M., & DeBra, E. (1997). *Women's colleges in the United States: History issues and challenges.* National Institute on Postsecondary Education, Libraries, and Lifelong Learning.

Hollins University. (n.d.). *Batten Leadership Institute.* Retrieved October 21, 2022, from https://www.hollins.edu/offices-and-services/batten-leadership-institute/

Horowitz, D. L. (1993). The challenge of ethnic conflict: Democracy in divided societies. *Journal of Democracy, 4*(4), 18–38. https://doi.org/10.1353/jod.1993.0054

Institute for Women's Leadership at Rutgers University. (n.d.). *Institute for women's leadership.* Retrieved October 20, 2022, from https://iwl.rutgers.edu/

Kim, M., & Alvarez, R. (1995). Women-only colleges: Some unanticipated consequences. *The Journal of Higher Education, 66*(6), 641–668. https://doi.org/10.2307/2943834

Komives, S. R., Owen, J. E., Longerbeam, S. D., Mainella, F. C., & Osteen, L. (2005). Developing a leadership identity: A grounded theory. *Journal of College Student Development, 46*(6), 593–611. https://doi.org/10.1353/csd.2005.0061

Leath, S., & Chavous, T. (2018). Black women's experiences of campus racial climate and stigma at predominantly White institutions: Insights from a comparative and within-group approach for STEM and non-STEM majors. *Journal of Negro Education, 87*(2), 125–139. https://doi.org/10.7709/jnegroeducation.87.2.0125

Lewis, J. A., Mendenhall, R., Harwood, S. A., & Huntt, M. B. (2013). Coping with gendered racial microaggressions among Black women college students. *Journal of African American Studies, 17*(1), 51–73. https://doi.org/10.1007/s12111-012-9219-0

Linder, C. (2011). Exclusionary feminism: Stories of undergraduate women of color. *Journal About Women in Higher Education, 4*(1), 1–25. https://doi.org/10.2202/1940-7890.1066

Loyola University Chicago. (n.d.). *Gannon scholars: Gannon center for women and leadership.* Retrieved October 21, 2022, from https://www.luc.edu/gannon/gslp.shtml

Marthers, P. P. (2013). Did the women's colleges founded in the progressive era represent a new model? Connecticut College for Women as a case study. *American Educational History Journal, 40,* 221–239. https://eric.ed.gov/?id=EJ1144437

Mary Baldwin University. (n.d.). *Virginia women's institute for leadership.* Retrieved October 21, 2022, from https://marybaldwin.edu/vwil/#:~:text=Get%20ready%20for%20a%20lifetime,leadership%20training%20on%20the%20sidelines.

Meredith College. (n.d.). *Leadership programs.* Retrieved October 21, 2022, from https://www.meredith.edu/leadership-service/leadership-programs/

Miller-Bernal, L., & Poulson S. L. (Eds.). (2006). *Challenged by coeducation: Women's colleges since the 1960s.* Vanderbilt University Press.

Mount Holyoke College. (n.d.). *Student involvement studio.* Retrieved October 21, 2022, from https://offices.mtholyoke.edu/studentprograms/leadership/studio

Nanney, M., & Brunsma, D. L. (2017). Moving beyond cis-terhood. *Gender & Society, 31*(2), 145–170. https://doi.org/10.1177/0891243217690100

Notre Dame of Maryland University. (n.d.). *Bonner leaders.* Retrieved October 21, 2022, from https://www.ndm.edu/student-life/service-community-engagement/bonner-leaders

Palmieri, P. A. (1987). From Republican motherhood to race suicide: Arguments on the higher education of women in the United States, 1820–1920. In C. Lasser (Ed.), *Educating men and women together: Coeducation in a changing world* (pp. 49–64). University of Illinois Press.

Pennsylvania State University. (n.d.). *Leadership initiative.* Retrieved October 21, 2022, from https://hhd.psu.edu/undergraduate/leadership-initiative

Perkins, L. (1997). The African American female elite: The early history of African American women in the seven sister colleges, 1880–1960. *Harvard Educational Review, 67*(4), 718–757. https://eric.ed.gov/?id=EJ556456

Portland State University. (n.d.). *Undergraduate program women's leadership.* Retrieved October 21, 2022, from https://www.pdx.edu/academics/programs/undergraduate/womens-leadership-certificate

Rutgers University. (n.d.). *Women build.* Retrieved October 21, 2022, from https://myrbs.business.rutgers.edu/mentoring/women-build

Saint Mary's College. (n.d.). *Center for women's intercultural leadership: Saint Mary's College, Notre Dame.* Retrieved October 21, 2022, from https://www.saintmarys.edu/cwil

Salem College. (n.d.). *Leadership & service clubs.* Retrieved October 21, 2022, from https://www.salem.edu/clubs/leadership-service#:~:text=Leaders%20in%20Training%20is%20a,leadership%20legacy%20at%20Salem%20College

Scripps College. (n.d.). *LASPA fellowship: Scripps college in Claremont, California.* October 21, 2022, from https://www.scrippscollege.edu/laspa/programs/laspafellowship

Simmons University Institute for Inclusive Leadership. (n.d.). *Courses & learning journeys.* Institute for Inclusive Leadership. Retrieved October 21, 2022, from https://www.inclusiveleadership.com/courses-learning-journeys/arrive-thrive/?gclid=Cj0KCQjwhsmaBhCvARIsAIbEbH42NqZ6mtGTG6BkP8L0lYt12puCJy7xG75yog7UFuJU1Wd-MRmQilUaApQfEALw_wcB

Smith, D. G. (1990). Women's colleges and coed colleges: Is there a difference for women? *The Journal of Higher Education, 61*(2), 181–197. https://doi.org/10.1080/00221546.1990.11775104

Soares, L. (2013). *Post-traditional learners and the transformation of postsecondary education: A manifesto for college leaders* (pp. 1–18). American Council on Education.

Solorzano, D., Ceja, M., & Yosso, T. (2000). Critical race theory, racial microaggressions, and campus racial climate: The experiences of African American college students. *Journal of Negro Education, 69*(1–2), 60–73. https://psycnet.apa.org/record/2002-10183-005

Strange, C. C., & Banning, J. H. (2015). *Designing for learning: Creating campus environments for student success.* Jossey-Bass.

The College of New Jersey. (n.d.). *Women in learning and leadership (WILL).* Retrieved October 21, 2022, from https://will.tcnj.edu/

The University of Denver. (n.d.). *CWC leadership scholars.* Retrieved October 20, 2022, from https://academicaffairs.du.edu/cwc

The University of Texas at Austin. (n.d.). *College of Liberal Arts: The University of Texas at Austin.* Retrieved October 21, 2022, from https://liberalarts.utexas.edu/cwgs/projects-initiatives/inspire-leadership-program/index.html

Towson University. (n.d.). *Women's leadership collective.* Retrieved October 21, 2022, from https://www.towson.edu/about/administration/president/scholar/womens-leadership-collective.html

Tulane University. (n.d.). *Newcomb scholars program.* Retrieved October 21, 2022, from https://newcomb.tulane.edu/scholars

Tyson, M. (2019). Cultivating campus environments to support diverse student populations. In C. Akens, R. Wright-Mair, & J. Martin Stevenson (Eds.), *College students and their environments: Understanding the role student affairs educators play in shaping campus environments for student success* (pp. 88–111). Charles C. Thomas Publisher.

Tyson, M. (2021). Perspectives of adult undergraduate women working towards a degree. *Journal of Adult and Continuing Education, 27*(2), 248–266. https://doi.org/10.1177/1477971420934820

University of Maryland. (n.d.). *Home: Adele's circle of women.* Retrieved October 21, 2022, from https://adelescircleofwomen.umd.edu/

University of Michigan. (n.d.). *Women in learning and leadership (WILL).* Retrieved October 21, 2022, from https://umdearborn.edu/casl/life-casl/women-learning-and-leadership-will

Vaccaro, A., & Camba-Kelsay, M. (2016). *Centering women of color in academic counterspaces: A critical race analysis of teaching, learning, and classroom dynamics.* Lexington Books.

Watkins, S. R. (2020). *Contributions of student affairs professional organizations to collegiate student leadership programs in the late twentieth century* [Doctoral dissertation, Florida State University]. https://eric.ed.gov/?id=ED590037

Women's College Coalition. (2023). *Directory of Women's Colleges & Degrees.* https://www.womenscolleges.org

Wright-Mair, R. (2019). Creating a culture of inclusion in the classroom. In C. Akens, R. Wright-Mair, & J. Martin Stevenson (Eds.), *College students and their environments: Understanding the role student affairs educators play in shaping campus environments* (pp. 132–154). Charles C. Thomas Publisher.

Yosso, T. J., Smith, W., Ceja, M., & Solórzano, D. (2009). Critical race theory, racial microaggressions, and campus racial climate for Latina/o undergraduates. *Harvard Educational Review, 79*(4), 659–691. https://doi.org/10.17763/haer.79.4.m6867014157m707l

CHAPTER 3

THE MEANING TO OUR METHODS

Trisha Teig
Maritza Torres

Ignored, skipped over, presumed confusing: research methodology is often perceived as the unloved section of research writing. Alternatively, we hope you dig into this chapter to understand that the scaffolding of this book stands upon our methodology and methods. We have undertaken a significant challenge to upend traditional, dominant narratives of leadership. To manifest this hopeful disruption, we employed thoughtful implementation of narrative research methodologies (our overarching approach to the project) and methods (how we collected data and analyzed it) as well as theoretical and conceptual frameworks.

This chapter serves as an overview of paradigms, methodology, theoretical and conceptual frameworks, and research methods for the entire text. We share a review of how this study aligned across a large umbrella of narrative methodologies and within lenses that allowed the researchers/authors to co-explore the participants' narratives with intentionality. In this chapter, we also share the story of our collaborative process, including how we came together over several sessions to share ideas, thoughts, and inspiration. We examine all these steps through our conscious process to build a foundation for the book based on previous qualitative, narrative explorers.

A COMMON PURPOSE

As introduced in the preface, the foundations of the book began with a powerhouse team of leadership educator-scholars who shared excitement over gathering and sharing women's narratives of leadership. As researchers, we did not "find" or create these narratives ourselves. We did, however, participate in the process of their creation and interpreted their concepts in thematic chapters to learn across the narrative ideas. Our purpose was not to create just one account of women's lives in leadership; rather, we hoped to co-create a spectrum of truths and to leave our readers with excitement for what can be further explored. Riessman (2008) explained, "Narrative truths are always partial—committed and incomplete" (p. 186). We love the interwoven, complete incompleteness of the stories in this collection of narratives for the possibilities they represent, the hope they engender, and the unknown where they bravely venture.

Qualitative narrative methodology directly aligns with our purpose for this book—to dive into stories of women's lived experiences and how they examine, explore, and articulate those experiences in leadership in relationship to their salient identities. We recognize no story stands alone and therefore must be considered from its context and for its possibilities to understand the world in a new way.

> Stories operate within "interpretive communities" of speakers and hearers that are political as well as cultural actors. They build collective identities that can lead, albeit slowly and discontinuously, to cultural shifts and political change. Personal stories thus often operate as bids for representation and power from the disenfranchised. (Squire, 2008, p. 15)

In response to Squire's (2008) notation, we contend the collection and interpretation of these narratives is framed with the intention to emphasize that the personal is political (Lorde, 1983) and within that perspective, these narratives have liberatory power for the writers' agency to discuss and claim leadership narratives for themselves.

RESEARCH PROCESS

The book is based on a multi-site research project collecting narratives of women and their descriptions of understanding leadership. All sites received IRB approval at their institution to gather, analyze, and disseminate the narratives. All sites employed an electronic consent form for participants to choose to participate in the study. Each site had a research coordinator who facilitated the IRB, consent, and data collection process.

The Stellar Six

In Spring of 2021, our starting group of 12 met to discuss the possibility of co-creating a book that would capture women's narratives of leadership across a multitude of locations and participants. In our first meetings, the creative energy and excitement about the need for this project spurred our passion to move forward. The iterative, collaborative brainstorming led to decisions to collect the narratives at five different research sites and include one additional research project collaborator. These are listed in Table 3.1.

TABLE 3.1 Research Site Descriptions

Research Site/ Study	Program or Course	Research Site/ Study Coordinator	Participant Info
Florida State University	Leadership Learning Research Center—Undergraduate Leadership Studies Certificate: Gender and Leadership Course	Brittany Devies	Undergraduate college students
George Mason University	Women and Leadership Course	Julie Owen	Undergraduate college students
Rutgers University	Institute for Women's Leadership	Sasha Taner	Undergraduate college students
Rutgers University	Institute for Women's Leadership	Sasha Taner	Alumnae of the Leadership Scholars Certificate Program[*]
Texas State University—Alumnae from University of San Diego	Longitudinal Research Project of Women and Leadership	Paige Haber Curran	Alumnae 10 years post-undergraduate
Tulane University	Newcomb College Institute—Newcomb Scholars Program on Feminist Leadership	Julie Henriquez Aldana	Undergraduate college students
University of Denver	Colorado Women's College Leadership Scholars Program	Trisha Teig	Undergraduate college students

[*] Some data from Rutgers University was from a previously collected study. These data and collection methods are described further in the data collection section.

All participants listed in Table 3.1 were considered research site coordinators. In addition to this role, each site coordinator also served as a chapter author. In total, we have 18 chapter authors who contributed to the book. In addition to the chapter authors, 39 narrative authors are included in the volume. Narrative authors are the women who responded to our research prompt at each of the research sites. Each chapter integrates 3–5 narrative author stories as well as a narrative from the chapter author(s).

METHODOLOGY

We decided on narrative as a methodology because we were directly asking women to share their written narratives and wanted analytical tools to best understand the individual and collective stories we collected. We implemented specific tools of critical narrative methods in critical feminisms and counter-storytelling to analyze the narratives. Each chapter author employed a specific method of narrative within one of these frames. The authors collectively agreed to implement qualitative narrative methodology and narrative methods, but chose to implement distinct theoretical and/or conceptual frameworks based on the theme of their chapter.

Narrative methodology is an in-depth exploration into "stories lived and told" (Clandinin & Connelly, 2000, p. 20). In qualitative research, narrative methodology expanded in the 1980s and 1990s in direct response to educational research focused primarily on quantitative analytical formats of research (Clandinin & Connelly, 2000). Narrative methodologists do not all agree on a central perspective of narrative research; rather, the methodology is shaped by the discipline of the project, the perspectives of the researchers and participants, and the examination of narratives as part of the process of co-creating an understanding of larger meaning or grand narratives (Boje, 2001; Wortham, 2001).

In our project, the researchers/chapter authors are leadership educators, women, and leaders. We all have navigated our own experiences of opportunities and barriers in learning about, defining, developing in, and accessing positions of leadership. Clandinin and Connelly (2000) expressed, "Narrative is the best way of representing and understanding experience" (p. 18). Our goal was to share women's understanding of leadership from across a multitude of identities and spaces. These frames assisted the researchers in exploring the narratives of the participants in this study in their individual contexts and as aggregated larger themes.

Critical Perspectives on Narrative Methodology

The chapter authors employed critical narrative methodology (Dillard, 2020; Souto-Manning, 2014) across several theoretical foundations. Dillard

(2020) notes the intentionality of critical perspectives on narrative methodology as a framing and response to systemic inequity:

> With the introduction of the power of personal (and counter-) narratives, this type of research can focus on and highlight how individuals can share their own stories and narratives to begin to make new meaning that challenge and resist dominant narratives. (p. 49)

While narrative researchers, as a whole, are interested in analyzing the storied experience of individual lives, a critical lens to narrative furthers this conversation by implementing methods that center marginalized voices, question inequitable systems, and integrate questions about social location and positionality as factors in how a person creates, frames, and shares their story (Brockmeier & Carbaugh, 2001; Dillard, 2020). Further, we follow the tradition of narrative methodologies to "treat narratives as modes of resistance to existing structures of power" (Squire et al., 2013, p. 5) thereby activating a social justice response through the act of creating and exploring the narratives within the book.

Feminist Narrative Methodologies

Chapter authors also grounded their work in feminist narrative methodology. Feminist methodologies are rooted in feminist theories and practices that a researcher integrates into their work in research as praxis. These include the importance of acknowledging and investigating the profound, intricate lives of women, the recognition and continued challenge to address inequity for women in our society, and how women's intersecting identities in race/ethnicity, sexualities, and other salient social identities directly inform women's complex interactions within their worlds (hooks, 2000).

Bloom (1998) encourages narrative researchers to note "master scripts" from hegemonic narratives as well as validate and uplift counter-stories to this dominant, masculine-normative script within women's stories. She notes, "If feminists have an attraction to narrative, it is not the attraction to the traditional narrative, but the attraction to the feminist project of rewriting the master script" (Bloom, 1998, p. 70). We are excited to share work that builds on this disruption and reclaiming process through all narratives shared in this book.

FRAMEWORKS

In addition to the narrative methodologies used above, chapter authors implemented a theoretical frame to inform their exploration of the narratives. The pairing of the narrative and method with a theoretical lens allowed the researchers to understand the narratives in the chapter through critically applied microscopes, examining themes, connections, and new conceptualizations across the women's narrative experiences as singular entities. Theories employed in this process include critical race theory (CRT), critical feminisms, and intersectionality. These frames are described below in summary for reference.

Critical Race Theory

Developed as a lens to examine and highlight race in inequitable systems in law and policy, CRT (and subsequent additional critical race-gendered epistemologies) have since been applied in education and leadership scholarship (Delgado Bernal et al., 2012; Ladson-Billings, 1995; Magdaleno, 2021; Solorzano & Yosso, 2001, 2002). CRTs must (Solorzano & Yosso, 2002):

1. center race and the intersections of other social identities as important factors in recognizing the multiple, interlocking, unique experiences and layers of oppression in our systems;
2. emphasize capturing and supporting experiential knowledge as a crucial piece of knowing (Delgado Bernal et al. (2012) noted, "Experiential knowledge also allows researchers to embrace the use of counterstories, narratives, testimonios, and oral histories to illuminate... unique experiences" [p. 110]);
3. respond to and disrupt dominant ideologies;
4. be transdisciplinary and consider multiple perspectives across academic and professional sectors; and
5. stem from and push an agenda of social justice to purposefully disturb and deconstruct historic inequities in creation of a more just society.

In consideration of narrative methods, the perspective of multiple consciousnesses serves as a primary tool to implement theoretical analysis for CRT. Delgado and Stefancic (2001) clarified the concept:

> Multiple consciousness... holds that most of us experience the world in different ways on different occasions, because of who we are. If we pay attention to the multiplicity of social life, perhaps our institutions and arrangements will better address the problems that plague us. (pp. 55–56)

Critical Feminisms

Feminist theory represents a broad range of conceptualizations across disciplines. Primary perspectives include ideas from radical, liberal, critical, and postmodern perspectives (Dentith & Peterlin, 2011). Each of these feminisms offers unique insights on how to employ tools for systemic change.

Similar to CRT, feminisms recognize and emphasize the need to consider historical oppression and current contexts of sexism and genderism as structural, cultural factors in perpetuating inequities. Feminisms center gender in examining the roots of these inequities while also considering racialization, class, and other important social identities (Blackmore, 2006, 2013). For this book, we employ critical race feminism.

Berry (2010) employed critical race feminism (CRF) to emphasize centering Women of Color as primary knowledge-holders experiencing life in dominant culture. She noted, "CRT and CRF adherents like myself utilize narrative or storytelling as counterstories to the master narrative, the dominant discourse" (Berry, 2010, pp. 23–24). Leadership through an analysis of critical feminisms analyzes "gendered power relations that impact on social justice" (Blackmore, 2006, p. 186).

Intersectionality

Intersectionality theory asserts we must consider multiple, complex layers of social identities (race, ethnicity, gender identity, sexuality, etc.) in relationship to the interlocking systems of oppression that influence how different people experience the world (Collins, 2002; Crenshaw, 1992). A historically woven concept from Black feminist and Women of Color scholars and thought leaders, intersectionality as a phrase expanded in academic scholarship from the law to education to a multitude of spaces in the 20th and 21st centuries (Corlett & Mavin, 2014).

In relationship to our study, in her exploration of the intellectual history of intersectionality, Hancock (2016) describes narrative as "an especially useful discursive product, for it simultaneously empowers communication of specific intersectionality-like thought and serves as a strategy for acknowledging understanding and fixing failed solidarity" (p. 127). Authors in the study implemented intersectionality as a theoretical framework in relationship to narrative methods to question interlocking systemic oppressions across social identities to situate and understand narrative authors' articulation of self in relationship to their worlds (Museus & Griffin, 2011).

NARRATIVE METHODS

Narrative methods cover a dynamic and broad expanse of qualitative research across disciplines. Critical narrative analysis, considered an analytical process with emancipatory purpose, focuses our study further by enacting "critical meta-awareness" for social change through the power of narratives (Dillard, 2020, p. 49). Our authors employed critical narrative analysis through two narrative methods, counter-storytelling and feminist narrative analysis, and in some chapters, additional frameworks were used.

Counter-Storytelling

Critical race scholars emphasize counter-storytelling as a key method for disrupting dominant narratives that perpetuate harmful inequities in society (Bamburg & Andrews, 2004). As an intentional method of resistance, considering narratives from a lens of counter-storytelling can allow the researcher to see a person's story through the lens of disruption, activism, or change. Further, counter-storytelling aligns with the overall project goal to recognize how context informs the stories we share (Wagaman et al., 2018). To elaborate further:

> Dominant narratives were often taken for granted assumptions that go unquestioned. By intentionally bringing them to the forefront and naming them, participants [are] equipped to counter them with their own narratives, rather than devaluing their personal experiences because they did not fit the dominant narratives. (Wagaman et al., 2018, p. 9)

With a perspective on how the writers represented their stories in opposition to known, dominant ideas, our chapter authors employed this method to explore the multiple truths and complexities of the narrative authors' stories in relationship to their intersecting identities and contexts. These stories were then explored in how the storyteller deconstructed and remade the dominant ideology by first recognizing and then positioning their story in contrast to this "story most often told" (Dugan, 2017, p. 29).

Feminist Narrative Analysis

To apply feminist narrative analysis, researchers considered how the narratives may be unintentionally created to reify patriarchal structures because of women's lived experiences in a patriarchy itself (Bloom, 1998). The chapter authors explored how to intentionally recognize feminist narrative analysis as a tool to "put themselves on the same critical plane as their research respondents" (Bloom, 1998, p. 53). This was accomplished through the integrative process of writing their own narrative and considering its implications from the lens of critical feminisms. Further, the chapter authors sought to understand the narratives through contextual factors of systemic sexism, genderism, and patriarchy (Bloom, 1998).

DATA COLLECTION

Data in the book represent these five research sites and one previously collected study*. The previously collected data was a qualitative study focused on oral histories for refugee women participating in a women and leadership program at Rutgers University. In addition to these data, Rutgers University also collected data for the project as a research site. The research process for all data outside of the previous study is detailed below.

First, narratives were collected as a pilot for the project at the University of Denver in Spring of 2021. All remaining sites (excluding Tulane University) collected data in the Fall of 2021. In the Fall of 2021, New Orleans experienced the devastating impact of Hurricane Ida. Unfortunately, this natural disaster affected the start date and course experience of students and faculty at Tulane University. They were unable to collect data for the project due to this crisis.

For the sites at Florida State University (FSU), George Mason University (GMU), Rutgers University, and the University of Denver (DU), participants learned about the project through their participation in a leadership course focused on women and leadership (GMU), gender and leadership (FSU), or as part of a women and leadership program (DU; Rutgers). In each course, the instructor integrated a writing prompt as an assignment that was required for all students. From there, researcher-instructors facilitated the prompt in their classes by sharing about the project and at some sites, researcher-instructors offered storytelling structure training materials created by Crystaline Randazzo (a storytelling consultant) at the beginning of the course. Instructors supported students' preparation for and reflection on how they wanted to approach the writing of their narrative and encouraged creativity, emphasis on telling a story, and on how the students' identities connected with their understanding of leadership. Participants across all sites were given the following prompt:

> Describe a moment in your life of coming to understand your definition of leadership. Include how your understanding of leadership is related (or not) to your gender identity and/or expression and how this also intersects with your race/ethnicity, and any other important social identities for you. Consider how you experienced this moment—What did you see, hear, feel, taste? Use descriptive and sensory language. This story can be written in prose or poetry—be creative! 1–2 pages double spaced. A first and final draft will be expected.

In the case of the longitudinal study through Texas State University, the participants were not in a current course or program. Rather, they were reflecting on their memories of a collective educational experience in a gender and leadership course from 10 years prior. These narrative authors were in varied professional and personal life phases.

In the case of the previously collected data from Rutgers University (all in Chapter 15), we utilized findings from interviews conducted with graduates of the leadership scholars certificate program within the Institute for Women's Leadership. These narratives were from alumnae in the classes of 2007–2015 who are 1.5 or second generation immigrant women. These data were collected for a grounded theory, feminist oral history (Bornat & Diamond, 2007) dissertation project facilitated by Sasha Taner. Sasha noted her work was created through feminist interviewing and oral history co-creations. She used the seminal works of Gluck and Patai (1991), and DuPlessis and Snitow (2007), to base her data collection and augment the philosophical grounding of using women's words as a counter-creation of mainstream knowledge production, with the aim to give voice and a reverence to immigrant women's stories. These narratives, included in Chapter 15, are direct cuttings from the interview transcripts that connect to the focus of the book—clarifying the women's understandings of leadership within their experiences in a women's leadership program.

Data Collection and Analysis

Data collection and analysis occurred from Spring 2021 through Summer 2022 and implemented a broad and complex process of collaboration. This section reviews the process for data collection and analysis across pilot, first, and second rounds.

Pilot Data Collection and Analysis

The pilot data collected in the Spring of 2021 allowed the research team an initial opportunity to analyze narrative data. Thirty-two narratives were collected in Spring 2021 from courses in a women and leadership program at the University of Denver; from these, five narrative authors consented to participate in the study from this pilot group. These narratives were shared with all researchers in the project to initiate a pilot analysis to identify themes for the larger analysis process (Saldaña, 2012). The pilot narratives also became data in the larger project.

In June 2021, the author team met to co-analyze the pilot narratives. All authors had read the five narratives and came to the meeting with their own identified emergent codes. The team then collectively categorized the narratives across themes. The themes identified from the pilot narratives included empower, authentic, imposter syndrome, disruption, systemic oppression, justice, growth, harms, conceptualizing leadership, enacting leadership, and leader identity.

First Round Data Collection and Analysis

Participants were invited to join the project in the Fall of 2021 across all research sites. In December 2021, the site coordinators served as the first level of analysis for the narratives—determining which narratives would move forward to the larger group. The research site coordinators were instructed to move forward all narratives that met the criteria for the study. All chapter authors were contacted to participate in the first-round analysis in January and February of 2022.

In this first step of the process, researchers instituted a thematic analysis (Riessman, 2008) of direct text. These researchers were given the following a-priori code descriptions to consider each narrative for inclusion in the book and for thematic analysis process which was developed based on the themes identified in the pilot analysis process.

At the end of February 2022, the entire author team gathered to participate in a data analysis retreat for all the narratives collected in the study. Before the retreat, all authors were assigned 10 narratives to read and thematically analyze using the rubric shared in Table 3.2. Each narrative was read by at least three chapter authors. Authors were instructed to code each

TABLE 3.2 A Priori Codes

Code	Description/Synonyms
Empower	Empowerment, being empowered, role models, mentors, becoming
Authentic	Authenticity, body image/embodiment, pride & connection to identity, finding space to lead authentically, claiming ownership/seeing self as leader, embracing identity, intersectional awareness of previous understanding of dominant narratives
Imposter Syndrome	Feeling imposter syndrome, encountering stereotypes/dominant narratives, overcoming imposter syndrome
Disruption	Disrupting/overcoming stereotypes, beyond great man/hero theories of leadership, challenging cultural leadership stereotypes
Systemic Oppression	White supremacy, patriarchy, colonization, intersectionality, heterosexism/normativity
Justice	Bringing margins to the center, leading by example, responding to injustice, advocacy, allyship
Growth	Healing and growth, strength and power, changing, gaining confidence, reclaiming power
Harms	Pressure, stress, anxiety, risks/danger, rage, shame
Conceptualizing Leadership	Collective, emergent, teams, definitions of leadership
Enacting Leadership	Statements of leadership action or intention of action
Leader Identity	Explicit or implicit statement of seeing (or not seeing) self as leader, discussion of leader capacity and/or efficacy

narrative under three a-priori codes (Saldaña, 2012) ranked first, second, and third. Then authors could add a fourth emergent code (Saldaña, 2012) if they felt the narrative content included ideas not represented in any of the existing themes.

At the retreat, the team reviewed the collected coding analysis document and discussed if the themes captured the data accurately (or if something needed to be added from the emergent code ideas represented). The team identified emergent codes through this process including family, role models, and mentors. These were added to the original list. It was also determined that some of the a-priori codes could be grouped together. We also considered inter-coder credibility (Saldaña, 2012) by affirming narratives identified in the theme buckets aligned across multiple coders.

Second Round Analysis

Directly after the analysis retreat, the three coeditors took the feedback from the team to define and clarify the chapter themes and place the narratives within the chapters accordingly. The final themes selected were systemic oppression, harms, family, role models, imposter syndrome, growth, conceptualizing leadership, authentic, leader identity, and enacting leadership. We then shared the chapter themes and narratives out to the chapter authors. Following the assignment of the narratives to specific chapters and authors (based on the first-round thematic analysis process), chapter authors were asked to employ critical narrative analysis and aforementioned narrative methods and theoretical frameworks to analyze how each narrative told both a small story and a larger, culturally contextual story (Dillard, 2020; Phoenix, 2008).

Honoring the Stories: Fidelity and Trust

Bloom (1998) approaches the complexity of power dynamics in researcher–participant relationships as a dynamic network of intersubjectivities and context. Across the research sites, each researcher site coordinator and narrative authors connected differently with the narratives. Five of the researchers served as instructors of record for the courses where the narratives were collected. This introduced a dynamic of power to be considered for the relationship of the student–teacher and participant–researcher. Feminist narrative methodologists note this power dynamic is often present in narrative research and must be attended to through ethical structuring of the research methods and through clarity in consent throughout the research process (Bloom, 1998).

Unusual for a research project, the team decided to offer narrative participants to use their name or a pseudonym if their writing was selected for the book. This decision allowed the narrative writers agency over how their work and their names were shared. All but one narrative author chose to use her real name in the text.

The qualitative research literature emphasizes the relevance of trustworthiness and reliability to how the analysis process is conducted (Andrews et al., 2008; Silverman, 2006). In considering this factor for the project, the research team first had to consider how the word *trustworthy* interacted with the very act of asking for narratives. The process of requesting a person to share their story requires a level of trust. Trust that the researcher will treat the author's story with respect and trust that the narrative will be seen both for its words as provided and its potential for impact beyond the words on the page. In undertaking this process, each person—the narrative writers and the chapter authors—asked for and gave the gift of trust to be able to co-create a powerful collective story beyond our individual memoirs.

Kim (2019) acknowledges the importance of considering fidelity, or "the bond between the teller and the listener (researcher), which takes place by honoring the told story and preserving the value and dignity of the teller" (p. 30). While each chapter author did not have a direct relationship with each narrative author, the relationship between the two still required a connection across words, a trust from the narrative author that the chapter author would thoughtfully consider and honor their words. The chapter authors integrated a reflexive process to ensure they stayed true to the words and experiences of the narrative author. Further, the chapter authors were instructed that the narratives would be kept whole, in their entirety, to fully capture the narrative within the text.

Following the process of narrative collection, analysis, and writing, the research team instituted a process of member checking by sharing the draft chapters of the book with one or two authors of the narratives from each research site. These authors shared feedback on how their narrative was explored and how the chapter shaped the overall understanding of the narratives in the group. In one instance of this, a narrative author from GMU articulated trepidation to Julie (the research site coordinator) over the use of her narrative in the book. She came to Julie much later in the research process and expressed concern about the level of vulnerability and rawness she'd incorporated into her story—she wasn't certain she wanted it to be shared. Julie affirmed the author's concerns and confirmed she could choose to remove her narrative from the book, but she also offered to have the participant be one of the authors who reviewed their chapter. When the narrative author read the chapter, she cried—and then shared with Julie how happy she was to see how her story was integrated into the theme and the other narratives in the chapter. She felt seen and heard. When we heard this story—we cried—and then took her feedback as affirmation of our work and the overall purpose of the project. We believe all of these avenues (incorporating the entire narrative, name agency, chapter author reflexivity, and member checking) created a greater collaborative culture to the project and addressed some concerns of the power dynamics in research noted by Bloom (1998).

While we all had different roles, every person in this book is a part of our collective story. Manifesting a tangible, living document out of an ephemeral idea requires diligence, structure, and methodological and theoretical direction. Building on these foundations to move into the next section, we are excited to share the narratives, their interpretations, and what we have learned together.

REFERENCES

Andrews, M., Squire, C., & Tamboukou, M. (Eds.). (2008). *Doing narrative research*. SAGE. (Originally published in 2008)

Bamburg, M. G., & Andrews, M. (Eds.). (2004). *Considering counter-narratives: Narrating, resisting, and making sense*. John Benjamins Publishing Company.

Berry, T. R. (2010). Engaged pedagogy and critical race feminism. *Educational Foundations, 24*, 19–26. https://files.eric.ed.gov/fulltext/EJ902670.pdf

Blackmore, J. (2006). Social justice and the study and practice of leadership in education: A feminist history. *Journal of Educational Administration and History, 38*(2), 185–200. https://doi.org/10.1080/00220620600554876

Blackmore, J. (2013). A feminist critical perspective on educational leadership. *International Journal of Leadership in Education, 16*(2), 139–154. https://doi.org/10.1080/13603124.2012.754057

Bloom, L. (1998). *Under the sign of hope: Feminist methodology and narrative interpretation*. State University of New York Press.

Boje, D. M. (2001). *Narrative methods for organizational and communication research*. SAGE.

Bornat, J., & Diamond, H. (2007). Women's history and oral history: Developments and debates. *Women's History Review, 16*(1), 34–35. https://doi.org/10.1080/09612020601049652

Brockmeier, J., & Carbaugh, D. D. (Eds.). (2001). *Narrative and identity: Studies in autobiography, self, and culture*. John Benjamins Publishing Company.

Clandinin, D. J., & Connelly, F. M. (2000). *Narrative inquiry: Experience and story in qualitative research*. Jossey Bass.

Collins, P. H. (2002). *Black feminist thought: Knowledge, consciousness, and the politics of empowerment*. Routledge.

Corlett, S., & Mavin, S. (2014). Intersectionality, identity and identity work: Shared tenets and future research agendas for gender and identity studies. *Gender in Management: An International Journal, 29*(5), 258–276. https://doi.org/10.1108/GM-12-2013-0138

Crenshaw, K. (1992). Race, gender, and sexual harassment. *Southern California Law Review, 65*(3), 1467–1476. https://scholarship.law.columbia.edu/cgi/viewcontent.cgi?article=3872&context=faculty_scholarship

Delgado, R., & Stefancic, J. (2001). *Critical race theory: An introduction.* New York University Press.

Delgado Bernal, D., Burciaga, R., & Carmona, J. F. (2012). Chicana/Latina testimonios: Mapping the methodological, pedagogical, and political. *Equity & Excellence in Education, 45*(3), 363–372. https://doi.org/10.1080/10665684.2012.698149

Dentith, A. M., & Peterlin, B. (2011). Leadership education from within a feminist ethos. *Journal of Research on Leadership Education, 6*(2), 36–58. https://doi.org/10.1177/194277511100600201

Dillard, N. (2020). Designing research to dismantle oppression: Utilizing critical narrative analysis & critical participatory action research in research on mothering and work and beyond. *Journal of International Women's Studies, 21*(7), 47–60. https://experts.umn.edu/en/publications/designing-research-to-dismantle-oppression-utilizing-critical-nar

Dugan, J. P. (2017). *Leadership theory: Cultivating critical perspectives.* Jossey-Bass.

DuPlessis, R. B., & Snitow, A. (Eds.). (2007). *The feminist memoir project: Voices from women's liberation.* Rutgers University Press.

Gluck, S. B., & Patai, D. (Eds.). (1991). *Women's words: The feminist practice of oral history.* Routledge.

Hancock, A. M. (2016). *Intersectionality: An intellectual history.* Oxford University Press.

hooks, b. (2000). *Feminism is for everybody: Passionate politics.* South End Press.

Kim, J. H. (2019). *Locating narrative inquiry in the interdisciplinary context in understanding narrative inquiry: The crafting and analysis of stories as research.* SAGE.

Ladson-Billings, G. (1995). Toward a theory of culturally relevant pedagogy. *American Educational Research Journal, 32*(3), 465–491. https://doi.org/10.3102/00028312032003465

Lorde, A. (1983). The master's tools will never dismantle the master's house. In C. Moraga & G. Anzaldua (Eds.), *This bridge called my back: Writings by radical women of color,* 98–101. Kitchen Table.

Magdaleno, K. R. (2021). Preface: Tenets of critical race theory. *Journal for Leadership, Equity, and Research, 7*(3), 1–6. https://journals.sfu.ca/cvj/index.php/cvj/article/download/161/309

Museus, S. D., & Griffin, K. A. (2011). Mapping the margins in higher education: On the promise of intersectionality frameworks in research and discourse. *New Directions for Institutional Research, 2011*(151), 5–13. https://doi.org/10.1002/ir.395

Phoenix, A. (2008). Analysing narrative contexts. In M. Andrews, C. Squire, & M. Tamboukou (Eds.), *Doing narrative research* (2nd ed., pp. 64–77). SAGE.

Riessman, C. (2008). *Narrative methods for the human sciences.* SAGE.

Saldaña, J. (2012). *The coding manual for qualitative researchers.* SAGE.

Silverman, D. (2006). *Interpreting qualitative data: Methods for analyzing talk, text, and interaction* (3rd ed.). SAGE.

Solorzano, D. G., & Yosso, T. J. (2001). Critical race and LatCrit theory and method: Counter-storytelling. *International Journal of Qualitative Studies in Education, 14*(4), 471–495. https://doi.org/10.1080/09518390110063365

Solorzano, D. G., & Yosso, T. J. (2002). Critical race methodology: Counter-storytelling as an analytical framework for education research. *Qualitative Inquiry, 8*(1), 23–44. https://doi.org/10.1177/107780040200800103

Souto-Manning, M. (2014). Critical narrative analysis: The interplay of critical discourse and narrative analyses. *International Journal of Qualitative Studies in Education, 27*(2), 159–180. https://doi.org/10.1080/09518398.2012.737046

Squire C. (2008). *Approaches to Narrative Research*. ESRC National Centre for Research Methods Review Paper.

Squire, C., Andrews, M., & Tamboukou, M. (2013). *Doing narrative research?* SAGE. https://doi.org/10.4135/9781526402271

Wagaman, M. A., Obejero, R. C., & Gregory, J. S. (2018). Countering the norm, (re)authoring our lives: The promise counter-storytelling holds as a research methodology with LGBTQ youth and beyond. *International Journal of Qualitative Methods, 17*(1), 1–11 https://doi.org/10.1177/1609406918800646

Wortham, S. (2001). *Narratives in action: Strategies for research and analysis*. Teachers College Press.

PART II

EXPLORING THE NARRATIVES—CONTEXT

Art by Prasamsha

Society has taught women we are no more than what we can give. Even as a child I was an older sister first . . . I will now change the narrative and write my own meaning to being their older sister as that was written for me but by society. We are more than mothers, daughters, sisters, and wives. We are leaders who are authoritative, creative, ambitious, and fearless.

—Bianca, Chapter 6, p. 98

CHAPTER 4

"ME! I AM LEADERSHIP!"

Evolutions and Disruptions by Black, Indigenous, and Women of Color

Sharrell Hassell-Goodman
Aoi Yamanaka
Kristen Pender
Neda Kikhia

> *On campus, I've found warm waters that have helped me wade into my being. My experiences in shark tanks and kiddie pools have equipped me with the confidence necessary to know that sometimes I just have to paddle harder when confronted with choppy waves. Sharks will lurk and the ocean is fickle but sinking has never been an option.*
>
> —Pam

Black, Indigenous, and Women of Color (BIWOC) are often not the first group of people one thinks of when it comes to leadership. In fact, BIWOC are often rendered invisible or unrecognizable as leaders. Our hope throughout this chapter is to increase awareness of the impacts of systemic oppression within the larger context of leadership. We examine the ways in which BIWOC come to know themselves as leaders through the exploration of four narratives. Not only do these narratives reveal instances of racism, sexism, misogynoir, colonialism, and the like, but further examination of systemic oppression reveals the extent of endemic injustices present for BIWOC in leadership. Through counter-storytelling (Solórzano & Yosso, 2002) we describe the ways women have served as disruptors of systemic oppression and instead exhibited inclusive practices around leadership and opportunities for transformation and liberation. As we examined the narrative authors' stories, leadership was obviously and systematically denied to women because of their multiple minoritized identities. Their stories were a reclaiming of their humanity and of their ability to lead. As authors, we first offer our own counter-stories of systemic oppression in leadership before we delve into making meaning of student narratives.

> "Are you kidding me! This is not happening right now." I (Sharrell) was frantically talking to myself as I stood in front of a group of 40 volunteers after an older white male cut me off for the third time that meeting. In fact, I was smiling politely as he went on and on about the good old days and complained about the current expectations for volunteers. While I tried to respond and return the conversation back to the meeting agenda, he just continued to overtalk me. Other volunteers looked irritated or laughed and looked at me awkwardly as if to suggest that they too noticed his behavior; however, they did not intercede. He then went on to direct a specific question towards my white male supervisor, instead of deferring the question to me as the facilitator of the meeting. I stood there embarrassed that I was not able to effectively redirect the conversation and insulted that this volunteer did not trust my judgment to answer the question. While I recognize that the volunteer was from the baby boomer generation and a retired military man, likely socialized to identify the man with the most amount of power as the expert in the room, I couldn't help but feel silenced in that moment as a leader. A few women came up to me after the meeting, expressing their frustration for his male entitlement and my supervisor even made a joke about how this volunteer meant well but he couldn't really read the room.
>
> At first, I saw this situation as a slight or example of a microinvalidation in which a white male publicly interrupted and silenced my voice. As I thought about this in more detail, I realized this was a situation in which larger structural inequities create spaces for his behavior to be placated. My presence was erased temporarily for the purposes of not making anyone feel awkward. Further, by failing to acknowledge these seemingly small slights, we were making space for an exclusive environment in which other volunteers may too be afraid to share, as this incident could have established an unintentional precedence around expectations of whose perspective was most valuable. I felt the pressure to shrug it off. As a Black woman, I needed

> to "take the high road" for fear of confirming the "angry Black woman" stereotype. As a woman, I felt the need to demonstrate my ability to remain professional rather than appearing emotional or vulnerable. I learned to act in certain ways for fear of ridicule.

APPROACHING THE NARRATIVES

Throughout this chapter, critical race feminism (CRF; Wing, 2003) and counter-storytelling (Solórzano & Yosso, 2002) served as the theoretical framework and narrative method respectively to examine the impact of historically minoritized women's experiences in leadership. Both CRF and counter-storytelling are closely aligned with critical race theory (CRT), an interdisciplinary framework to understand the impact of systemic racism on society and within institutions such as housing, education, healthcare, and the legal system (Delgado & Stefancic, 2012).

CRF, a derivative of CRT, focuses on a race intervention in feminist discourse, or more specifically, "embraces feminism's emphasis on gender oppression within a system of patriarchy" (Wing, 2003, p. 7). CRF offers recognition of the breadth and depth of women's perspectives beyond a monolithic experience for BIWOC (Wing, 2003). CRF highlights and centers the experiences of Women of Color to interrupt essentialist norms and expectations (Wing, 2003), embracing a deeper examination of BIWOC's lived experiences and deeper consciousness (Doharty & Esoe, 2022; Evans-Winters & Esposito, 2010). CRF concerns multiple forms of oppressions and discriminations (e.g., White patriarchy) experienced by BIWOC, which differ from the experiences of Men of Color and White women (Evans-Winters & Esposito, 2010). The term intersectionality (Crenshaw, 1989) best describes the specific type of discrimination of the double marginalized identities of both race and gender (Combahee River Collective, 1986; Dill & Zambrana, 2009; Rosenthal, 2016). Intersectionality, a hallmark of CRF, describes the interlocking oppressive structures that overlap to create a more nuanced form of discrimination based upon one's place in society or one's social identities (Crenshaw, 1989).

Counter-storytelling is a technique that acknowledges the experiences of people of minoritized identities (Solórzano & Yosso, 2001, 2002); critical race methodology is concerned with intersecting oppression present in research and is intended to transform conditions that maintain oppressive aspects of research. The technique of storytelling is a healing practice for communities and serves as a tool for maintaining and preserving persistence while marginalized individuals work to move beyond deficit perspectives and racial injustice (Goessling, 2018; Ladson-Billings & Tate, 1995; Solórzano & Yosso, 2002). Counter-storytelling focuses on impacts of structural inequities present in leadership and is a form of resistance, as it creates solidarity and confronts White supremacy as dominant narratives (Goessling, 2018; Solórzano & Yosso, 2002). Not only does counter-storytelling, a critical narrative tool, humanize the experience of BIWOC, it builds on the fundamental exploration of CRF to better understand BIWOC's relationship with power beyond the notions of race and gender. Collectively, CRF and counter-storytelling will assist in the exploration and deconstructing of various forms of oppression within the context of leadership in this chapter.

EXPLORING THE NARRATIVES

Our aim with this chapter is to engage in a CRF approach, using narrative analysis of counter-storytelling to explore systemic oppression within the larger context of leadership. The narratives below explore how BIWOC experience systemic oppressions in leadership, and how they come to acknowledge themselves as leaders. For the purposes of this chapter, we examine four narratives to better understand the ways several BIWOC explored leadership. Further, we utilize an intersectional lens to examine the barriers present in leadership and acknowledge the complexities of real-world experiences and systemic power structures that exclude BIPOC from leadership.

Pam: "Bite Me"

This first narrative is the story of Pam, a Latina college student managing her disability, womanhood, and status as a first-generation college student (FGCS), navigating a predominantly White male space in the academy.

> My lungs, heart, and brain are crucial components of my livelihood. Every thought, breath, and pump of blood throughout my body are effortlessly completed. Yet, the moment I get a headache, or can't catch my breath, my body's response is immediate and I become hyper-aware that something is amiss. It is the context of these situations that make me fixated entirely on the specific area of my body that is somehow not functioning like the rest. This hyper fixation exists in other parts of me: my identity. I am Latina and I become so aware of this when everyone around me is white and doesn't even know the difference between Colombia the country and Columbia the school in New York. I have a chronic illness and I become so aware of this at the start of every year when my medical insurance renews and I just have

to pray that no new laws or company policies are going to impact my coverage. I am a first-generation college student and I become so aware of this when my peers always have job security postgraduation because their parents own a company. I am all these things at once and it makes my identity multifaceted. All these categories intertwine effortlessly to make my being; however, I often become confronted with situations that easily untangle my interconnected identities and cast a spotlight on one facet of my being. My experience with leadership has caused me to become hyper-aware of my gender—this is something that I've grown to manage in the many waters I've encountered and prepare myself for the pools I've yet to enter.

I joined the National Speech and Debate Association my freshman year of high school. Here, I learned that the stereotype of lawyers being sharks is rooted in the training tanks that were crucial to building their icy fierce exterior: a debate team. The turbulent waters of being on a debate team required hours of preparation, research, and drilling. Going into a round with the confidence of a great white, I had my perfectly crafted argument just for an even stronger team to destroy it with a tsunami of rebuttals and counter evidence. The competitive nature of debate is given. What I had not been prepared for was the overwhelming feeling of discomfort when I would walk into a room and be the only girl present—this did not deter me, until it did. During partnered questionings, somehow, I was left out of crucial discussions despite the valid points I made. Somehow, my voice was never loud enough. Somehow, my voice was never strong enough. Somehow, my arguments were never acknowledged; that is, until my male partner repeated them. Soon, I realized I was not the only one to feel this. The girls on the team shared their experiences and we spoke to our coach about how we felt. It was outright disrespectful to work for several hours and give up a weekend to attend a debate tournament just to receive a judge's comment form with one word on it: "pretty." My teammate fumed over her judge's response. My other teammate was irritated that another had the audacity to write about her professional attire being too flashy. We were judged on components that had nothing to do with our public speaking nor the content we were presenting. Our male teammates thought we were being dramatic.

It's been 6 years since I competed on a debate team. I've since found solace in my womanhood. In my sorority, full of women; in the Women in Pre-Law Society, the Hispanic Latinx Student Association, and more—I've found comfort in my intersectionality. On campus, I've found warm waters that have helped me wade into my being. My experiences in shark tanks and kiddie pools have equipped me with the confidence necessary to know that sometimes I just have to paddle harder when confronted with choppy waves. Sharks will lurk and the ocean is fickle but sinking has never been an option.

Pam's narrative illuminates systemic issues of colonialism, xenophobia, racism, sexism, patriarchy, ableism, and classism. Pam stated that everyone around her is White and does not even know the difference between Colombia, the country, and Columbia, the school in New York. LatCrit theorists (Mutua, 1999; Shelton, 2018; Solorzano & Yosso, 2001) argued that the colorized system of racial oppression has been the principal racial system, which has significantly influenced how individuals think about race in the United States. This indicates that White individuals have the power to categorize and oppress racial groups, to develop the system of identifying Latinx individuals as foreign and attempt to eliminate them. This notion of "foreign" is essentially the issue of xenophobia. Thus, the fact that individuals cannot distinguish between Colombia—the country—and Colombia—the school in New York—is rooted in colonialism, xenophobia, and racism.

Pam's narrative also indicates FGCSs' struggles in leadership. Pam discussed the issue of access to resources (for her, it was health insurance coverage and professional and social networks). As Pam has learned to manage her struggles and has become prepared for the future, many FGCSs have learned to manage how to cope with being "presumed incompetent" (Harris & Gonzáles, 2012, p. 1). Pam described this, stating, "I've grown to manage in the many waters I've encountered." In a society where colonialism, xenophobia, racism, and classism are pervasive, many FGCSs with multiple marginalized identities, such as Pam, are more vulnerable to systemic oppressions.

White people and males possess power related to race and gender, while BIWOC like Pam, are dehumanized by systemic issues. Pam embraces her multifaceted identity, but experiences of marginalization create a sense of separateness for her. These are the moments in which she expressed feeling othered. Pam's narrative begins with a whole-bodied description of awareness, informed by her chronic illness, of when something seems off. She knows these truths in her brain and her heart; feels the pain of being othered through a somatic experience in her body. A debate team judge recognized her as a second-class citizen and had lower expectations for her, as shown when Pam and her debate team received a judge's comment form with one word on it: "pretty." Due to these biases and experiences of microaggressions, Pam felt socially isolated or invisible and perceived greater pressure to perform and to prove her capabilities (Solórzano et al., 2000; Turner, 2001). These experiences were also taxing in terms of her energy, time, and productivity, making her cautious about possible consequences and requiring her to defend herself (Owen, 2020). Like Pam, historically marginalized individuals are required additional time, energy, and emotional and cognitive labor—this is called the "inclusion tax" according to Melaku and Beeman (2022, p. 1)—to navigate White spaces or resist White norms (Melaku, 2019; Melaku & Beeman, 2022). This inclusion tax influences Pam's experiences in navigating the overarching systemic oppressions of patriarchy, misogyny, and ableism as well as Whiteness. In the end, Pam recognized strength in her intersectional identities and found herself, through the embrace of spaces filled with the love and support of other women—"I've found warm waters that have helped me wade into my being."

Mia: "My Gender and Leadership Journey"

Like Pam, Mia, a cisgender Black female, also experienced biases and microaggressions in circumstances where her voice was not heard.

> As a college Senior, I have experienced many different instances of leadership situations and opportunities. George Mason University is the second university I have attended, so I have been able to meet and work with many diverse groups throughout the years. In the college setting, we tend to be assigned a lot of group assignments where we must all work together to reach a common goal. The purpose of these assignments is to likely gather many different insights, and to get students more comfortable collaborating within a group setting. Although these assignments are designed to take students out of their comfort zones, sometimes these situations can be uncomfortable, especially given some particular circumstances.
>
> I would like to tell a story about an instance that occurred during my freshman year of college at my past university. A little background about myself before I begin: I am a cisgender black female, but I am of a very light complexion, so sometimes my race goes under the radar and people are sometimes too nervous to pose the question: "What are you?" I was a student in a Communications 101 class, and we had a group project that was going to be due within the upcoming weeks. I cannot remember the particular details of the assignment (obviously something about communicating,) but I do remember that I was assigned to a group including four cisgender, white males. "Great," I thought to myself, as I could already smell the entitlement from this group, and I was right. These four guys barely asked my opinion about what kind of project I thought would be best, however they wanted me to document (or be the notetaker) for everything that they said??? And when they didn't quite get the gist of whatever reading we were to do for the assignment, then they would ask me kindly, "did you do the reading?" or in layman's terms: please tell us everything you read so we can pretend that it was us who gathered this information! Please!!! I felt utterly disgusted and used by this group, and that is when I realized that men are not always the leaders they were "born" to be, and just because they were born male does not mean they were born a leader.
>
> Since then, I have been able to be a part of a few all-female group assignments and the case is always much different from the story above. Women like to hear each other out, weed out what's good or bad from EVERYONE'S viewpoint and take on roles that best suit their individual personalities. The

> case is always extremely different in a group of all women and one man, the male tends to be submissive and pretends that they do not know anything and just "goes with the flow."
>
> Conclusively, these occurrences have taught me exactly what this class puts into words which is: Leadership is not a trait that people are born with, leadership is taught and ANYONE (no matter their race, gender, class, religion, or any other intersection) can be a leader. A good leader takes on many different viewpoints, stances, and opinions to lead everyone involved towards a positive direction. It does not matter if someone was born George Washington's great-great-great-great grandson/granddaughter, if they were not taught good leadership qualities, then they cannot be a good leader.

Mia's male counterparts expressed misogynistic perceptions by asking her to do the labor (course readings and note taking) without considering her opinion. This misogyny indicates that not only are BIWOC expected to be submissive, but they are also still perceived as inferior to White male counterparts. Additionally, Mia's narrative addresses the issues of dominant norms of leadership and gendered leadership. Mia mentioned, "I realized that men are not always the leaders they were 'born' to be, and just because they were born male does not mean they were born a leader." This statement addresses the fact that current narratives of leadership are still dominated by ideas and norms created by and for White, male, cisgender, and heterosexual individuals (Guthrie & Chunoo, 2018). While Mia did not address this explicitly, it is possible that she developed the dominant norms of "who should be a leader" from socialization (please see Chapter 12 for more discussions of how socialization influences leadership identity development). Mia began to question her progressions of understanding of "who should be a leader." When the male group members required Mia to serve as a notetaker and took undue credit for her work, she recognized an exploitation of labor resulting from buying into the myth of "men are automatically leaders."

Associating leadership with gender is dangerous. Mia mentioned, "Women like to hear each other out, weed out what's good or bad from everyone's viewpoint and take on roles that best suit their individual personalities." The way Mia described women's leadership was tinged by her internalized oppressions, and she described leadership in gendered ways because her definitions were aligned with certain notions of women's leadership, such as that "women tend to lead in more participatory or democratic styles" (Owen, 2020, p. 167). However, the gender approach is based on cisgender, heterosexual perspectives and excludes transgender, nonbinary, and intersex individuals as well as individuals whose leadership styles are not aligned with gender stereotypes (Owen, 2020). Thus, degendering leadership is important (Katuna, 2019). However, Owen (2020) also argued that individuals' identities and bodies are not separable in leadership spaces, and that instead of degendering leadership, it is important to reevaluate how individuals' multiple identities and embodied selves influence how they lead and how their leadership is perceived (Butler, 2006). In this sense, regendering instead of degendering leadership may be the correct path, because regendering leadership examines "how our embodied selves shape how we lead and how that leadership is shaped" (Owen, 2020, p. 167). While Mia acknowledged that anyone can be a leader, and that a good leader takes on various viewpoints, stances, and opinions, she unconsciously associated leadership with gender, and thus she could oppress others who do not fit into the gender norms. Mia ultimately incorporated a more inclusive viewpoint of leadership; however, tension exists between her gendered argument and her more expansive view. In light of this tension, she started to be more critical about how gender shapes individuals' practice in leadership.

Isabel: "Benevolent Sexism"

Similar to Mia, Isabel became more critical about associating leadership with gender. Isabel described how she became a feminist throughout this reflection below. After taking a gender and leadership course, she developed an attitude around agency and her interest in learning and examining her experience around leadership advanced.

> My inspiration also came from a recent experience at work where I am forced to turn on my camera at 9:00 a.m. for a daily meeting. To understand my reflection, first, some background. I am currently a single mother to an 8-year-old girl, I work full time, and I go to school full time. In addition, I am heavy set, and while that is not impacting my health too much currently, it is affecting my sleep, rest, body aches, and self-esteem. I feel that my male counterparts can roll out of bed, wear a hoodie sweatshirt, and baseball cap. They don't have school-aged children and don't mind getting up for work at 5:00 a.m. I, on the other hand, am typically up until 2:00 a.m. doing schoolwork. I get up at 7:00 a.m. at the latest to get ready for the day. Get my child ready, make breakfast and lunch, and drop her off at school when the doors open between 8:30–8:40 a.m. By the time I am rushing home to jump on the call, I may or may not have brushed out my unruly hair and put on make-up. My boss once commented that I looked tired. I knew I wasn't tired but realized that I "looked tired" if I didn't have a winged liquid liner on my eyelid.
>
> It's because of these unfair expectations of women that I thought of this concept of the dual female both day and night. We must be all four or more

in one person. It's not fair, it's not right, but that's what our society believes. Luckily for me, I received a nice response from my boss regarding being on camera. While the war is not over, a small battle has been won. I still must get on camera each morning, but so does everyone else. Including managers who were not doing so previously.

Taking this course has changed my thought process in a few ways. The first is through knowledge. There are certain concepts that I didn't know were a "thing." One of the most interesting concepts to me is that of "benevolent sexism." According to Owen (2020), benevolent sexism refers to a more understood type of prejudice in which women are stereotyped as affectionate, delicate, and sensitive (p. 184). This reminds me of the times when my boss uses curse words and then apologizes to me because I'm the only female on the team. It's as if I can't handle hearing some attitude and temper and terms that are used for emphasis because of my gender.

I learned that as a woman, I would like to lead through adaptive leadership with adaptive solutions. That means that I will mobilize people who report to me, or to whom I have influence over to solve issues. By leading even when I am not a manager or someone's direct supervisor, I can create positive organization, systemic, or social change in the workplace, school, community, and even at home. Critical theory, which according to Owen (2020) is the social theory oriented toward critiquing and changing society as a whole, in contrast to traditional theory...I would also like to learn through emotionally intelligent leadership. I believe that it's important to have a consciousness of the following three: self, others, and contexts.

Another way in which this course has changed my attitude is through agency. I will know my empowerment and be proud of what I bring to the table. I will not think of myself as less worthy or an imposter. Instead, I will focus on my leadership self-efficacy. As a woman, I will surely face some additional obstacles to becoming a leader in the workplace. Some of these obstacles include the sticky floor, the concrete wall, maternal wall, glass ceiling, glass cliff, double bind, leaky pipeline, microaggressions, and even the gender pay gap. I will do what I can to avoid burnout by using skills that I learned in my other integrative course this semester. For example, through meditation, mindful meals, gratitude, and so on. In this way, I can maintain critical hope when I face adversities.

I find that the only sure way to continue to develop leadership abilities and insights is through my love of learning. I firmly believe that knowledge is power, and ignorance is bliss (or epistemic privilege when folks take advantage of that ignorance). Being a lifelong learner doesn't necessarily mean that I will continue formal education, although that is the goal. However, I can learn through reading textbooks, watching Ted Talks, being a mentor, or personal observations.

The most important concept I've learned about this semester is that I am a feminist. Being a feminist in the wave now means that I don't have to be

> perfect. My thoughts, ideas, and morals may not perfectly align with everyone else. Albeit I am a feminist through and through and proud of it! (Even if I'm a bad one...)

Isabel shared examples of how systems create expectations about performance or ways in which she experienced bias as a woman in the workplace. Isabel was subject to a specific type of benevolent sexism when her supervisor apologized for using foul language, an indication that she was too delicate or sensitive to hear it (Owen, 2020). Although Isabel shares frustration for "unfair expectations of women" regarding physical appearance, she is still beholden to them when she expressed relief that she "received a nice response from my boss regarding being on camera." The work environment that suggests that Isabel is fragile is still hostile in that Isabel must adhere to physical standards in order for her to be favored. As long as she maintains her supervisor's approval, she will benefit from her current working environment; however, her long-time success will be predicated on her ability to maintain this performance. This indicates that systems create conditions for ways in which women show up in professional settings that differ in comparison to their male counterparts.

Isabel, a nontraditionally aged student, managed the tug and pull from both the educational and work environments in which she had to balance the taxing demands of coursework and her job. There was a pressure to navigate these spaces that compromised her wellness, but they are required for her to advance her occupational opportunities as a single mother. Isabel's recognition of the microaggressions that she experienced created a sense of empowerment for the future, and she demonstrated a desire to persevere in the future. Although this sounds promising, it continues to promote grit ideology, personal attributes, and characteristics that allow you to overcome adversity (Duckworth et al., 2007), in which she is responsible for overcoming these hardships, instead of holding the system accountable for creating additional barriers that women must persist in navigating. While Isabel recognizes that systems are not meant for her, she continues to increase her grit by bolstering strategies for perseverance as she finds herself unable to change the system. Isabel is still evolving as a feminist and holds herself captive to expectations when she calls herself a "bad feminist," indicating her continuous evolution.

Camiya: "Thank You, Colonization"

Both Isabel and Camiya strive to be a better leader, but Camiya, a Native and queer-identifying student, acknowledges the issues of colonialism and the intersectional oppression she experiences as a result of her Indigenous and LGBTQ+ identities. Through sarcasm, Camiya mocks larger social structures that inhibit her ability to lead. This points to the irony in leadership that is situated to advance liberatory approaches to leadership but that continues to suppress and control BIWOC.

> Thank you, colonization.
> I love you so much.
> For the stereotypes of how I should be as a Native,
> For telling me I am not Native "enough" because of my lighter skin,
> For not living on the rez, for being a city Native,
> For not growing up immersed in my culture.
> So, how could I lead despite not following your ideas of being Native?
> Thank you, I appreciate it so much I could marry you.
> However, I am grateful I can lead a group of People of Color as a queer person, so actually, thank you for the opportunity.
>
> I at first was a confused teenager when handling leadership.
> In the Native club, a participant, solely there as a presence.
> Later, the vice president, helping plan events and volunteering more in my community.
> Because I wanted to learn more about myself, my people, my community as a city Native.
> Another year later, president of Indigenous peoples united,
> My first test at my leadership skills.
> What even was that?
> Learning how to lead a group of people with a common interest? Dictatorship?
> I do all the work?
> I was unsure.
> The mixture of very few people, lack of confidence, and my limited knowledge
> Resulted in a lot of pressure on myself
> A very stressful and draining time.
>
> After some reflection and discussion with mi oso mámá,
> I realized it should be a TEAM effort,
> Not me doing all the work, that adds stress.
> So, because of mi oso mámá, I was able to better myself as a leader for my last year as president.
> Less pressure!
> Less stress!
> Teamwork!

> The moment I learned how I could better myself even more?
> Being asked,
> What is leadership?
> The warm fall day,
> With a purple marker and paper,
> Writing in BIG letters,
> ME!
> I am leadership.
> And everyday, I work to better myself
> So I can help my community, My people
> My Native American people
> My Mexican people
> My LGBTQ+ people.
>
> I give thanks to The Creator,
> With a bundle of sage in my hand, the powerful scent lingering around me,
> For the opportunities I have been given to lead myself and others.
> Even though I am still at times a confused person handling leadership.

Camiya described the ways in which systems of oppression collide and create inequities that are counteractive to her Indigenous leadership approach. Centering the needs of people in the community takes precedence over individuals' needs. Showing respect to the land, ancestors, and the Creator, and maintaining collective ideologies counter Western ideas of leadership (Merculieff & Roderick, 2013). Camiya called out to her elders, mi oso mámá, for strength and inspiration to lead beyond the constraints of colonial expectations. The omnipresence of colonial and Western ideals shows up and situates leaders in positional roles such as president and vice president. However, Camiya disrupted them through the implementation of a team and provided space for humility. Camiya disrupted White supremacist, patriarchal, and heteronormative expectations around single leaders' expectations by demonstrating a value for a community of leaders: "I realized it should be a TEAM effort. Not me doing all the work."

Camiya's regular use of sarcasm throughout (e.g., "Thank you, colonization. I love you so much... Thank you, I appreciate it so much I could marry you") serves as a mechanism to disrupt normative expectations around leadership and how leaders should present themselves and who they should be. In the end, she recognized there will always be times of confusion and uncertainty and that she should have gratitude for the opportunity. When she says, "I give thanks to The Creator" she is indicating a larger connection to nature and spirituality. Even though Camiya described herself as "still at times confused," she also recognizes the opportunities granted to her and sees a way forward as she explores leadership by breaking boundaries and challenging systemic discrimination against women who look and identify like her.

WEAVING THE NARRATIVES

Numerous overlapping themes are apparent among the four narratives featured in this chapter. Each narrative addressed a misalignment between the narrative authors' multiple identities, including gender, and dominant norms of leadership. For example, Camiya struggled to reimagine or imagine leadership in ways that are inclusive of her lived experiences as an Indigenous and LGBTQ+ woman. Camiya, like others, wanted to break free from leadership roles that are centered on colonial and patriarchal approaches and are constraining and oppressive in nature. These women desired communal expectations regarding leadership that differed from hierarchical structures and that instead focused on community obligations and valued community elders. With a focus toward advocating for and with others, these women shared their hopes and desires for the future centered around ways they might be able to enact their leadership, free from assumptions based on their identities that dictate how society expects them to show up as leaders. However, in Mia's case, she unconsciously associated leadership with gender, and this also indicates that traditional roles of women bind how they can enact leadership; thus, this limits how women approach and respond as leaders and engage in leadership.

One of the most notable struggles that all the participants experienced was how their voice was a mechanism for interpreting assumptions about leadership, and many are still reconciling how to advocate for themselves and for others. Each of the women's unique environments created a particular type of constraint as they navigated oppressive structures in leadership: Isabel was bound by work expectations, whereas Pam's restrictive school environment created a challenging dynamic. Camiya discussed larger social structures such as colonialism and heteronormativity that continue to impact her environment and how she showed up as a leader. Mia felt silenced and used in a group of privileged, young men. Ultimately, it was a struggle to reimagine leadership in ways that were inclusive of their lived experiences (Liu, 2020; Owen, 2020). Leadership based on racism, sexism, colonialism, classism, heterosexism, ableism, and xenophobia fosters oppressive constraints. To interrupt these systemic issues, we need to emphasize liberatory and transformational approaches to leadership.

APPLYING THE NARRATIVES

> I (Aoi) sometimes become extremely tired of my effort to fit into U.S. society and academia as a Japanese, non-native English speaker. When I was a student, some American students were reluctant to work on group projects with me because they thought that I would not be able to contribute to the groups and that my lack of knowledge or English skills (based on their perceptions) would jeopardize their grades. Also, I have experienced numerous situations where my voice was not heard or valued. At the same time, throughout my academic career, I have learned not to vocalize my opinions explicitly as a Woman of Color. Because of these experiences, I purposely started to avoid being the first person to speak up on any occasion. By doing this, I could take the time to articulate my thoughts thoroughly so that my voice would be valued, and I could avoid vocalizing my opinions too explicitly. However, I recently noticed that my avoidance of being the first speaker actually reinforces stereotypical views of Asian women (e.g., submissive, passive, docile, invisible). Furthermore, my actions could also reinforce stereotypical views of other Women of Color. However, being a foreigner whose English is not native requires me to develop more self-esteem to be the first person to speak up, and I have been gradually developing my self-esteem and being the first speaker whenever the opportunity arises.
>
> Recently I had an opportunity to work professionally with another Japanese professional in my native language, Japanese. I did not know what I had been missing until this moment regarding being truly comfortable with the environment and authentic to myself. Then I had an "aha" moment: "This is probably what many professionals, especially dominant groups, feel." To be honest, this is something that I did not want to know because I realized that I have been forcing myself to fit into the dominant culture of professional life and I need to continue to do so as a Japanese, non-native English speaker. But I sometimes become extremely tired of my effort to fit into the dominant culture. Now, I keep code-switching by analyzing environments and occasions and negotiating with systems and power dynamics in the professional field.

As we see through all reflections in this chapter, without the critical acknowledgment of colonized cultures and power dynamics, systems reinforce prioritizing privileged communities and excluding minoritized communities by maintaining social control over their daily lives and opportunities (Dugan, 2017; Guthrie & Chunoo, 2018). In applying a CRF lens, we see how leadership continues to promote Western ideals of leadership in ways that are problematic but particularly troubling for women engaging in leadership (Collinson, 2011; Dugan, 2018; Soria & Johnson, 2020). Leadership practices are not only concerning but also inaccessible as we consider communities that are most often excluded based on historical legacies and expectations around knowledge (Teig & Dilworth, 2021). Although leadership identity development is often measured on an individual level, there is a need to consider the impact of larger overarching systems of power (Bitton & Jones, 2021; Turman et al., 2018). This is helpful to understanding the concept of leadership as a process of self in relation to others (Guthrie et al., 2013; Ostick & Wall, 2011; Owen et al., 2017). Further, by paying close attention to the environment as a barrier for inclusion, we can begin to negotiate racial and gender dynamics and involvement in leadership (Ely et al., 2011). Thus, culturally responsive conceptualizations of leadership should question Western civilization's reliance on colonialism and disrupt existing power differences between BIWOC and dominant groups.

As authors, we could resonate with the four narratives we analyzed based on our own experiences. We found similarities; yet each narrative author provided viewpoints of systemic oppressions in leadership based on their multiple identities. For many of the participants, the pathway for leadership often included recognition of the myths of leadership and analysis of how BIWOC were not often identified as a leader. BIWOC were also required to either increase their grit or disrupt White norms. All of them, whether they engaged in disruptions of the systemic oppression experienced or not, were required to reconcile stereotypes and expectations placed upon them. There was a need among these narrative authors to reconstruct inclusive leadership, to redesign, reimagine, and reconstruct BIWOC as leaders, "Me! I am a leadership!"

We, as BIWOC, hope that leadership educators find ways to decenter Whiteness in our interpretation and adoption of leadership and center BIWOC ways of knowing and enacting leadership. Leadership is complex and thus as we work to create more socially just approaches to leadership, we must be adaptive and be ready to manage the tensions around leadership that seeks to disrupt while all that same time reimagining leadership that is accessible to BIWOC.

REFERENCES

Bitton, A. L., & Jones, S. R. (2021). Connecting social class and leadership learning through intersectionality. *New Directions for Student Leadership, 2021*(169), 61–68. https://doi.org/10.1002/yd.20421

Butler, J. (2006). *Gender trouble: Feminism and the subversion of identity*. Routledge.

Collinson, D. (2011). Critical leadership studies. In A. Bryman, D. Collinson, K. Grint, B. Jackson, & M. Uhl-Bien (Eds.), *The SAGE handbook of leadership* (pp. 179–192). SAGE.

Combahee River Collective. (1986). *The Combahee River Collective statement: Black feminist organizing in the seventies and eighties* (1st ed.). Kitchen Table: Women of Color Press.

Crenshaw, K. (1989). Demarginalizing the intersection of race and sex: A Black feminist critique of antidiscrimination doctrine, feminist theory, and antiracist politics. *University of Chicago Legal Forum, 1989*(1), 139–167. https://chicagounbound.uchicago.edu/cgi/viewcontent.cgi?article=1052&context=uclf

Delgado, R., & Stefancic, J. (2012). *Critical race theory: An introduction.* New York University Press.

Dill, B. T., & Zambrana, R. E. (2009). Critical thinking about inequality: An emerging lens. In B. T. Dill & R. E. Zambrana (Eds.), *Emerging intersections: Race class and gender in theory policy and practice* (pp. 1–21). Rutgers University Press.

Doharty, N., & Esoe, M. (2022). 'Demonstrable experience of being a mammy or crazy Black bitch' (essential). A critical race feminist approach to understanding Black women headteachers' experiences in English schools [Advance online publication]. *Race Ethnicity and Education, 26*(3), 318–334. https://doi.org/10.1080/13613324.2022.2122520

Duckworth, A. L., Peterson, C., Matthews, M. D., & Kelly, D. R. (2007). Grit: Perseverance and passion for long-term goals. *Journal of Personality and Social Psychology, 92*(6), 1087–1101. https://doi.org/10.1037/0022-3514.92.6.1087

Dugan, J. P. (2017). *Leadership theory: Cultivating critical perspectives.* Jossey Bass.

Dugan, J. P. (2018). Critical perspectives on capacity-building for international leadership. *New Directions for Student Leadership, 2018*(160), 31–39.

Ely, R., Ibarra, H., & Kolb, D. M. (2011). Taking gender into account: Theory and design for women's leadership development program. *Academy of Management Learning & Education, 10*(3), 474–493. https://doi.org/10.5465/amle.2010.0046

Evans-Winters, V. E., & Esposito, J. (2010). Other people's daughters: Critical race feminism and Black girls' education. *The Journal of Educational Foundation, 24*(1–2), 11–24. https://files.eric.ed.gov/fulltext/EJ885912.pdf

Goessling, K. (2018). Increasing the depth of field: Critical race theory and photovoice as counter storytelling praxis. *The Urban Review, 50*(4), 648–674. https://doi.org/10.1007/s11256-018-0460-2

Guthrie, K. L., Bertrand Jones, T., Osteen, L., & Hu, S. (2013). *Cultivating leader identity and capacity in students from diverse backgrounds.* John Wiley & Sons.

Guthrie, K. L., & Chunoo, V. S. (2018). Opening up the conversation: An introduction to socially just leadership education. In K. L. Guthrie & V. Chunoo (Eds.), *Changing the narrative: Socially just leadership education* (pp. 1–8). Information Age Publishing.

Harris, A. P., & González, C. G. (2012). Introduction. In G. G. Muhs, Y. F. Niemann, C. G. González, & A. P. Harris (Eds.), *Presumed incompetent: The intersections of race and class for women in academia* (pp. 1–14). Utah State University Press.

Katuna, B. (2019). *De-gendering leadership in higher education.* Emerald Publishing.

Ladson-Billings, G., & Tate, W. F. (1995). Toward a critical race theory of education. *Teachers College Record: The Voice of Scholarship in Education, 97*(1), 47–68. https://doi.org/10.1177/016146819509700104

Liu, H. (2020). *Redeeming leadership: An anti-racist feminist intervention.* Bristol University Press.

Melaku, T. M. (2019). *You don't look like a lawyer: Black women and systemic gendered racism.* Rowman & Littlefield.

Melaku, T. M., & Beeman, A. (2022). Black women in White academe: A qualitative analysis of heightened inclusion tax [Advance online publication]. *Ethnic and Racial Studies, 46*(6), 1158–1181. https://doi.org/10.1080/01419870.2022.2149273

Merculieff, I., & Roderick, L. (2013). *Stop talking: Indigenous ways of teaching and learning and difficult dialogues in higher education.* University of Alaska Anchorage.

Mutua, A. D. (1999). Shifting bottoms and rotating centers: Reflections on LatCrit III and the Black/White paradigm. *University of Miami Law Review, 53,* 1177–1217. https://digitalcommons.law.buffalo.edu/journal_articles/435

Ostick, D. T., & Wall, V. A. (2011). Considerations for culture and social identity dimensions. In S. R. Komives, J. P. Dugan, J. E. Owen, C. Slack, W. Wagner, and Associates (Eds.), *The handbook for student leadership development* (2nd ed.; pp. 339–368). Jossey-Bass.

Owen, J. E. (2020). *We are the leaders we've been waiting for: Women and leadership development in college.* Routledge.

Owen, J. E., Hassell-Goodman, S., & Yamanaka, A. (2017). Culturally relevant leadership learning: Identity, capacity, and efficacy. *Journal of Leadership Studies, 11*(3), 48–54. https://doi.org/10.1002/jls.21545

Rosenthal, L. (2016). Incorporating intersectionality into psychology: An opportunity to promote social justice and equity. *American Psychologist, 71*(6), 474–485. https://doi.org/10.1037/a0040323

Shelton, L. (2018). "Who belongs": A critical race theory and Latino critical theory analysis of the United States immigration climate for undocumented Latinx college students. *Journal of Critical Thought and Praxis, 7*(1), 123–147. https://doi.org/10.31274/jctp-180810-95

Solórzano, D., Ceja, M., & Yasso, T. (2000). Critical race theory, racial microaggressions, and campus racial climate: The experiences of African American college students. *Journal of Negro Education, 69*(1–2), 60–73. http://www.jstor.org/stable/2696265

Solórzano, D., & Yosso, T. (2001). Critical race and LatCrit theory and method: Counter-storytelling. *International Journal of Qualitative Studies in Education, 14*(4), 471–495. https://doi.org/10.1080/09518390110063365

Solórzano, D., & Yosso, T. (2002). Critical race methodology: Counter-storytelling as an analytical framework for education research. *Qualitative Inquiry, 8*(1), 23–44. https://doi.org/10.1177/107780040200800103

Soria, K. M., & Johnson, M. R. (2020). A conceptual framework for evidence-based leadership development practices. *New Directions for Student Leadership, 2020*(168), 9–17. https://doi.org/10.1002/yd.20404

Teig, T., & Dilworth, D. (2021). *Dismantling the cool kids table: Growing an inclusive leadership educator community in student affairs. Part 1: Our current status.* ACPA. https://developments.myacpa.org/dismantling-the-cool-kids-table-growing-an-inclusive

Turman, N. T., Garcia, K. C. A., & Howes, S. (2018). Deepening attention to social location in building leader and leadership efficacy. *New Directions for Student Leadership, 2018*(159), 65–76. https://doi.org/10.1002/yd.20298

Turner, M. R. (2001). Don't forget about the women. *Black Issues in Higher Education, 18*(6), 34–35. https://www.diverseeducation.com/demographics/african-american/article/15077691/dont-forget-the-women

Wing, A. K. (2003). *Critical race feminism: A reader* (2nd ed.). New York University Press.

CHAPTER 5

"UNTIL WE COULDN'T FLY"

Bitches, Scars, Breath

Trisha Teig

It plucks the feathers from my kind, one by one, until we couldn't fly
—Prasamsha

I (Trisha) came home every day and cried; deep, soul-searching sobs. It was a clear indication I needed to leave, but I ignored the warnings. I was the Title IX coordinator—the person responsible for adjudicating cases of gender-based violence, and somebody had to lead the change. For one year I stuck it out, I created educational programming, co-created policy, attended trainings, and listened to heart-wrenching stories of sexual assault and dating violence. I bent and folded myself into a version of the leader I thought the institution needed. My body screamed at me with tension, headaches, exhaustion—begging me to see that leading from a place not aligned with my values was leading at all. I told them I was not the right person for the job—to be "impartial" and determine a "finding" that follows "policy." I am a survivors' advocate. I believe the stories. I believe women. I believe Queer folx. I believe People of Color. We reside in a system set up against and

> not built for survivors of violence. I realized I was an active participant and perpetrator of this system. I exhaled a long sigh of relief the day I decided to prioritize my truths and leave my role and the institution. Sometimes leadership is not standing up, it is walking away.

What does it mean to be able to fly; to soar towards your wildest dreams, unimpeded and unencumbered by the weight of societal roles and expectations? The process of becoming a leader and seeing your role in the action of leadership is directly informed by the experiences and interactions you have in relationship to others. Lived experiences in our bodies inform our (actual and perceived) ability to take flight towards passions to influence change, aka... leadership (Sinclair, 2019). We cannot understand distinct framings of leadership without considering how unique narratives capture experiences of limitations to leading. The narratives in this chapter consider internal and external barriers to leadership as well as tools of resistance to address them.

In the process of interacting with four narratives (as well as considering my own), sinking deeply within them, I found myself profoundly struck by the distinctive, yet parallel stories of frustration and rage, objectification, acts and threats of violence, and emotional, agentic power articulated. We all responded to the same writing prompt—and our interpretation of "telling a story of understanding leadership" was intensely informed by direct interactions with the harms our world perpetuates against women, against women's bodies. These narratives do not sugarcoat; they have little patience for bullshit. They represent brutal truth-telling of the impossibilities faced in accessing or enacting leadership in a world that tells, or more aptly, screams: women cannot and should not be—leaders.

APPROACHING THE NARRATIVES

For this chapter, I implemented a feminist narrative analysis (Woodiwiss et al., 2017) from a critical feminist (Qin, 2004), embodied perspective (Alcoff, 2013). Qin (2004) noted in considering critical feminism, "The self is grounded in *heterogeneous* and critical cultural contexts along differing positions of power in a larger social structure" (p. 298, emphasis in original). We must consider women's bodies and lived experiences as multidimensional and complex within intersectional and socially constructed identities of gender, race, and class. Building on these concepts, in my analysis, I considered how the narrative authors articulated gender and leadership while framing gender as "a hierarchical structure of opportunity and oppression as well as an affective structure of identity and cohesion" (Ferree, 1995,

p. 125). Finally, I analyzed conceptualizations of embodiment through emotional expression and description of bodies. Fraser and MacDougall (2017) described "emotions [as] important sources of embodied knowledge" (p. 245). I considered ideas of embodiment as a feminist philosophical and scholarly tool to delve deeper into analysis beyond the mind-centric, positivist perspective of research (Woodiwiss et al., 2017).

EXPLORING THE NARRATIVES

In this section, I examine the places where authors of two poems (Prasamsha and Maddie) grapple with the truths of being and living in the body of a Woman of Color in society. In Chapter 4, the authors explored how socialization informs our understanding of self in relationship to others. In Prasamsha and Maddie's words, I noticed how emotions, expectations of bodies, and conversations of violence and control arose.

Prasamsha: "The Female Body"

First, let me introduce you to Prasamsha, a first-generation American, Nepali immigrant. Prasamsha is a beautifully skilled artist whose drawings are included throughout the book. She was a first-year, first-generation college student at the University of Denver when she penned this piece.

> The female body
> The weaker sex
> Used, abused, and accused
> How have they survived
> Without losing all hope?
>
> You can see them passing by
> Everywhere, everywhere
> Where there is joy
> And success and peace
>
> And fraudulent eyes see them too
> They look into the ones
> That carry a thousand stories
> And grope them, loot them
> Shoot them

A few are lucky like me
They cover themselves in the shadow
Begrudgingly but willingly wear a shackle
If they were to fly
They would see the punishment

In a classroom illuminated by yellow lights
Closed off for privacy
For discussion, for agendas
Of the brightest minds
By the selected officers

There are five such specimen
And one man
Who whisper of a robbing
Of their dear sister
Purest flower of the tree

The robber they also knew
But how could it be
That such a fine lad
Could commit a misdemeanor

Fear overpowers truth
Where the power is
the perpetrator is
More culprits are still innocent, unmarked
Why is this circumstance different?

One blood, same red, shimmering for a decade
Now boiled and erupted
It spread like wildfire, uncontrolled, unsuppressed
Do we not hold the reigns, the scale, the scythe, the future in our palms?

Sit down, a shadow tells me
Who do you think you are?
What is your status, your place, your authority?
It questions, not stopping to breathe, spitting again and again and again

It reaches out to slap consciousness into me
And I turn
Into my mother, into my sister, into my daughter

Into every other energy that has been scolded
For stepping out of line, from the kitchen, from their homes, from their words

The figure steps into the light and reveals itself
To be my father, my brother, my son
To be an entity that puts my energy back in it's said place
It plucks the feathers from my kind, one by one, until we couldn't fly

But today, under the roof that held learners, not genders, together
The soul of my tormented sister conjoined with my own
How could I disregard her pain, my pain
Our pain

I shed tears, not of sorrow anymore, but of rage
If rage is what motivates the change
The change that has been far too long pushed and shoved
Then so be it

Channeling the raw emotions is hard
The people call it weak
We are not humans though
We are animals
Have you ever seen a beast roar, protect, fight?

Once one beast growls, others growl along
All the fire needed was ignition
Before it consumed every part
Of the castle so intricately built
To show and uphold the reign of shadows

We crackle, slip, break
As we push ourselves with fervor
From the mold that held us in, from the fear that binds us.

Maddie: "Women in Leadership"

Our next narrative author is Maddie, a biracial, cisgender woman and undergraduate student at George Mason University. In the reflection of her thoughts when writing this poem, she noted influences from Roxanne Gay's (2014) *Bad Feminist* and her consistent frustration with mixed messaging around women's empowerment and feminism in contrast to the continued violence and sexual assault against women's bodies.

> I am angry.
> I don't hate all men but sometimes I'm scared of all men (and that's close)
> I'm not very friendly to everyone all the time
> I express my anger and sometimes I let it get the best of me
> I'm outspoken
> I'm bitchy
> I ask too many questions
> I am not perfect, I do not have to be
> But yet I'm expected to be perfect and smile and to shhhhh...
> Which makes me just want to be WORSE
> But it isn't really worse,
> It's better, it's more powerful.
> The more I keep asking too many questions and the more I keep saying "I was speaking" when interrupted and keep being a bitch and keep being angry...?
>
> Well actually, that doesn't seem powerful at all.

For both Prasamsha and Maddie, high emotions of anger, rage, and disgust are apparent in their assessment of our current world. They have seen and felt rejection and objectification, pain and violence, invisibility and frustration. In the strength of these emotions, I found both authors grappled with concepts of power, both in the traditional and inaccessible sense based on their social location as Women of Color, and in the agentic sense—a determination to create a new understanding from what they have been told. Prasamsha exclaimed, "I shed tears, not of sorrow anymore, but of rage, if rage is what motivates the change." The authors wrestled with their emotions because oppressive external factors elucidate a catch-22 of women's responses to unequal access to leadership: Anger can be powerful, but only if it is also purposeful. And who decides?

Both pieces also centered women's bodies as places of castigation. Feminist leadership scholars, building on feminist literature across disciplines (Alcolff, 2013), have analyzed how gendered bodies and role expectations overlap with leadership interactions, expectations, and outcomes (Ladkin, 2013; Sinclair, 2005; Sinclair & Ladkin, 2020). In each poem, the authors described how the proverbial male gaze (Pontorotto, 2016) creates a liminal space for women to embody, neither allowed to be nor *not* allowed to be fully herself. Maddie's expectations of perfection (just smile!) intertwine with visceral descriptors from Prasamsha about how women's bodies are treated—groping, looting, shooting, pain, blood. Maddie opened with the stark statement, "I don't hate all men but sometimes I'm scared of all men (and that's close)." The harsh tone surrounding experiential descriptors of women's bodily subjugation allows us to be present in the authors' unmitigated truths: there is violence against women, always present, always lingering as a dark shadow over the hopeful flight each woman dreams to take. Prashamsha's and Maddie's words also rang true with my own narrative reflection, affirming even in the leader role of responding to dating violence and sexual assault in the college environment, the reality of this work often reifies instead of mitigates violence. The depths of despair and rage in all our words highlight the unerring reality of our world—we require deep societal, community change to make spaces of safety and growth for women. This change includes recognizing how bodies and gendered, racialized bodily performance is an influential factor in leadership (Sinclair, 2005).

Both women continued to consider power and did not reach certainty in their reflections. Prasamsha acknowledged power tends to lie with the person who causes harm: "Where the power is, the perpetrator is." Maddie, in an additional reflection that accompanied her poem (full reflection not included in this chapter), struggled to understand messaging around women's empowerment: "I feel as though sometimes behavior that can seem empowering really isn't when you take a step back and look at the big picture; my behavior is being controlled by my oppressor; therefore, it is inherently not empowering." We can learn from these women the consistent practice to question our current existence by honestly stating the harm it perpetuates. Further, we can question how even feminist perceptions of "empowerment" do not agenticly create spaces for the woman herself to be in power in her own way. We (feminists, leadership educators) discuss empowering others by giving voice, sharing space, and encouraging other women to become leaders. However, does the very framing of "giving" others "access" to leadership through the act of 'empowerment' perpetuate the system it claims to dismantle?

Ariana: "Bearing Scars"

Next, I unpack Ariana's and Amna's narratives focused on acknowledging the scars we bear while growing together towards seeing and owning power and beauty. I also consider how solidarity with other women committing to healing is an act of collective leadership. Ariana, a first-generation Latina undergraduate student from the University of Denver, created a poem centered around scars. She asks us to reflect on the beauty of taking ownership of our scars as an act of leadership.

I own scars in my eyes;
Those you can barely see,
but also the ones that don't let me breathe.
The ones keeping my tears from being set free.
Tears that are slowly drowning me,
as slow as a faucet dripping into the sink
causing a flooding within me.
A flooding that keeps rising.
Rising so high it won't stay down below,
and half of my lungs are already dull.
So dull it has evoked rotting.
And the tears are filling up every single cranny,
and the salt in the midst of the tears has now ignited.
The burning has turned me psychotic,
now my blood is scorching with pain
and my flesh is part of the rain.
The rain creating a storm.
A storm of crimson and bloodshed,
lured in times of restrain.
To think I was once a perfect soul;
But the damage is done.
I have been branded.
Scars do not vanish,
And scars are what I own.
They have shown my true home,
So wherever I roam I place a piece of my soul.
I implant it into the sweet Earth,
It's true home.
From where it was sculpted from dirt,
By hands so warm.
The ones I now return myself to
Because dirt I once was, And
Dirt I will become.
With time I have been defined,
By these marks of my own.
These words each their own meaning.
They all come together like a freshly baked cake.
I give anyone a slice
To better their mind,
To help them grow.
In order for them to open their alluring eyes
And own the scars that make them struggle to survive;
So they too can find their true home.
Amidst the storm of crimson and bloodshed

> Present on this dirt of the Earth
> That we can all halt.
> By recognizing that we were once perfect souls
> But the damage is done.
> We have been branded.
> Scars do not vanish,
> And beautiful scars are what we own.

Amna: "Reflection in Healing"

In our final narrative of the chapter, Amna from Rutgers University, brings us along to a poignant moment of self and collective realization. Amna was a graduating senior as she shared this story. An active student leader, Amna reflected on her shared experience in a night of reflection with other Women of Color who were all leaders in a student organization. She weaved her experiences as a first-generation American, South Asian woman into her story of coming to understanding leadership in a new, collective light.

> It was a Saturday night that changed my entire life. I met up with two friends that were part of the same senior leadership organization. Here we were in the lobby of a dorm room, just a Pakistani, Nigerian, and Indian American girl reflecting on the complexities of our time at Rutgers. We were all selected to be a part of this organization for our extraordinary academics, leadership, character, and service. Before this girl's night, I was processing an immense amount of grief coupled with anxiety about the future after graduation. This time, which was supposed to be about making final memories, became so difficult to enjoy. As a first-generation college student, getting through these 4 years required perseverance, and as I approached the finish line, I simply became exhausted. I had seen and gone through many things the past few years that I never truly gave myself the space to breathe, or more accurately, I felt like I couldn't. I carried a burden that I owed it to my family and the people who came before me to keep pushing through no matter how hard it got.
>
> But talking to these two girls was a breath of fresh air. I left the dorm that night with a lighter heart and a deep-felt connection between two Women of Color who overcame so many barriers to reach this point. We reflected on the ways our identities shifted depending on the space we occupied. This shift was oftentimes related to the power relations we were navigating. In other words, the push and pull between our race, religion, education, and everything else that makes us who we are, became a site of contestation at some point during our college careers.

> At the end of it all, we realized there was still a whole lot of generational trauma to unpack. "Our history is in our present" and all three of our commitments to leadership were grounded in our personal experiences of overcoming social and institutional barriers. For me, despite generational trauma, my grandmother's resilience in my blood allows me to fearlessly stand up for what I believe in, particularly, when it comes to women's human rights. My two friends also channeled their frustrations into advocacy work, raising their community's voice in the political process. More importantly, they learned to take care of their heart and mind. To let yourself breathe. While there will always be grief and loss, there is also love and life and the beginning of new friendships. Leadership, for me that night, became a commitment to healing. By remembering and honoring each other's truths, we were reclaiming ourselves and our identity. Through these acts of remembrance, healing becomes social change.

Ariana and Amna's narratives present similar themes from Prasamsha and Maddie—harm, pain, and overwhelming experiences. These descriptions offer direct examples of explicit embodied experiences. Ariana's scars limit her ability to breathe, to cry the tears that seek to drown her. Amna described her and her peers' identities as Pakistani, Nigerian, and Indian American women as "sites of contestation"; they learned to "shift" themselves, their bodies, their truths based on environmental power dynamics (Wright et al., 2022).

However, they also build on these ideas to consider, "Now what?" The action of owning our scars can be considered a process of self-leadership—leading others through examples to notice, accept, and recognize the beauty in our scars. In a reflection that accompanied her poem, Ariana shared,

> Through recognizing my scars and true identity, I learned how to use leadership and become a leader by connecting what I know about leadership and who I am...the way I think I was meant to be a leader is to be willing to give everyone a piece of myself in order to make room for all the pieces others give me. I want to be represented as a leader who embodies a mosaic and uses everything they have learned to show others that it's ok to have scars.

Another key takeaway from Ariana and Amna is the process of discovering beauty in difficulties and finding connection with others who understand similar challenges (see also Chapter 10). Ariana highlighted, "In recognizing our scars we can accept who we are and use that for good in this world where we will find where we belong." Resilience arises as a critical tool to process trauma in healthy, purposeful ways. Amna recognized, "We have a whole lot of generational trauma to unpack." Yet, the skillset of recognizing the need and undergoing this process of unpacking, particularly with other women who can be a support community, stands as a historical and current tool for women as leaders (Einwohner et al., 2021). Amna described it as a "breath of fresh air." Both authors realized the overcoming of systemic oppression and the scars born from the circumstances must be considered, appreciated, and implemented. Further, Amna emphasized we must learn resilience with and from other women in order to collectively succeed in our efforts of change. She shared, "By remembering and honoring each other's truths, we were reclaiming ourselves and our identity." In profound insight, Amna teaches us leadership as healing equates to social change.

In a follow-up email conversation with Amna, who served as a member-checker for the project, she noted that while resilience can be seen as a tool for community healing, she questions how much we should emphasize or rely on it for our future. Specifically, she expressed wanting to move "past the concept that Women of Color need to be resilient." She pushed against the perspective that Women of Color must look at their trauma and only draw strength.

WEAVING AND APPLYING THE NARRATIVES

The tone and content of each narrative in this chapter may cause discomfort; these authors do not wrap their views of leadership in optimistic or meritocratic platitudes ("If you just try hard, you will make it!"). Instead, they offer to and demand from us a realization that we have not achieved our goals of equality or equity in leadership. We are still working within a system not built for everyone and simply "leaning in" (hooks, 2013; Sandberg, 2013) will not solve the complex challenges we face. Asian Australian leadership scholar Helena Liu (2020) agreed with our narrative authors' call: We must deconstruct and reimagine leadership in order to redeem it.

Aligning with Liu's (2020) reconceptualization of leadership in relationship, the women provide creative possibilities for how to move forward—through community in solidarity. Prasamsha described this solidarity through empathy, "I turn into my mother, sister, daughter; Her pain, my pain, our pain." Maddie pushed us to break the mold together, to keep being a bitch, to question our notions of "empowerment"; Ariana encouraged us to understand how to give and take pieces of ourselves from others to co-create beautiful mosaics. Finally, Amna noted we can find spaces to breathe in a community of others who hold our pain and give love. She urged us to consider "leadership as a commitment to healing." How can we apply these pieces of brilliance to our co-created understanding of leadership? I implore us to see the nuanced insights our authors brought to light in these pieces:

- We must acknowledge and address our pain as a part of our process in becoming leaders; our emotions are tools for change.
- Systemic gendered and racialized violence and objectification of women's bodies directly inform women's ways of leading and our perceptions of others in leadership.
- We cannot assume leadership is accessible for everyone; we have not arrived in a just world.
- We must push back against narratives that expect "Communities of Color to carry [expectations of resilience] on their shoulders in order to move forward." (Amna)
- We can learn to self-lead and heal as a process and tool of leadership.
- We must learn to lead in community and solidarity.
- We must create "a world where the next generation doesn't have to be resilient and can just live and breathe." (Amna)

Prasamsha's warnings inspired my reflection: We cling to a narrative of girls and women who can dream of leading, yet we allow others to pluck their feathers before they can fly. Movement outside of this detrimental cycle begins by mirroring our narrative authors in truth-telling and disruption. We can co-create leadership (see more in Chapter 10) to be a space for everyone to fly, but we must grapple with the harms and barriers women face in community and solidarity as a significant part of the process for healing and change.

REFERENCES

Alcoff, L. M. (2013). Luce Irigaray Cluster—Editor's introduction. *Hypatia, 28*(3), 417–418, https://doi.org/10.1111/hypa.12041

Einwohner, R. L., Kelly-Thompson, K., Sinclair-Chapman, V., Tormos-Aponte, F., Weldon, S. L., Wright, J. M., & Wu, C. (2021) Active solidarity: Intersectional solidarity in action. *Social Politics: International Studies in Gender, State & Society, 28*(3), 704–729. https://doi.org/10.1093/sp/jxz052

Ferree, M. M. (1995). Beyond separate spheres: Feminism and family research. In G. Bowen & J. Pittman (Eds.), *The work and family interface: Toward a contextual effects perspective* (pp. 122–137). National Council on Family Relations.

Fraser, H., & MacDougall, C. (2017). Doing narrative feminist research: Intersections and challenges. *Qualitative Social Work, 16*(2), 240–254. https://doi.org/10.1177/1473325016658114

Gay, R. (2014). *Bad feminist*. Harper-Perennial.

hooks, b. (2013, October 28). Dig deep: Beyond lean in. *The Feminist Wire*. https://thefeministwire.com/2013/10/17973/

Ladkin, D. (2013). From perception to flesh: A phenomenological account of the felt experience of leadership. *Leadership, 9*(3), 320–334. https://doi.org/10.1177/1742715013485854

Liu, H. (2020). *Redeeming leadership: An anti-racist, feminist intervention*. Bristol University Press.
Ponterotto, D. (2016). Resisting the male gaze: Feminist responses to the "normalization" of the female body in Western culture. *Journal of International Women's Studies, 17*(1), 133–151. https://vc.bridgew.edu/cgi/viewcontent.cgi?article=1844&context=jiws
Qin, D. (2004). Toward a critical feminist perspective of culture and self. *Feminism & Psychology, 14*(2), 297–312. https://doi.org/10.1177/0959353504042183
Sandberg, S. (2013). *Lean in*. Alfred A. Knopf.
Sinclair, A. (2005). Body possibilities in leadership. *Leadership, 1*(4), 387–406. https://doi.org/10.1177/1742715005057231
Sinclair, A. (2019). Five movements in an embodied feminism: A memoir. *Human Relations, 72*(1), 144–158. https://doi.org/10.1177/0018726718765625
Sinclair, A., & Ladkin, D. (2020). Leading with embodied care. In L. Tomkins (Ed.), *Paradox and power in caring leadership: Critical and philosophical reflections* (pp. 63–73). Edward Elgar Publishing.
Woodiwiss, J., Smith, K., & Lockwood, K. (2017). *Feminist narrative research: Opportunities and challenges*. Palgrave Macmillan.
Wright N. L., Longerbeam S. D., & Alagaraja, M. (2022). Chronic codeswitching: Shaping Black/White multiracial student sense of belonging. *Genealogy, 6*(3), 2–19. https://doi.org/10.3390/genealogy6030075

CHAPTER 6

"THEY MADE ME WHO I AM"

How Family Shapes Leadership Identity Development for Women of Color

Lauren Contreras

> My (Lauren's) mom grew up in poverty and was the first person in her family to graduate from college. She changed the trajectory of our family. As an educator herself, my mom has always been my inspiration. Though she never wanted to take on a formal, positional leadership role, my mom showed me leadership by working hard every day to ensure she supported the students in her classroom and their families, and by ensuring my brothers and I had all the resources we needed to be our best selves. My mom's sacrifices and dedication have changed families, including our own. In our family now, we are nearly all college graduates, and many of us work in education just like my mom. Unfortunately, the way in which my mom leads, I lead, and many Women of Color lead, though supporting others and caring for family is not valued and recognized as leadership.

As I read through their narratives, I observed that the leadership identities of Bianca, Kat, Negin, and Sophia, who are featured in this chapter, were also shaped by their families. They too had learned leadership from observing their family members. They too learned leadership through the lens of their gender, race, ethnicity, and their roles in their families. They too wanted to honor their families through their leadership. In their narratives shared in this chapter, Bianca, Kat, Negin, and Sophia share how they were influenced by their family experiences, both the positive and the negative, and by their family responsibilities to become the leaders they are today.

APPROACHING THE NARRATIVES

For this chapter, I drew from Yosso's (2005) theoretical framework of community cultural wealth (CCW). Yosso developed CCW to challenge the deficit-based beliefs that People of Color do not possess resources and capital within their communities. Drawing from critical race theory (see Chapter 3), CCW is defined as "an array of knowledge, skills, abilities and contacts possessed and utilized by Communities of Color to survive and resist macro and micro forms of oppression" (Yosso, 2005, p. 77). Yosso identified six forms of CCW, including familial capital, the primary focus of this chapter. Yosso defined familial capital as, "the cultural knowledge nurtured among familia that carry a sense of community history, memory, and cultural intuition" (p. 79). Familial capital encompasses the stories and lessons shared by family members about caretaking, providing, and coping. The actions, values, behaviors, and emotions of Students of Color are informed by familial capital (Matos, 2015; Shapiro, 2018). Previous research has demonstrated how Communities of Color have an abundance of familial capital that inspires them to pursue higher education and that helps them to navigate and to persevere through challenging higher education environments (Contreras & Kiyama, 2022; Matos, 2015; Sáenz et al., 2018; Shapiro, 2018). In this chapter, Bianca, Negin, Kat, and Sophia demonstrate how familial capital, in the form of family experiences and lessons, shaped their leadership identities.

The leadership displayed by Women of Color is often overlooked because it does not fit the traditional narrative about leadership, which comes from a White, male perspective (Liu, 2020). Furthermore, Communities of Color, in general, are viewed from a deficit perspective as though they do not possess assets and strengths. Women of color have an abundance of leadership qualities that are often shaped by the experiences and lessons learned within their families (Matos, 2015; Shapiro, 2018). To challenge the dominant narrative regarding the leadership of Women of Color, this chapter utilized counter-storytelling, defined as "a tool for exposing, analyzing, and challenging the majoritarian stories of racial privilege" (Solórzano & Yosso, 2002, p. 32). Counter-stories are stories of those on the margins that can lead to the transformation of established beliefs. For more information on counter-stories, see Chapter 3. Through their counter-stories, Bianca, Negin, Kat, and Sophia, all Women of Color, share how they possess familial capital that has influenced their leadership identities.

From their research, Komives et al. (2005) learned that college student leadership identity development is composed of six stages which are connected to developmental influences, including influential adults who are members of the student's family. For the student leaders in their study, family members were "very important in building confidence and being an early building block of support" (Komives et al., 2005, p. 596). Komives et al. also found that in the first stage of leadership identity development—"awareness"—family members played a significant role. Awareness is the stage during which students recognize that leadership exists, in some part due to their experiences of leadership within their homes through familial examples. The student leaders often recognized their parents as those that exhibited leadership qualities they wished to emulate. While Komives et al. noted that gender was an important factor in leadership identity development, their study did not focus on gender. More recent work has further explored how leadership identity development for women and girls is shaped by their gendered experiences (Le Ber et al., 2017; McKenzie, 2018; Ricks-Scott et al., 2017; Shetty, 2020). See Chapter 12 for a more detailed analysis of women's leadership identity development. In recent scholarship on leadership and leader identity development, "leadership" and "leader" are both used for various semantic and philosophical reasons. For the purpose of remaining succinct and clear in this chapter, I used the term "leadership identity development" to be inclusive of both terms.

In more recent leadership identity development scholarship and research, family emerged as an important factor that shaped early leadership identity development for women and girls. In their construction of a women's leader identity development model through the use of their own leadership narratives, Ricks-Scott et al. (2017) discovered that family members often affirmed, valued, and uplifted the leadership of young girls by providing them opportunities and recognizing their leadership qualities. This is significant as role models (see Chapter 7 for a more detailed analysis on the significance of role models), such as parents, can enhance or deter a woman's leadership identity development (Le Ber et al., 2017). For example, Le Ber et al. (2017) noted that those who were told by family members that they were good at leadership readily accepted opportunities to develop their leadership identities. In her study on young Black women's leader identity development, Shetty (2020) found that mothers or othermothers, specifically, were the most important influence in Black womens' leadership identity development. Mothers (or female caretakers) are the first example of leadership in a Black woman's life; mothers are the example of leadership to emulate. Mothers also provide the encouragement and support young Black women need to aspire to leadership and to gain confidence as a leader.

According to the studies by Le Ber et al. (2017) and Ricks-Scott et al. (2017), the context of family was also important for women as it provided opportunities, especially those who were the eldest child, to assume responsibility in caregiving for siblings. Family circumstances, such as the absence of a parent, divorce, and other family difficulties also impacted leadership identity development because it gave further responsibilities to girls in the family (Le Ber et al., 2017; Ricks-Scott et al., 2017). For some women, these responsibilities provided them strength and a feeling of importance. However, not all women had this same experience. For some women, these family dynamics did not have a positive impact on their childhood experiences. In particular, women who experienced loss and change in their family dynamic when they were girls were often given greater responsibilities that impacted their leadership identity development (Ricks-Scott et al., 2017).

While previous studies provide context for how family shapes the leadership identity of women, these studies do not account for how Women of Color experience family in unique ways that shape their leadership identity development. Previous research has found the experiences of Women of Color and immigrant women are greatly shaped by their families' values and expectations (Matos, 2015; Onorato & Musoba, 2015; Shapiro, 2018; Sy & Romero, 2008). For Women of Color and immigrant women, their families often expect them to adhere to traditional gender roles that include putting their family first, being submissive to the men in the family, taking on household responsibilities, getting married, and having children (Onorato & Musoba, 2015; Shapiro, 2018). Previous research on Latina women, in particular, found that even though family members were supportive of them pursuing higher education, they still expected for them to engage in household responsibilities, including caretaking for younger siblings (Sy & Romero, 2008). While this expectation diminishes once they are in college, Latinas still desired to give back and to support their families.

In their research that focused on the leadership identity development of 11 Latina student leaders at a Hispanic serving institution, Onorato and Musoba (2015) found that messages from family members, including gender role expectations, shaped the values, ethics, and behaviors of the Latina student leaders in their study. While some women have received messages around traditional gender roles and patriarchal family structures, previous research also found that Women of Color were given messages from their family members that encouraged them to be more autonomous and focus on their own goals (Liang et al., 2017; Onorato & Musoba, 2015; Shapiro, 2018). In their study, Onorato and Musoba found that family members encouraged Latina student leaders to be anything they desired.

Furthermore, Latinas learn from their mothers' actions and messages how to balance traditional gender roles with independence (Liang et al., 2017; Onorato & Musoba, 2015). Their mothers often encouraged them to be more autonomous and wanted more for their daughters than they were able to do or to have in life. Similarly, research focused on refugee students found that parents cleared the path for their children to pursue educational and extracurricular opportunities by negotiating their family roles and responsibilities (Shapiro, 2018).

As demonstrated by existing research, family members and family context are important influences in the lives of Women of Color. Family members can help to encourage and inspire their daughters to be leaders. Additionally, the family context provides Women of Color with roles and responsibilities that influence their leadership identities. Their experiences with their families can be both positive and negative, and collectively, these experiences impact how Women of Color develop as leaders.

EXPLORING THE NARRATIVES

The four narratives in this chapter connect ideas of family experiences with understandings and conceptualizations of leadership. The narrative authors explore trauma in family relationships, applications of healing as a leadership practice, and the contexts of familial influences in shaping their identities as leaders.

Healing Family Trauma as Leadership

In this section, I share the leadership narratives of Bianca and Kat. Bianca and Kat were both impacted by the trauma experienced in their families to become the leaders they are today. As college students, they were developing into the leaders they wished their parents would have been to them during their childhood. While family plays an important role in the leadership identity development of women and girls, their family context is not always one that is positive and can sometimes be filled with family difficulties (Le Ber et al., 2017). For Bianca and Kat, their family experiences forced them to grow up faster and to take on the responsibilities their parents did not want or could not assume due, in part, to their own marginalized identities. Previous research indicates that challenging experiences within childhood, such as that of taking on additional responsibilities because of an absent parent, can create resilience. Resilience is a strength of leaders that allows them to overcome challenges (Le Ber et al., 2017). Similarly, for Bianca and Kat, their family experiences helped them to develop resilience and to grow as leaders. Through their leadership narratives, they shared how their childhood helped them to become strong and capable of leading for themselves and for others.

Bianca: "It's in Her Nature"

The first narrative is by Bianca, a biracial (African American and White) heterosexual woman, who shared about her experience taking on caretaking responsibilities within her family.

> For as long as I can remember, I have always been a second mother. Caring for my younger siblings was just "in her nature" as some would say. Older siblings take on many roles and have many responsibilities. Why did I feel as if I had more just because I am a girl? Starting at the age of 11 I was learning how to cook and clean. These abilities aided me in my daily activities as a second mother. Oh, the groans I would give to my mom as she would ask me to help my siblings for the 20th time that week. As I got older, I would pick my siblings up from school, take them to practice, help with assignments, and teach them basic life skills. Although I am grateful for the memories these responsibilities have brought me, I feel I had to grow up faster than most. I never knew how to explain my family dynamic to people as I found it complicated myself. I grew up with a single mother along with occasional visits and calls from my dad. Most calls with my dad would consist of how my siblings and I were doing... nothing more and nothing less. One day as I was chatting with my friends over the phone, I suddenly got a call from my dad. The first thing I hear is "your sister says she is hungry, cook her some food." I responded with, "she is old enough to cook her own food now" in which he responded, "you're her older sister, that's your job." Society has taught women we are no more than what we can give. Even as a child I was an older sister first. My siblings and I have a wonderful relationship. I am their role model, shoulder to cry on, best friend and much more. I will now change the narrative and write my own meaning to being their older sister as that was written for me by society. We are more than mothers, daughters, sisters and wives. We are leaders who are authoritative, creative, ambitious, and fearless.

Bianca's family influence and context impacted how she developed her own leadership identity (Le Ber et al., 2017; Ricks-Scott et al., 2017). In her narrative, Bianca shared her family context was one where she was expected to be a caretaker because she was raised by a single mother. Gender roles often force girls and women to be caretakers and to sacrifice for their family members (Komives et al., 2005; Ricks-Scott et al., 2017). As the oldest female in her family, Bianca was given greater responsibilities and was expected to make sacrifices to take care of her siblings. While this experience provided Bianca with opportunities to develop her leadership identity, Bianca also described it as a harmful experience that caused her to grow up faster than others. See Chapter 5 for a more detailed analysis on how harm impacts the leadership development of women. This is demonstrated when Bianca's father demanded her to make food for her sister when she was on the phone with her friends. In this moment, Bianca longed to be a teenager without caretaking responsibilities.

Similar to ideas presented in previous research, Bianca was experiencing a contradiction related to the influence her family experiences had on her leadership development (Onorato & Musoba, 2015; Ricks-Scott et al., 2017). On the one hand, she often felt burdened by familial responsibilities imposed on her by her parents. On the other hand, by providing caretaking for her siblings, she was given responsibility and the opportunity to test her leadership skills. Though not often recognized as an asset, Bianca was cultivating familial capital through her caretaking role (Yosso, 2005). Bianca was also able to pass on familial capital in the form of care and support to her siblings. By being her siblings' caretaker, Bianca was able to make a significant impact in the lives of her siblings and to be a role model for them.

In her narrative, Bianca provides us a counter-story that pushes back against the caretaking role while also acknowledging its power. Bianca wanted to be acknowledged for more than just her caretaking responsibilities. Bianca had a desire to break free from the gender roles that had been placed on her as a caretaker of her siblings. She wanted to be known for being "authoritative, creative, ambitious, and fearless." Bianca understood that women, mothers, daughters, sisters, and wives have additional strengths and deserve to be recognized for being more than caretakers; in the same breath, she also described a desire to reclaim what it means to be a female sibling, caregiver, and family member. Being a caregiver can be empowering, too. She is dismantling and rebuilding definitions of leadership through her counter-story that recognize the complexities of caretaking and familial responsibilities.

Kat: "Better for Her"

Kat, a Latina woman, also experiences the influences of family context on her leadership identity development. Kat, a sexual assault survivor, felt betrayed by her mother for staying with her stepfather, who was her abuser. Kat held resentment towards her mother for not protecting her and for not being the leader she needed during her childhood. These childhood experiences impacted Kat's leadership identity development because she did not see leadership displayed through her mother's actions and wanted a leader to whom she could turn for guidance and support. Through a series of letters addressed to her mother, Kat demonstrates how she is becoming the leader she needed as a child and a leader of whom she is proud.

BETTER FOR HER
Katherine
06/18/2018
Dear Mom,
I graduated high school today,
I'll be starting as a first-
generation college student with
already $6,000 of debt. I hate
that you're undocumented.

You weren't there for me when I
was a kid and now you still
aren't there. I don't trust
women because of you and I can
only ever seem to find the ones
who take advantage of my
kindness.

How do I move on?
I need a hero,
I'm waiting for a leader
Someone to guide me.

BETTER FOR HER
Katherine
05/30/2020
Dear Mom,
So much has happened between us
and to us. I've learned so much
about myself and your identities
and struggles. I've come to
understand so many things that I
couldn't when I was younger and
forgive you for so much. But, not
everything some things I can't let
go of yet.
Guess what though? I started to
learn about how to work better in
a group and how to trust other
people! That's a step up from
thinking everything is out to get
me, right?
I'm slowly becoming happier, I
have so many passions here at

school. I can't wait to see where
they lead me. I just hope to be
better for her one day, to show
her it wasn't her fault and that
she has so much more to live for
now.

BETTER FOR HER
Katherine
12/08/2021
Dear Mom,
I've learned so much more about myself since the
last time I wrote about you in my journal. I'm slowly learning to heal myself in order to
move on with my life. I know I want to have a
relationship with you now.

In the time that I have been afforded
opportunities on and off campus, I have broken
so many glass ceilings and continue to battle
imposter syndrome with resiliency and fierceness.

I had the chance to revive an on campus
organization that seeks to empower and uplift
women. I was able to pass that down to someone I
have mentored for the last year.

I think I'm doing it, Mom.
I'm finally becoming a better version of her,
for her. I'm finally showing myself that it
wasn't my fault. I built my dreams on clouds I
thought I'd never reach and now I'm on my way to
catch them.
I think I'm finally becoming the leader I've
been waiting for.

For Kat, her family context during her childhood was one of harm, violence, and abandonment. This family context ultimately impacted Kat's leadership identity development because she did not view her mother's actions as one of a leader. In Kat's first letter, she suggested that she did not view her mother as a model of leadership. By stating, she was "waiting for a leader," it is evident that Kat's mother also did not encourage Kat's leadership. As such, Kat was left questioning what leadership was and who would be the leader in her life.

In Kat's first letter she revealed that her mother is undocumented. As an undocumented woman in the United States, Kat's mom faces systemic oppression that limits her opportunities. See Chapter 4 to learn more about the impact of systemic oppression on women's leadership. In Kat's second letter, Kat shared how she has learned more about her mother's situation and the challenges facing undocumented women. Through this realization, Kat begins to understand her mother better and why she may have made certain choices in her past. However, she does not forgive her mother for all of the harm that was caused in her childhood. The experiences of her mother as an undocumented woman, although not positive, were familial capital that Kat was able to draw upon to become her own leader. Due to her childhood experiences, Kat cultivated familial capital in the form of essential coping and survival skills (Yosso, 2005).

While Kat's childhood experience may have delayed her leadership identity development, it did not deter it. In Kat's final letter, she demonstrates growth from her experiences and revealed she has become a leader on her campus and a leader for herself. While Kat's experiences in her childhood caused trauma, she persevered and was ultimately able to find healing. This healing allowed her to become the leader she wished she would have had in her childhood. In her final letter, Kat also shared how she was uplifting, empowering, and mentoring other women on her college campus. This demonstrated how Kat was sharing her familial capital, lessons of survival, and coping skills with others. Kat's narrative is not the dominant way in which the literature shares how family contributes to leadership identity development (Ricks-Scott et al., 2017). However, Kat provided a counter-story that demonstrates how even a traumatic family situation can lead to a positive leadership identity development. Learn more about Kat's experience of growth as a leader in Chapter 9.

In their narratives, Bianca and Kat both shared how they experienced hardship and trauma within their families during their childhood. Similar to the experiences of participants in previous research, for both Bianca and Kat, their challenging family contexts had a significant impact on their leadership identity development (Le Ber et al., 2017; Onorato & Musoba, 2015; Ricks-Scott et al., 2017). Both Bianca and Kat demonstrated how they were able to overcome adversity during their childhood to become leaders. While their family contexts were challenging, Bianca and Kat cultivated an abundance of familial capital, including lessons of caretaking, survival, and coping. Bianca describes this learning well when she wrote, "Even as a child I was an older sister first. My siblings and I have a wonderful relationship. I am their role model, shoulder to cry on, best friend and much more. I will now change the narrative and write my own meaning to being their older sister as that was written for me by society." As leaders, they were then able to share this familial capital with others, including their siblings and other students at their colleges. Both Bianca and Kat offered their narratives as counter-stories to demonstrate how lessons of caretaking, survival, and coping impact leadership identity development.

They Made Me the Leader I Am

In this section, I share narratives by Negin and Sophia, both women born in immigrant families, both who were inspired by their family's life stories of sacrifice and perseverance to become the women and leaders they are today. As previously mentioned, family members are often the earliest examples of leadership seen in childhood (Komives et al., 2005). In the case of Negin and Sophia, their parents displayed qualities such as hard work, sacrifice, providing for family, strength, and resilience, that they wanted to emulate throughout their lives, and that they ultimately identified as important aspects of leadership.

Negin: "You Hold All the Keys"

First, I share the narrative of Negin, an Iranian American immigrant, who shared her journey to understanding leadership through a poem.

> Leadership is a journey.
>
> I am a first-generation immigrant, split between two homelands.
> Leaving one at the age of six for a better life in the other.
> Leaving behind family, traditions, and culture.
> For the pursuit of the American dream.
>
> Growing up I watched my parents struggle, knowing money was short.
> Living paycheck to paycheck was our typical norm.
> I felt their stress more times than I can count.
> Yet they never gave up their hustle to provide all they could amount.
> Adversity leads to growth.
>
> They made me who I am, as did the immigrant experience.
> Wake up. Work hard. Focus on your education.
> They've provided the foundation.
> The grind should never stop.
> Do that and you will make it to the very top.

> Put myself through school, I am still drowning in debt.
> Never became a doctor, it made my parents upset.
> But I hustle just as they did. I know I'll make them proud.
> If not for them, then for myself I vowed.
>
> Got a corporate job, I'm working nine to five.
> This Iranian American woman is keeping her dream alive. Leadership is a journey, measured by what you make of it.
> It's not always a title or position that makes one seem more legit. Leadership is a choice—it starts with you, just commit.
> And do it authentically, for you hold all the keys if you admit.

As Negin reflected on her journey to leadership, she realized that leadership is not a "title or position," it is measured by the actions you take. This type of leadership was cultivated in Negin's early experiences watching her parents, as Iranian immigrants, struggle, hustle, and stress to ensure she and her family had all they needed to pursue an education and to achieve the "American dream." The lessons of survival and hard work Negin witnessed in her family were examples of their familial capital. Previous research indicates that immigrant and refugee family members' stories about survival and perseverance inspire their children "to invest in their education as a way to honor their parents' hard work and sacrifice" (Shapiro, 2018, p. 339). Like her parents, Negin continued to work hard, sacrifice, and pursue her education, and is now working in a corporate job. While the dominant leadership narrative often leaves out immigrants, Negin's narrative offers a counter-story that demonstrates how her parents' hard work and sacrifice did contribute to Negin's leadership identity development and to success in her corporate job as a product manager. Immigrant parents have high expectations for their children, which can sometimes cause stress for the child (Shapiro, 2018). Likewise, Negin noted that she had not become a doctor like her parents hoped. However, Negin did utilize the familial capital in the form of lessons learned from her family to achieve her goals, and to make herself proud. In all likelihood, her parents were proud of her too.

Sophia: "The Kind of Woman and Leader She Was"

Similar to Negin, Sophia—a White Hispanic, Cuban, Catholic, and heterosexual woman—shared how her family's immigrant experiences impacted her leadership identity development. Sophia was grateful for her parents' and grandparents' hard work and sacrifice, which inspired her to be a leader. Sophia's narrative is an essay that seamlessly weaves in her family's story with her own leadership story, demonstrating the strong impact her family has on her own leadership identity development.

> I grew up in Miami, FL with a brother, sister, and two loving parents. Growing up, I went to catholic school for my whole life which definitely put me in a bubble. That being said, I'm super grateful for my bubble and what my parents were able to provide for me because I know they worked so hard to give me the life and things they had. That kind of motivation and dedication to provide for your family has been instilled in me since I was young.
>
> I come from a family of immigrants and being Cuban American is something so essential to who I am. My grandparents came to this country with nothing but the clothes on their backs and their two kids by winning a Cuban "lottery." This lottery allows you and your family to leave communist Cuba on the condition that the man of the household works for the Cuban army for 1 year. My grandpa worked in treacherous conditions to be able to escape this terrible regime. He woke up with rats on his face, worked in muddy fields that were up to his knees, and had to be away from my grandma and his kids for a whole year, unable to even contact them. His hard work paid off and the Cuban authorities let my family leave, but not without seizing all their belongings first. From Cuba, my grandparents went to Puerto Rico and opened a very successful security business where they put bars on peoples' windows due to the heavy crime there. However, because of this heavy crime my grandfather became a target and was held at gunpoint multiple times. Feeling unsafe, my grandparents ultimately decided that it was best to move the family to Miami where they had my mom. In Miami my grandparents worked very hard to open a successful grocery store and were able to send their three kids to catholic private school like they had always dreamed. My grandparents did all this and more with no college degrees or even understanding of the English language. They knew what kind of life they wanted for their kids and that the world wasn't going to just hand it to them. So, they worked hard to do just that and instilled that kind of leadership in me. In addition, through these actions and hearing these stories, this showed me how strong a woman can be at a young age. My grandma worked so hard alongside my grandpa to create this better life and was the heart of their businesses. This only proved to me that as a girl I could do the job any man could do and that nothing was off limits for me no matter what anyone else said.
>
> As a child I was always very outgoing and made friends easily. I was a natural born leader of the group and always wanted to be in charge. So, when middle school elections came around and I was still the same outgoing girl I had always been it seemed like a natural fit for me to run, right? Wrong. Despite every part of me wanting to run for student council I was too scared to run against my male classmates and friends. I would have been so embarrassed if I lost against/in front of the guys and I was so sure that they

> would win simply because they're boys. I think the reason I believed these things was because growing up the boys were usually the ones celebrated in school. They were always the ones to move the chairs when a teacher needed "someone strong" to help and I guess I saw them more as leaders because in the society I was growing up that was the case. This led me to seeking more confidence in myself and my gender that I hadn't previously realized I was lacking.
>
> When the time came for me to go to high school, I decided to attend the all-girls catholic high school that my mom went to instead of the coed one that my dad and sister went to. I think the main reason I did this was because I was searching for a place that I could go to every day and just feel comfortable and accepted at without having to worry about impressing anyone. I found just that and more in my school. My freshman year, I decided to run for student council without the fear I previously had in middle school. Since it was all girls, I wasn't scared about embarrassing myself in front of my crush or guy friends because there were no guys in sight. So with the encouragement of my parents, I decided to take a leap of faith and actually ended up winning. I continued to run and win for the next 3 years of high school. Being in student government was so essential to my growth as a person and leader because it taught me how to listen to people but also how to understand that you have to take the people's ideas and adjust them to feasible things that can realistically come to be. It also taught me a lot of self-confidence and surrounded me with a strong community of women who became my best friends for life. My experience at an all-girl school changed my life and I'm so grateful for the sister and friendships it left me with, but I wouldn't be the person or leader I am today without a strong female in my life showing me how to be.
>
> My mom is and forever will be my biggest inspiration in life. She showed me not only how a woman should be, but a person too. I couldn't give a presentation or write a paper about the girl I am and how I became this way without talking about her. She was the perfect example of how you don't have to be this big over the top person to be a leader, you just need to be kind and respected. Unfortunately, I very unexpectedly lost her this summer, but I will forever strive to be the kind of woman and leader she was.

For Latina immigrants, like Sophia, family plays an important role in their identity development and their own goals. Latinas from immigrant backgrounds often invoke an immigrant narrative in which they recognize the sacrifices their families have made and their families' experiences with labor exploitation (Conchas & Acevedo, 2020). Influenced and motivated by their families' experiences, Latina's desire to honor their families by attending college and achieving academically (Aragon, 2018; Kiyama, 2018). Sophia was also invoking the immigrant narrative by sharing stories about how her grandfather endured treacherous working conditions. She also shared how both of her grandparents, despite not having college degrees or knowing English, worked hard in the United States to provide for her and for the rest of their family. The rich stories shared by Sophia are examples of familial capital that was cultivated during her childhood. Though the immigrant story is not often recognized as leadership, Sophia's narrative offered a counter-story. Sophia believed her grandparents' hard work and perseverance instilled important leadership qualities within her which she hoped to emulate.

The leadership identity development of Latinas is greatly influenced by the other women in their families, including their mothers and grandmothers (Torres, 2019). Sophia's narrative offers a counter-story that demonstrates the prominent influence the women in her family, her grandmother and mother, had in shaping her as a leader. Latina women are often subject to gender roles influenced by the Latina/o/x value of *marianismo*, which encompasses the beliefs that women should be humble, submissive to men, make sacrifices for their families, and embody the characteristics of the Virgin Mary (Castillo et al., 2010). However, the matriarchs of Latina/o/x families also hold important roles and demonstrate qualities of hard work, strength, and sacrifice (Liang et al., 2017; Torres, 2019). While Sophia's mother and grandmother did make sacrifices for their families, Sophia also saw them as equals to the men in the family. From seeing their mothers and grandmothers be caretakers and make sacrifices, Latinas learn how to be independent and how to balance family expectations (Liang et al., 2017). Sophia also learned from her grandmother and mother how to challenge traditional Latina gender roles and believed she could "do the job any man could do."

However, Sophia shared how she did not initially see herself as a leader when it came to middle school student council elections at her coed school. Despite what she had observed in her family, Sophia felt the boys in her school were preferred for leadership positions. This influenced Sophia to attend an all-girls high school. Once there, she felt comfortable and ran for student council and won 3 years in a row! Similar to previous research (Onorato & Musoba, 2015) that found family members encouraging Latinas to take on leadership roles, Sophia shared how she was encouraged by her family to run for student council at her high school. However, Sophia notes how she was not comfortable with this until she was at an all-girls school. Previous research has found that it is important to have spaces where women can learn about leadership separate from men (Contreras et al., 2022; Eagly & Carli, 2007). Sophia's story emphasizes the importance of also having spaces for women and girls to enact their leadership separate from males, particularly as women have been found to support each other's leadership development (Contreras et al., 2022; Onorato & Musoba, 2015). See Chapter 14 to learn more about the impact of women and leadership programs.

Family members are important role models (see Chapter 7) in childhood because they are often the first leaders that children see and wish to emulate (Komives et al., 2005; Ricks-Scott et al., 2017). As we see through their experiences, Negin's and Sophia's leadership identity development was influenced by their family members' actions and behaviors. Furthermore, Negin's and Sophia's leadership identity development are closely connected to the familial capital, stories and lessons of sacrifice, and perseverance cultivated within their families. Deficit perspectives about Communities of Color and immigrants suggest they are uninvolved in their children's education. Their sacrifice and ability to overcome adversity is often not seen as a strength that they possess that can support their children. For Negin and Sophia, their families' ability to overcome adversity resulted in familial capital that was passed on to them and allowed them to achieve their own goals. Influenced by her family, Negin was committed to showing up every day as herself, which meant leading by working hard and honoring her family's sacrifices. Similarly, Sophia gained strength and confidence from her family and was encouraged and motivated by them to take on positional leadership roles.

WEAVING AND APPLYING THE NARRATIVES

For all of the women in this chapter, Bianca, Kat, Negin and Sophia, their family played an important role in their leadership identity development. As mentioned, previous research has indicated that family is important for Women of Color (Matos, 2015; Shapiro, 2018), and these narratives demonstrate that family experiences and family influences are also important for their leadership identity development, specifically. However, as the narratives demonstrated, Women of Color do not always have monolithic experiences within their families. For some women, like Bianca and Kat, their family experiences are traumatic and force them to mature quickly and to learn how to be leaders for their families. For other women, like Negin and Sophia, their family members role modeled leadership qualities they aspire to emulate.

In their narratives, Bianca, Kat, Negin, and Sophia all discussed the role of gender in their families and how this impacted their leadership development. Each of the women felt there were gendered expectations on how they should act and what they should become. Bianca was expected to be a caregiver for her family members. Kat was expected to stay silent about her sexual abuse. Negin was expected to fulfill her family's wishes. Sophia was expected to be lacking in self-confidence. None of them were expected to be leaders. As such, they all shared how they were reluctant to become leaders and were on a journey to understanding themselves as leaders.

As demonstrated by their narratives, Bianca, Kat, Negin and Sophia connected their familial capital to their leadership identity development. The dominant narrative does not share how the lessons, such as caretaking, coping, and survival, cultivated in Communities of Color can be seen as leadership. The narratives offered in this chapter are counter-stories that demonstrate experiences and lessons learned within Communities of Color influence the leadership identity development of Women of Color. The lessons learned by Bianca, Kat, Negin and Sophia within their families helped them to become leaders who were determined and able to overcome adversity. Komives et al. (2005) described the final stage of leadership development as integration and synthesis. They explained it as "a time of continual, active engagement with leadership as a daily process—as a part of self-identity" where leaders were "increasing in internal confidence and were striving for congruence and integrity" (p. 607). While they have not yet reached integration and synthesis, their narratives demonstrate that Bianca, Negin, Kat, and Sophia were growing in their leadership identity development. They were becoming more confident and beginning to see themselves as leaders. The narrative authors also shared how they hoped their leadership would make their families proud. By becoming leaders in their schools, work, and families, they demonstrate to their families that their hard work and sacrifices did not go unnoticed.

To support Women of Color with their leadership identity development, it is important to understand the role family plays. The narratives shared in this chapter clearly demonstrate for Women of Color their leadership identity development is first cultivated in the home and within the family context. Families within Communities of Color are rich with stories, experiences, and lessons of caretaking, survival, and coping that impact leadership identity development, and they should be acknowledged. Thus, those working with Women of Color should strive to understand their family influence and context and help Women of Color to make the connection between their family experiences and their leadership experiences.

The narratives in this chapter support existing research that demonstrates how family influences the leadership identity development of women and girls (Le Ber et al., 2017; Ricks-Scott et al., 2017). However, these narratives provide a more nuanced understanding of how the intersections of gender, race, ethnicity, class, and immigrant status impact how leadership is developed, conceptualized, and enacted. Future research should utilize an intersectionality framework to understand how multiple forms of oppression based on gender, race, ethnicity, class, and sexuality overlap and compound to impact the leadership identity development of Women of Color.

Lastly, the narratives shared in this chapter, including my own, were counter-stories to the dominant leadership narrative that revealed there is an abundance of familial capital within Communities of Color. The stories and experiences cultivated within the families of Women of Color include lessons of caretaking and providing for family members, and how family members are role models of sacrifice and perseverance. The narratives clearly demonstrate that these lessons impact the leadership identity development of Women of Color. However, the familial capital of Communities of Color is not often seen as leadership. As we support Women of Color, we must acknowledge and value the familial capital of Communities of Color and see it as leadership.

REFERENCES

Aragon, A. (2018). Achieving Latina students: Aspirational counterstories and critical reflections on parental community cultural wealth. *Journal of Latinos and Education, 17*(4), 373–385. https://doi.org/10.1080/15348431.2017.1355804

Castillo, L. G., Perez, F. V., Castillo, R., & Ghosheh, M. R. (2010). Construction and initial validation of the marianismo beliefs scale. *Counselling Psychology Quarterly, 23*(2), 163–175. https://doi.org/10.1080/09515071003776036

Conchas, G. Q., & Acevedo, N. (2020). *The Chicana/o/x dream: Hope, resistance, and educational success.* Harvard Education Press.

Contreras, L. R., & Kiyama, J. M. (2022). "There are obstacles...but we can do it": Latina/o/x activate community cultural wealth and funds of knowledge in the college transition. *Journal of the First-Year Experience & Students in Transition, 34*(1), 9–26. https://www.ingentaconnect.com/content/fyesit/fyesit/2022/00000034/00000001/art00001

Contreras, L. R., Teig, T., & Tyson, M. (2022, April 21–26). *More than just learning leadership: A women's leadership program as a counter-space at a predominantly White institution* [Paper presentation]. AERA 2022: Cultivating Equitable Education Systems for the 21st Century, San Diego, CA.

Eagly, A. H., & Carli, L. L. (2007) Women and the labyrinth of leadership. *Harvard Business Review, 85*, 62–71. https://hbr.org/2007/09/women-and-the-labyrinth-of-leadership

Kiyama, J. M. (2018). "We're serious about our education": A collective testimonio from college-going Latinas to college personnel. *Journal of Hispanic Higher Education, 17*(4), 415–429. https://doi.org/10.1177/1538192717709583

Komives, S. R., Owen, J. E., Longerbeam, S. D., Mainella, F. C., & Osteen, L. (2005). Developing a leadership identity: A grounded theory. *Journal of College Student Development, 46*(6), 593–611. https://doi.org/10.1353/csd.2005.0061

Le Ber, M., LaValley, J., Devnew, L., Austin, A., & Elbert, C. (2017). Tracing the developmental precursors of leadership during childhood and adolescence: A collaborative autoethnographic study of women's leader identity development. In J. Storberg-Walker & P. Haber-Curran (Eds.), *Theorizing women and leadership: New insights and contributions from multiple perspectives.* (pp. 225–248). Information Age Publishing.

Liang, C. T. H., Knauer-Turner, E. A., Molenaar, C. M., & Price, E. (2017). A qualitative examination of the gendered and racialized lives of Latina college students. *Gender Issues, 34*(2), 149–170. https://doi.org/10.1007/s12147-016-9163-8

Liu, H. (2020). *Redeeming leadership: An anti-racist feminist intervention*. Bristol University Press.

Matos, J. M. D. (2015). La familia: The important ingredient for Latina/o college student engagement and persistence. *Equity & Excellence in Education, 48*(3), 436–453. https://doi.org/10.1080/10665684.2015.1056761

McKenzie, B. L. (2018). Am I a leader? Female students leadership identity development. *Journal of Leadership Education, 17*(2), 1–18. https://doi.org/10.12806/V17/I2/R1

Onorato, S., & Musoba, G. D. (2015). La líder: Developing a leadership identity as a Hispanic woman at a Hispanic-serving institution. *Journal of College Student Development, 56*(1), 15–31. https://doi.org/10.1353/csd.2015.0003

Ricks-Scott, H. I., Yeager, K. L., Storberg-Walker, J., Gick, L. M., Haber-Curran, P., & Bauer, D. (2017). Theorizing leadership identity development in girlhood through collaborative autoethnography and women's ways of knowing. In J. Storberg-Walker & P. Haber-Curran (Eds.), *Theorizing women and leadership: New insights and contributions from multiple perspectives* (pp. 265–289). Information Age Publishing.

Sáenz, V. B., García-Louis, C., Drake, A. P., & Guida, T. (2018). Leveraging their family capital: How Latino males successfully navigate the community college. *Community College Review, 46*(1), 40–61. https://doi.org/10.1177/0091552117743567

Shapiro, S. (2018). Familial capital, narratives of agency, and the college transition process for refugee-background youth. *Equity & Excellence in Education, 51*(3–4), 332–346. https://doi.org/10.1080/10665684.2018.1546151

Shetty, R. I. (2020). *The leader identity of Black women in college: A grounded theory* [Doctoral dissertation, University of Georgia]. https://esploro.libs.uga.edu/esploro/outputs/doctoral/The-Leader-Identity-of-Black-Women/9949365960702959

Solórzano, D. G., & Yosso, T. J. (2002). Critical race methodology: Counter-storytelling as an analytical framework for education research. *Qualitative Inquiry, 8*(1), 23–44. https://doi.org/10.1177/107780040200800103

Sy, S. R., & Romero, J. (2008). Family responsibilities among Latina college students from immigrant families. *Journal of Hispanic Higher Education, 7*(3), 212–227. https://doi.org/10.1177/1538192708316208

Torres, M. (2019). *Ella creyó que podía, así que lo hizo: Exploring Latina leader identity development through testimonio* [Doctoral dissertation, Florida State University]. https://diginole.lib.fsu.edu/islandora/object/fsu:722587

Yosso, T. J. (2005). Whose culture has capital? A critical race theory discussion of community cultural wealth. *Race, Ethnicity and Education, 8*(1), 69–91. https://doi.org/10.1080/1361332052000341006

CHAPTER 7

MIRROR, MIRROR ON THE WALL

College Women Leaders Reflect on Their Role Models

Simone A. F. Gause

> OMG! I (Simone) am having a fangirl moment! As I am sitting at the table in a quarterly meeting, I found the room filled with various organizational leaders, including the very few women leaders in a male-dominated field. For a young female and new professional, it was rare for me to see myself reflected in the upper echelons of leadership. One woman was the organization's second in command and unbeknownst to her, she was my role model. The way she carried herself professionally was with a firm but calming grace. I would hear rumblings about how strict and no-nonsense she was, but that just made her even more appealing for me. From my vantage point, her presence commanded respect and was felt before she even spoke a word. At the time, I thought... She is everything I want to be in life! As we are assigned breakout groups, I walk towards my professional exemplar, and my stomach is doing flips. I take a deep breath and tell myself... You got this!

> I courageously introduce myself and was surprised at the welcoming smile that responded and beckoned me to join her table. That was the beginning of a lifelong relationship with her—built by finding community, shared identity, bilateral support, and sage advice on navigating the male-dominated leadership of higher education.

This is the power of one. All it takes is one person to express their belief in you, one person to offer words of encouragement, or one person to embody what you see in yourself. This is the power of role models. Whether you meet one by happenstance or set out on an intentional path to meet your inspirational model—we all have role models that have influenced us in some way. I write this chapter as an ode to the many influential women in my personal and professional lives. It was with their collective love and support that I have succeeded and thrived against all odds. In a full circle moment, where my aspirations have now become inspirations, I give a similar love and support to the next generation of women leaders. It is my hope that by reflecting on role models, this glance in the rearview mirror will allow others to see that their leadership journey is not traveled alone. In the era of likes and followers, it is not necessarily about quantity but more so about the quality of interactions that truly matter.

The power of mentor networks, mentorship, and role models cannot be overstated. Having a "champion" in one's corner bolsters confidence, provides validation, and steels you against obstacles that will undoubtedly appear in your personal and professional journey. The personal narratives highlighted in this chapter underscore the need for women to work with and in support of each other. Much like the previous chapter highlighted, we learn this initial skill of leading and modeling within our family unit.

APPROACHING THE NARRATIVES

The motivational theory of role modeling (Morgenroth et al., 2015) is a new framework that coalesces disparate literature on role models and motivational theory. The motivational theory of role modeling highlights three distinct functions of role models: role models (a) act as behavioral models, (b) represent what's possible, and (c) are inspirational. The theory further highlights the how and when role aspirants engage with role models. Role aspirants are individuals who "makes active, although not necessarily always conscious or deliberate, choices about whose footsteps to follow based on their own values and goals" (Morgenroth et al., 2015, p. 466). In other words, role models do not exist without role aspirants. Much like the mentor–mentee relationship, a role model needs a role aspirant for the relationship to be sustained and balanced. Being a role model can be an overlapping identity with being a mentor. In fact, for this chapter, we consider how role modeling is one type of mentoring relationship. With this in mind, the theory presumes the role model has an active role in the relationship. Otherwise, it would be more akin to idolism or hero worship on the part of the aspirant, where there is not necessarily a direct engaged relationship or an agreement to mentor.

The concept of role modeling has been utilized across broad scholarly contexts to examine how they can convey core knowledge, skills, and abilities (e.g., Paice et al., 2002). For example, studies show role modeling affects the underrepresentation of women in the hard sciences (e.g., Stout et al., 2011; Wang, 2012). The extant literature also provides us with important and interesting insights into the various factors that may impact the effectiveness of role models such as shared identity and group membership (Hoyt, 2013; Lockwood, 2006), shared professional similarities or trajectory (Wang, 2012), as well as the level of role model success and the attribution of this success by the role aspirant (Hoyt, 2013).

Role models provide role aspirants with support in goal embodiment, attainability, and desirability (Morgenroth et al., 2015). In practice, role models model vital experiences in formal leadership, including organizational strategy, financial management, personnel management, and fundraising (Bosma et al., 2012). Across academic and professional disciplines, role models can help bolster one's visibility in their organization that could lead to other opportunities for advancement (Bosma et al., 2012). In the higher education sector, role models serve as an advocate for all students, especially disenfranchised women and minoritized students (Kofoed & McGovney, 2019). Seeing reflections of oneself in professors or in middle and upper management are associated with improved sense of belonging, sense of accomplishment, and an affirmative outlook on the future (Haynes & Block, 2019; Kofoed & McGovney, 2019). Such is the case for Faith, Ameena, Emma, and Anahi.

EXPLORING THE NARRATIVES

From the four narratives below, we see their sources of inspiration, empowerment, and awe as leaders in various organizations, including, academics, athletics, community services, and their own families. In each of the narratives, the women delineate who their role models are, what characteristics or traits were emulated, and how they made the impossible seem possible.

Faith: "Coaches as Role Models"

At the time she wrote her narrative, Faith was a college student majoring in the business field. She is an active member of the first and only Asian-interest sorority on campus. She also identifies as queer, Filipino-American, and White.

> To tell my story properly, I have to introduce you to my family. I was raised in a nuclear household—a mother, father, son, and daughter—the ideal family structure. Throughout my life, my parents have loved me fiercely, supported me through every new passion, and pushed me to be the strongest woman I could be. But growing up wasn't all smooth rides and rainbows. There came a time in my life when I discovered I was queer. And like most young queer people, I was eager and excited to explore a whole new world of culture and history that had just opened up to me. Though I was curious to learn and embrace my newfound identity, I knew my queerness was not accepted in my home. My mother is from the Philippines and was raised with strong Catholic values, and my father is a former marine who grew up with just his father. While I knew they loved me dearly, I also knew that because of their traditional and old-fashioned ways of thinking, they didn't fully understand who I was, why I was gay, and why I couldn't conform to the same conservative values that they held. Yet, on the other side, I felt like I couldn't be my whole true self at home, keeping my romantic life and queer identity a secret for as long as I could.
>
> Still, I discovered my sexuality entering the key formative years of high school and I was determined to know more about the colorful world of the LGBT+ community. I wanted to know more about myself, affirm my identity, and explore what the world had to offer the queer youth of 2014. Another important part of my identity at this time in my life was lacrosse. I started playing the sport at the age of 11 and going into high school I knew I wanted to join my school's team. So I tried out, made the team, and was introduced to my new coaches—two confident, respectable women who also happened to be in a relationship with one another. The more I got to know my coaches, to see them live their day-to-day lives, be accepted by the people around them, and be loud and proud about who they were, the more I admired these women.
>
> Throughout my 4 years on the team, my coaches gave me copious amounts of advice on and off the field. One of my coaches, in particular, was a queer Asian woman, which really resonated with me as I had not seen many queer Asian people in my community. This coach could always read me like a book, and when she pulled me to the side I knew a pep talk was coming, but it was always welcome. I remember the thing she always told me when I was unsure of myself—that I had all the tools to succeed, and she would give me the good juju to go forth and do what I needed. I applied my coach's advice to everything in my life. She instilled the confidence in me

> to go out into the world as the unwavering, proud, queer woman that she inspired me to be.
>
> Having my coaches on my side of the ring gave me the confidence to lead my team as a captain going into my senior year. They taught me how to lead with passion and loyalty and emphasized the importance of being a unit as one and listening to all individuals in the group. Not only that, but they led as an example to show how to share a leadership role as I had a co-captain. My co-captain was also my romantic partner at the time. You can see how the parallels of the dynamic of my relationship and that of my coaches were very significant to me, as I felt like their mirror in a sense. Their presence in my life during these formative years allowed me to see a queer relationship in the later stages of life and gave me an insight into my own possible future. My identity as a queer Asian woman was finally validated and affirmed and being confident in my gender expression allowed me to grow into a strong, thoughtful leader and woman.

Faith shared her struggles in navigating traditional nuclear familial and gender roles and sexuality. She opened her narrative with what she describes as growing up in the ideal family structure of heterosexual parents with two children—a girl and a boy. Compounding that ideal family structure were the religious influences of the family's Catholic faith and in her father's military background, as well as her mother's Filipino cultural perspectives. All these contexts framed Faith's exploration of her sexuality in her family environment from a negative or restrictive viewpoint. Although she knew her parents loved her, Faith had no example or outlet for her burgeoning queer sexuality. Being queer was starkly juxtaposed against the conservative household she described, nor was it accepted at home. However, having a place in two seemingly incongruent worlds did not prevent Faith from authentically embracing her true self. On her path of self-discovery, she found support and community within her lacrosse team.

Faith found inspiration in her two lacrosse coaches. She shared several intersectional identity markers with one coach in particular: Asian, woman, and queer. Not only did the coach serve as a racially familiar role model (Haynes & Block, 2019), but she also instilled the confidence to explore her sexuality fully. Faith was able to witness her coaches stand at full attention in who they were without hiding or shrinking for specific audiences and receive the full support of those around them. The encouragement from the coaches was not limited to lacrosse, as they provided unencumbered support on and off the field. As Faith shared, the pep talks sprinkled with positive affirmation reminded her that she already possesses all the tools needed to be successful. Faith was able to identify these talks as sage advice she could take along in all aspects of life. No longer confined by the traditional conservative gender/

racialized/religious roles of her familial upbringing, Faith now had the confidence to embody her true self-image and self-worth.

For Faith, the coaches demonstrated what leadership can look like in a queer-affirming way. The passion and loyalty the coaches shared with the team emanated from their shared leadership and strength. Faith's formulation of leadership was definitively influenced by witnessing a successful queer intimate partnership and shared team facilitation leadership roles. Almost mirroring her coaches, she too was engaged in a personal relationship with her co-captain, while also sharing the leadership role for the team. Unlike her home environment, the lacrosse team represented an inclusive familial space, one in which Faith saw a healthy queer relationship and what was possible for her future, as a queer, Asian woman. As these were Faith's formative years, she learned about love and leadership from role models that validated and reaffirmed her sexuality. Her coaches acutely represent the motivational theory of role modeling and its three distinct functions for role models: (a) act as behavioral models, (b) represent what's possible, and (c) be inspirational (Morgenroth et al., 2015). Faith affirmed at the end of her narrative she will take these learned skills to be a stronger leader for herself and others.

Ameena: "Teachers as Role Models"

At the time of writing her narrative, Ameena was a Middle Eastern senior double majoring in women's, gender and sexuality studies and journalism and media studies with a minor in political science. In her senior year in college, she was actively involved in student leadership roles including in her residence hall, hosting a weekly feminist discussion group on femme identity, and was the features editor of the campus newspaper, where she aimed to incorporate as many voices and stories from as many different individuals as possible. Ameena wrote:

> She always entered the classroom with a hurried air, her colorful dresses crunching with the quick movement, crossing the distance to the perched Red Bull at the edge of her desk. She would take a sip from a straw, turn to us grandly, and begin telling us the learning objectives of our class. Her name was Miss Whitfield and she taught the equivalent of seventh and eighth grade geography at the private school I attended in the United Arab Emirates.
>
> From the moment Miss Whitfield stepped into the classroom, all of our attention transferred to her. It was magnetic. She would stand in front of us and tell us excitedly about freeze thaw weathering and human migration patterns, as if there were nowhere else in the great wide world that she was

teaching us about that she would rather be. She would wear her hair the same everyday, without ever changing it—in a ponytail tucked into itself where the elastic sits, making the back of her head look like a chestnut waterfall. The front of her face was framed by bangs, sitting perfectly straight and ending at the top of her head. Miss Whitfield would match her dresses to what seemed like an endless collection of bright, similarly cut cardigans.

Whenever someone made an especially great point in our class, she used to take her left hand and close it into a vertical fist and say "you," then dramatically lift her right hand "the ball" before covering her fist and saying "on the ball!" The students in our class would laugh and tease her about that gesture outside of class, but secretly we all loved it, and the recipient of such praise would be flushed with pride for the rest of the class.

I can still remember the first time we learned about globalization. She talked to us about our ever-shrinking world, our technological "advancements," the great disparities in global wealth. For a room filled with students of expatriates whose parents had whisked them off to the UAE in search of better opportunities, understanding globalization helped contextualize our lived realities. She sometimes let me borrow her personal books to fertilize the ideas I would hesitantly tell her about post-class. Once she recommended I read *No Logo* by Naomi Klein. It soon became my Bible. Could she have known, even then, that just a few years later in a university miles away from that sacred classroom, that very author would be my professor?

But if I'm going to say anything about Miss Whitfield I have to tell you about her pink grin. Her smile was entirely conspiratorial, beginning at the corners of her mouth with a noticeable tug, and slowly transforming into a pleased smirk. It was a smile without teeth, just a thin line of pink to suggest her bemusement. It had to be in the curve of that knowing smile that told me everything I needed to know about leadership: that you could be patient and knowledgeable, energetic and kind, friendly and powerful.

Ameena described the quintessential woman when describing her role model, Miss Whitfield. Her description of her teacher seemingly conforms to stereotypical gendered imagery of femininity: dresses, matching cardigans, and wearing the same ponytail hairstyle every day. However, the stereotypical teacher diverges with mention of the academic subject of geography, a traditionally male field, and sips of Red Bull to begin her day. Her captivating persona made learning about geography and globalization even more engaging. Her ability to engage students in the current global activities helped them to make sense of their lived realities as expatriates in a foreign country. Ameena described her experiences in Miss Whitfield's class as magnetic and sacred.

All teachers are not the same. Some can be dry and dull while others have magnetic personalities. Such was the case for Ameena and Miss Whitfield.

Great teachers are those you remember for pushing your intellectual capacity. They provide educational spaces that challenge what you know and what you think you know. Their circle of leadership and influence is not just relegated to knowledge they impart but is inclusive of the sources and resources they introduce into the learning environment. As Ameena explained in her full circle moment, one of her professors in college was the author of a book she was exposed to by Miss Whitfield in high school.

Influential teachers as role models are like a ripple effect of a pebble thrown into a pond. The imagery projected of Miss Whitfield could rival a storybook or movie script—the mannerisms described emulate a humanistic transcendence of knowledge and quest for learning. What does not come across in the narrative is whether Miss Whitfield was a willing participant in the role model–role aspirant relationship or if she was aware of how she was inspiring students such as Ameena. The vulnerability required to be inspirational and actualize serving as a behavioral model (Morgenroth et al., 2015) is not articulated through the protracted admiration bestowed upon Miss Whitfield. However, we can infer that Miss Whitfield took special care to support Ameena, through sharing personal books and encouraging her to expand her understanding of the world. For Ameena, Miss Whitfield challenged traditional perceptions of leadership—authoritative, sharp, inflexible. It was through her interactions with Miss Whitfield that Ameena learned that leadership and femininity are not mutually exclusive.

Emma: "Entrepreneurs as Role Models"

Emma identifies as a White, heterosexual woman, born and raised in the southern United States. She grew up surrounded by women; she has three sisters and is the middle child. At the time of writing her narrative, she was a sophomore studying retail entrepreneurship.

> My story:
> In my female dominated household there were no gender stereotypes.
> I was taught that masculine roles also apply to women.
> Something as simple as going to the gym.
>
> Powerful women lead
> With their mind, body, and spirit.
> My mom believed in a healthy lifestyle for her family and others around her as well.
> She practiced what she preached and opened a female-positive fitness center.

> Rightfully so, her ambition taught me well at a young age.
> Quickly, she became the prototype of her brand,
> without the discrimination of her members.
> She maintained the image of determination, confidence, and radiated warmth with empathy.
>
> This all-inclusive female gym taught me about leadership.
> Strong women lead without fear of intimidation of males.
> Her defiance inspired me to achieve the same lifestyle.
> Moving through life, I carry my mom's ideals.
> Her aspirations made it easier to overcome once impossible obstacles.
> This was the fuel that started my fire of believing women had all the power.
> Powerful women are resourceful.
> I filled her shoes successfully and persistently.
> I have built trust within many aspects of my early life.
> Actively working to solve problems is the most effective leadership quality I radiate.
> This is from working at a design and architecture firm to being a captain of a cheerleading team.
> Having different experiences with a wide variety of people has helped me get to this point.
>
> Overall, my intentions range from searching for the best in people, especially women.
> When exuding confidence within myself, others around me lift and rise to the same level.
> This was taught through my mother and sisters and will lead into my future for children.
> It is very important to teach younger generations about confidence in every aspect of life.
> Success is within everyone, it is just the maze to find it lies within experiences.

Unlike Faith and Ameena, Emma is navigating nontraditional familial and gender roles. In her opening stanza, Emma described her nonnuclear family structure dominated by female heads of households. The absence of gender binaries and ascribed roles is evident in Emma's assertion that masculine roles also apply to women. For Emma, powerful women are creative and lead from within their mind, body, and soul. No one embodied this more than Emma's mother who successfully ran a women's fitness center. Ambition, body-positivity, and fearlessness were traits Emma learned early on just by observing her mom's entrepreneurial spirit.

Starting a business is no small feat, especially for women in a male dominated industry. The living example of Emma's mom taught her that there is a place for defiance, determination, and dogged pursuit of one's goals for women who embrace their power. Emma's mom represented what was possible (Morgenroth et al., 2015) for a woman with a dream and a plan. Emma was able to observe and emulate traits such as confidence, determination, warmth, and empathy. Emma's mother served as her behavioral model (Morgenroth et al., 2015). Her flourishing feminist leadership outlook was evidenced by the unapologetically pro-women stance. Powerful women can do the seemingly impossible. As a mirror reflection, Emma has fully embraced the ambitious goal setting and defying the odds in support of other women—fulfilling the role model–role aspirant requirements of the motivational theory. Emma is grateful for the investment of instilling confidence within, and it is the one thing she plans to pass down to (or build up within) future generations of women leaders. Emma learned from her mother to claim spaces that have been historically masculine and to lead in those spaces with power and strength. Emphasizing her leadership learning from her mother, she exclaimed, "Powerful women lead."

Anahi: "Community Leaders as Role Models"

Anahi identifies as a Latina, first generation college student. At the time of writing her narrative, she was a hospitality major and a member of a women and leadership program where she was exploring leadership skills and leadership styles.

> Growing up, my definition of leadership was always associated with a man. Presidents, dictators, famous CEOs, it seemed like they were always men and I did not understand that there was so much more to leadership than a title. As a Latina woman, my identities were prominent, but so was my idea of leadership. To me, it was generational and therefore somewhat traditional with engraved views of who men and women should be. It was not until I worked with Mrs. Marta Moreno that I aspired to make a difference in my community just as she has. I started volunteering for a nonprofit in Longmont called El Comite. I knew nothing of it, but my mom knew Marta after Marta helped her find a lawyer. El Comite is an organization that helps minorities and low-income communities with any problems they encounter whether with language barriers, legal necessities, or finding resources to succeed. On my very first day, a man walked in asking for Marta's help. He did not speak English and the factory where he worked was not paying him or any of the other minority employees the money they had worked to earn and needed to make a living. As soon as she heard this I remember Marta flaring up. I remember being in disbelief because I knew injustices were everywhere, but I was exposed to so

much more each time somebody would come in asking for help. Marta started making calls to the employer, the public services office, law enforcement, anyone you could think of to help. She was so outspoken and was not afraid to defend anyone who needed it. It scared me sometimes, hearing how loud she was and seeing how it was so effective. Her ability to command any room whereas I saw myself shrink every time I was confronted and did not feel like the room was big enough for all of my identities to belong. She spoke with a passion for what she stood for and whenever someone would come in with a problem she used all of the connections she had until a solution was found. That summer, I truly felt like I was making a difference in people's lives by helping with legal translation, citizenship classes, visiting retirement homes to help those financially struggling with a funeral plan and even set up and helped with community parades inviting all of the minority small businesses to participate. Now, every summer following I go to El Comite to volunteer alongside her. She taught me my true understanding of leadership, not by words but by example and action.

My understanding of leadership transformed as I began intersecting leadership with my identities of gender and ethnicity. Marta Moreno stood out to me because she was very purposeful and that changed my vision of true leadership. She was the first Latina woman I saw in a position like this and seeing the power she took into her hands to help not only our community, but all of the other minorities was something I admire. She was proud of our culture, showcased the work that we can do and she stood her ground despite being demeaned for being both a woman and Latinx. She was the opposite of what was expected of us Latina women. She was not "loud," she was confident and strong. She was humble, open, and honest. I could tell she really cared about what she did as she listened attentively to others' experiences. I wanted to feel fierce like her and raise my voice instead of staying silent. Her transparency taught me that leadership does not come from public figures flaunting for a camera or making empty promises for change, but rather from the people who are representative of all of their identities and embrace who they are while not being afraid to put in the tough work for the better.

For Anahi, traditional gender roles and cultural influences had a strong hold on her perception of who serves as leaders. Living in a patriarchal society and navigating a patriarchal, White dominant culture perpetuated the White, male dominated leadership archetype Anahi had heard about and experienced. It was not until Anahi met Ms. Moreno that she began to question and challenge dominant ideologies about leadership and the role of women. Ms. Moreno challenged what Anahi knew about Latina women! This underscores the importance for women of diverse backgrounds to see themselves in all facets of an organization (Haynes & Block, 2019). Latina women were not all loud and boisterous; Anahi's realization effectively liberated her from the stereotypes and tropes surrounding Latina women and allowed her to see what was possible (Morgenroth et al., 2015). Anahi learned about the quiet strength needed to engage in community support organizations and the openness and humility required to serve others. Anahi also got a first-hand lesson in authentic leadership by her role model's example and actions.

Working on behalf of others, you get to see the threshold between community and individuality. There is a strength in the collective that is inspirational and aspirational. Ms. Moreno inspired Anahi to fight for what is right, to use her voice for those less fortunate. As a result, Anahi aspired to give back to her community, using her knowledge and skills for the greater good.

Many organizations, including nonprofits (like the one Ms. Moreno and Anahi worked for), teams, education systems, families, and more are filled with role models and role aspirants. Organizations and groups inspired by a shared passion or shared cause, who are focused on the relationships that form, flourish, and push the organization forward will invariable check all the role model functions from Morgenroth et al. (2015), where role models: (a) act as behavioral models, (b) represent what's possible, and (c) are inspirational. By learning from the modeling of others, our narrative authors learned how leaders create a sense of belonging for themselves and others. We can learn from our narrative authors' reflections: When you truly feel like you belong, your contributions and sense of self-worth take on a fierceness that comes across as commanding, confident, and caring. By learning from role models, you begin to see your true self in the mirror.

WEAVING THE NARRATIVES

Although each narrative provides a unique perspective into the function of role models in one's leadership development, there are a few commonalities and distinctions worth noting. First, all the women were navigating familial influences, gender roles, and gender stereotypes. Many were going against the grain of dominant ideologies and finding grace within their role model relationships to circumnavigate what can be harsh terrain for women in developmental growth. As their backgrounds and intersecting identities came into play, they were all keenly aware that they were making sense of their own reflective journeys (the evolution of their own leadership identity) in relation to the world. Their reflections reveal the how and who influenced their leadership development thus far. Lastly, the women all in their own way concurred that leadership emanates from self-confidence. They all described being empowered to lead, to act, to embrace themselves. They learned from others how to think about themselves and who they want to be. Their leadership journey is a mirror reflection of their collective experiences influenced by external factors, including role models.

Each narrative was distinct in who served as a role model. Each woman's narrative convincingly shared the influential examples of leadership personified. When and where the seeds of leadership were planted varied, but the women all had a different terrain as role aspirants that was ripe for a role model to act as a behavioral model (Morgenroth et al., 2015). In each instance, the role model represented what was possible in a seemingly impossible world. Lastly, each narrative uncovered different reasons for why the role models were deemed inspirational and the timescale for the sphere of influence also varied greatly. Thus, a great role model can be found anywhere and have lasting impact on the future of their role aspirant.

APPLYING THE NARRATIVES

Role models are not only those in "positions of power" but rather those that touch and feed the most inner part of our identity development. Role models as mentors serve as a sounding board for students steeped in the growth and development phases of adolescence and young adulthood. The value of mentors and role models in identifying and developing diverse leaders is not a new discovery, but it is important to consider how this value is being intentionally addressed for strategic opportunity in our organizations. We can take the learning from these narratives to consider how purposeful integration of connection to and reflection on role models as mentors is a primary element of leadership learning in higher education and beyond.

With this purpose in mind, based upon the narratives, there are four integral components of a mentoring program that could be implemented in higher education or other organizations. These components are as follows: (a) provide training in leadership skills (Bosma et al., 2012), (b) provide participants with a national network for career opportunities (Kofoed & McGovney, 2019; Paice et al., 2002), (c) encourage participants to seek leadership opportunities (Lockwood, 2006; Stout et al., 2011), and (d) encourage community engagement to improve working relationships and professional communications (Haynes & Block, 2019).

Many traditional leadership development programs will pair you with a positional mentor. However, the narratives concur with the literature that role models serve various functions that are not necessarily positional (Hoyt, 2013). Having a mentoring program that is associated with a national network of peers or mentors will not only benefit incumbents with professional opportunities, but it will also broaden the reach and scope of an institution through alumni connections and a shared sense of belonging and community. Mentoring programs are designed to train the next generation of leaders; thus, it makes sense for such programs to identify and assist participants with pursuing new leadership opportunities as they arise and are applicable.

From a systems-change approach, the benefits of successful mentoring are increased intellectual capital through shared knowledge and increased opportunities for role aspirants to develop and advance their professional career trajectory. Furthermore, leaders who have benefitted from active role modeling relationships are likely to assist other women striving to push beyond perceived or institutionalized leadership limitations (Kofoed & McGovney, 2019). Aspiring leaders might also pursue participation in national professional development programs that affords mentees the rare opportunity to be formally partnered with a professional mentor who often remains a trusted confidant long after the professional development program concludes.

As women, we are often faced with various gender stereotypes and gender roles that, if left unchecked, could stymie ambition, innovation, and achievement. In learning from the narratives shared in this chapter, and the countless other stories yet told, we can have a greater appreciation for the role models in our lives that identify, encourage, support, and celebrate the leader within us. Like leadership, role models are not confined to positional places of power. The common thread amongst this group of role models was their generosity, strength in the face of challenges, and the impact they had on young women. As the role of women in society continues to evolve, so too do the challenges of gender conformity or nonconformity. Women work through these stereotypes and challenges as their multiple intersecting identities form, evolve, and take shape. One's leadership identity is therefore influenced by their personal and professional identity development and the role models that helped shape them. It is through our identity and leadership development that role models can help women fight against real and perceived obstacles, like imposter syndrome, which is further explored in the next chapter.

REFERENCES

Bosma, N., Hessels, J., Schutjens, V., Van Praag, M., & Verheul, I. (2012). Entrepreneurship and role models. *Journal of Economic Psychology, 33*, 410–424. https://doi.org/10.1016/j.joep.2011.03.004

Haynes, C., & Block, R. (2019). Role-model-in-chief: Understanding a Michelle Obama effect. *Politics & Gender, 15*(3), 365–402. https://doi.org/10.1017/S1743923X18000533

Hoyt, C. L. (2013). Inspirational or self-deflating: The role of self-efficacy in elite role model effectiveness. *Social Psychological and Personality Science, 4*(3), 290–298. https://doi.org/10.1177/1948550612455066

Kofoed, M. S., & McGovney, E. (2019). The effect of same-gender or same-race role models on occupation choice: Evidence from randomly assigned mentors at West Point. *Journal of Human Resources, 54*(2), 430–467. https://doi.org/10.3368/jhr.54.2.0416.7838R1

Lockwood, P. (2006). "Someone like me can be successful": Do college students need same-gender role models? *Psychology of Women Quarterly, 30,* 36–46. https://doi.org/10.1111/j.1471-6402.2006.00260.x

Morgenroth, T., Ryan, M. K., & Peters, K. (2015). The motivational theory of role modeling: How role models influence role aspirants' goals. *Review of General Psychology, 19*(4), 465–483. https://doi.org/10.1037/gpr0000059

Paice, E., Heard, S., & Moss, F. (2002). How important are role models in making good doctors? *BMJ, 325,* 707–710. https://doi.org/10.1136/bmj.325.7366.707

Stout, J. G., Dasgupta, N., Hunsinger, M., & McManus, M. A. (2011). STEMing the tide: Using ingroup experts to inoculate women's self-concept in science, technology, engineering, and mathematics (STEM). *Journal of Personality and Social Psychology, 100*(2), 255–270. https://doi.org/10.1037/a0021385

Wang, M. T. (2012). Educational and career interests in math: A longitudinal examination of the links between classroom environment, motivational beliefs, and interests. *Developmental Psychology, 48*(6), 1643–1657. https://doi.org/10.1037/a0027247

PART II

EXPLORING THE NARRATIVES—GROWTH

Art by Sam

Was I only given those positions because I was a good woman leader and not a good leader? . . . When did I even learn all of these labels and expectations?

This put a fire under me where I felt I had something to prove and wanted to show everyone I was a good leader. Not a "bad leader," not a good leader for a woman, but a good leader in any space.

—Katherine, Chapter 8, p. 135

CHAPTER 8

AM I DOING IT RIGHT?

College Women Leaders and Their Experiences With Imposter Syndrome

Adrian L. Bitton

My (Adrian's) hands are sweaty, my heart begins to race, intrusive thoughts start to permeate my mind—Who am I to advice on this topic? I'm not an expert. I'm just making it up as I go along most of the time. I stare blankly at the screen as the cursor blinks back at me. This is literally what happened when I sat down to write this chapter.

As a low-income, first-generation, Jewish woman, I was keenly aware that I did not fit the typical prototype of leader. My mother actively worked to combat this internalized belief by reinforcing messages that I could be or do anything. As a single mother, she knew all too well the trappings of imposter syndrome and wanted to ensure that I did not suffer the same fate. Building on the previous chapter about role models, my mother was my first and biggest role model. Her vocal encouragement was instrumental in building my confidence and courage and was a driving force in my pursuit of leadership opportunities.

As I stared back at my cursor, I reminded myself that although I am not

> an expert, I have experienced imposter syndrome at various points in my life and leadership journey, and I do have valuable insights to share that might resonate with others. My hope is that by writing about them, other people who experience imposter syndrome will feel less alone and recognize how the U.S. society, built upon White supremacy, socializes people, specifically those with marginalized identities, into doubting their capacity for leadership. Similarly, all three narratives below discuss how (real or prescribed) role models influenced their experiences with imposter syndrome.

APPROACHING THE NARRATIVES

Imposter syndrome is a term used to describe "a specific form of self-doubt where people fear being found out as less than worthy, or a fraud" (Owen, 2020, p. 194). Georgia State University psychologists Pauline Rose Clance and Suzanne Ament Imes are credited with studying what was first called "imposter phenomenon" in 1978 in a study about high-achieving women (Clance & Imes, 1978; Owen, 2020; Tulshyan & Burey, 2021). Their study included over 100 women ranging from undergraduate women, graduate students, medical students, women faculty with PhDs, and professional women from a variety of sectors. Despite their achievements, honors, degrees, and professional recognitions, these women did not feel an internal sense of success and instead described themselves as imposters. Clance and Imes (1978) elaborate, "Women who experience the impostor phenomenon maintain a strong belief that they are not intelligent; in fact, they are convinced that they have fooled anyone who thinks otherwise" (p. 241). This foundational study provided insights into the potential origins (e.g., familial dynamics) and persistence of imposter syndrome along with therapeutic interventions that could be used to disrupt these thought patterns (Clance & Imes, 1978).

Over the last 50 years, there has been a proliferation of research related to imposter syndrome with studies seeking to provide greater understanding on the ways in which imposter syndrome manifests and is related to other psychological phenomena (e.g., socialization, attributions, gender stereotyping, effortless perfection). Imposter syndrome has also become a common refrain to explain why women are underrepresented within leadership roles, particularly top leadership positions (Eagly & Carli, 2007).

However, attributing this trend to imposter syndrome alone is incomplete and does not take into account the structural and cultural barriers that may also affect a woman's attainment of a leadership position or even their motivation to lead. In order to better understand how leadership motivation and leadership enactment work in concert to shape women's experiences in leadership, we must first turn to the concept of leadership self-efficacy. Leadership self-efficacy is a term that builds upon psychologist Albert Bandura's concept of efficacy within social cognitive theory (Dwyer, 2019). Efficacy is the belief a person carries suggesting they can be successful in a particular task or domain (e.g., for leadership self-efficacy, it is the belief that one has the ability to be successful in leadership). The terms efficacy and confidence are often used interchangeably, however, it is important to note the distinction. Whereas confidence (or lack thereof) refers to one's overall sense of self, efficacy is contextually driven (e.g., a person can have high efficacy as a writer but simultaneously have low efficacy as a public speaker). Moreover, while leadership efficacy and leadership competency can be related, they are not necessarily aligned. In fact, according to the Multi-Institutional Study of Leadership, college women report lower levels of leadership self-efficacy than their male peers, despite reporting behaviors and demonstrating competencies related to socially responsible leadership at greater rates than their male peers (Calizo et al., 2007; Dugan & Komives, 2007; Haber-Curran et al., 2018; McCormick et al., 2002). These discrepancies are problematic and counter to the mission of many higher education institutions to develop active citizens and leaders (Devies & Guthrie, 2022; Guthrie & Chunoo, 2018). Therefore, many colleges and universities have commissioned reports regarding women's college experiences (e.g., Duke University's The Women's Initiative Report and Princeton University's Report of the Steering Committee on Undergraduate Women's Leadership).

Institution-specific data from reports like the ones mentioned above can be useful in conjunction with the efficacy literature in order to build programs and interventions that aim to increase women's leadership self-efficacy and address challenges of imposter syndrome. Bandura (1997) identifies four methods that are effective for building self-efficacy: mastery experiences (directly engaging in meaningful and practical domain-specific experiences), vicarious experiences (learning from role models and observing the example of others), verbal persuasion (positive, constructive feedback and support), and physiological and affective states (one's own sense of well-being and socioemotional health; Owen, 2020). Multiple studies have confirmed that these methods are effective for building women's leadership self-efficacy (Howes, 2016; Hoyt, 2005). For example, we know from the literature that women who are encouraged to participate in a leadership experience are more likely to participate than women who are not (Rupert, 2019). We also know the value of having a leader or role model who shares (some) of your social identities and having more women in leadership roles helps college women envision themselves as leaders (Lockwood, 2006).

Tushyan and Burey (2021) note many women-focused leadership development programs include conversations or sessions related to imposter syndrome. However, I caution that we must be careful with how imposter syndrome is presented and addressed in these leadership development programs. Although studies have shown that men also experience imposter syndrome (Clance & Imes, 1978; Pedler, 2011), it is still largely conceptualized and presented as a "women's issue." Furthermore, the language that is used to describe it (e.g., she *suffers* from imposter *syndrome*), and the framing of imposter syndrome as an individual issue (versus critiquing the systems and socialization that perpetuates it) continues to put the onus on women to adapt and to find a way to thrive within toxic environments rather than changing the toxic environments themselves (Haber-Curran et al., 2018; Owen, 2020; Tulshyan & Burey, 2021). In an effort to disrupt this entrenched practice, the narratives below are analyzed through the lens of critical perspectives in leadership (Dugan, 2017).

Critical perspectives in leadership are part of a larger trend to embrace socially just perspectives within the field of leadership education on college and university campuses. It shifts the focus away from skill-building and considerations of individual situations and contexts. Instead, critical perspectives in leadership foreground macro-level systems and structures of inequality within leadership and leadership education and invite critique of established leadership theories and models. Instead of reporting disparities among demographic groups and a deficit model approach to leadership education (e.g., lack of leadership efficacy, lack of leadership motivation, lack of leadership skill, or in this case, imposter syndrome), we are called to examine the ways in which the larger social context, socialization, and environments shape the beliefs, understanding, and practice of leadership (Barnes et al., 2018; Dugan & Humbles, 2018; Osteen et al., 2016).

EXPLORING THE NARRATIVES

In each of the three narratives in this chapter, the women described their experiences with imposter syndrome and how it has affected their leadership identity, capacity, and efficacy. However, when analyzing the narratives with feminist narrative methods (Bloom, 1998) and through the lens of critical perspectives in leadership (Dugan, 2017), we can consider how the narrative authors moved from an internal sense of doubt to rejecting societal norms and external expectations for them as leaders.

Katherine: "A Good Leader in Any Space"

First, we will consider Katherine's narrative. She identifies as a straight, White, Catholic woman.

Dance Marathon executive board member, honors colloquium leader, Torchbearer 100 inductee, student government vice president, student director of staff engagement and conduct for campus recreation, panhellenic recruitment counselor, print editor for *The Circuit* newspaper. You would think all of these titles I've held would allow me to believe that I am a good leader; however, no title stands out to me more than when my high school student government teacher told me I was a "bad leader."

Leader is a title I have been proud and privileged to hold throughout my whole life. Growing up, my mom was a huge role model to me because she has always been the leader everyone in our community looks up to. Her leadership style is to work tirelessly behind the scenes, but not feel the need to take credit for her work or prove her superiority to others. Because of her quiet self-confidence and the respect she was awarded from others, I learned to emulate her label as a quiet yet effective leader in every room I walked into.

In elementary and middle school, I had the privilege of receiving every leadership position I tried out for, in great thanks to the lessons my mom taught me. This meant that going into high school, I trusted my leadership abilities and tried out for positions even if it was scary for an introvert like myself. I still got every position I wanted, which is a huge privilege and should have been a sign that I was doing something right as a leader, but instead, I started to doubt myself. This was the moment my student government teacher labeled me as a "bad leader." Even though I was doing everything that was asked of me and more, she gave all the credit to my male counterpart because he was so outspoken and took all the credit despite my effort behind the scenes. This was the turning point I realized the positions I held had always been in female dominated spaces and not male dominated ones. I began to question everything I ever thought about my leadership abilities. I felt like my hard work up to this point had been for nothing. I was embarrassed, disheartened, and emotionally crushed. Was I only given those positions because I was a good woman leader and not a good leader? Would I only be a good leader in my Girl Scout troop or yearbook class and not in spaces where men also held positions? Do I need to be loud and pushy to be a leader? Should I have looked up to my dad instead of my mom to shape my idea of leadership? When did I even learn all of these labels and expectations?

This put a fire under me where I felt I had something to prove and wanted to show everyone I was a good leader. Not a bad leader, not a good leader for a woman, but a good leader in any space.

In order to prove to my teacher and myself that I could be a good leader on my own terms, I came to college and instantly got involved with every leadership opportunity I could. I was successful at this challenge, and because of my skills, I kept getting promoted in all of my involvements. However, no matter how many titles and accolades I accumulated, it still didn't feel like I was doing enough. The doubt, criticism, shrinking, and

> silencing from myself and others led me to have a mental health breakdown, ultimately forcing me to step down from my biggest and most treasured leadership position in college.
>
> While I wish I could have kept my leadership position, taking a step back has taught me how critical it is for women to believe in themselves and to build each other up as leaders. Whether we are quiet and nurturing or loud and outspoken, we all deserve to be treated with respect and recognized for the unique assets we bring to the space in which we lead.
>
> Does this make me a bad leader or simply a woman who has faced too much pressure to prove to the world that I am capable of leading?

Katherine's narrative begins with an expansive list of leadership positions that she has held. Each position is presented as if it is proof of her leadership capacity and skills. However, just like in Clance and Imes's (1978) study, this "evidence" is discounted immediately as she recalls being labeled a bad leader by her high school student government teacher. In listing her leadership positions and reflecting on her early and consistent attainment of leadership roles throughout her K–12 and undergraduate experiences, Katherine is describing leadership as positional and conferred through the authority that is granted through formalized roles. Indeed, this is how many people conceptualize leadership and leaders. Ashford and DeRue (2012) complicate this notion by asserting that "leader" is an identity that can be both self-proclaimed and granted by others. Initially, Katherine's identity as a leader was largely contingent upon others' perception of her as a leader and the positive feedback loop of acquiring more and more leadership positions. These mastery experiences (i.e., leadership positions) were instrumental in building her leadership efficacy. However, her leadership efficacy plummeted when Katherine's student government teacher deemed her a bad leader. This is an example of how feedback (or verbal persuasion) from others can be harmful to one's leadership efficacy and have negative repercussions for one's physiological and affective states. She describes how she began to question her identity as a leader as she navigated overwhelming feelings of doubt as well as her feelings of being "embarrassed, disheartened, and emotionally crushed." She became keenly aware of how her government teacher favored her male counterpart who was more outspoken and quick to take credit for efforts or achievements that involved her.

Through her self-reflection (see Chapter 10 for more on this reflection), she noted how her democratic and communal style of leadership was stereotypical of how women lead. This led her to question whether she "was a good woman leader and not a good leader?"—demonstrating the pervasiveness of the dominant leadership narrative of "think leader, think male" (Hoyt, 2005). She also realized the different ways that leadership was valued within single gender versus mixed gender contexts. Initially these realizations were motivation for her to double down on her efforts and involvement when she entered the collegiate setting. However, this was not sustainable and ultimately, the need to prioritize her mental health and relinquish one of her leadership positions served as a major shift in Katherine's conceptualization of leadership. She reframed the criticism of being a bad leader from a personal failure to a rejection of the dominant, gendered narrative of leaders and leadership. At the end of her narrative, she makes an impassioned call for inclusive and expansive leadership that honors the contributions of all people.

Stephanie: Love Freely, Be Me Unapologetically

Building off of Katherine's call for inclusive leadership, Stephanie's narrative below beautifully illuminates how her identities as a queer, Latina, college-aged woman is inextricably linked to her values, practices, and identification as a leader.

> I think I've always known I was a leader, just didn't know what it meant to truly be one. Growing up I was always the bossiest one out of all of my cousins. They would always listen to what I said, but a part of that was definitely me being older than most of them. I felt like a leader in my family, but not in any other aspect of my life. I always felt different than my cousins but I wasn't really sure of why that was. Some of my cousins were really smart and they excelled at school. They were expected to do well in school as they were undocumented. Some of my cousins were really "good girls" and loved to cook and clean the house, really taking care of their family. They were expected to be that way. I never fell into either/or.
>
> Growing up I never felt enough. So I decided it was up to me to decide what I was really good at. I started doing makeup for fun and thought I had finally found the one thing I was really good at, but once my love for makeup had vanished I again felt like I wasn't enough. I was so unsure of who I was and what I wanted out of life. I was tired of trying to meet the standards of my family until I eventually stopped caring and stopped yearning for their approval. I stopped trying to meet their exhausting standards and for once, started listening to my own thoughts and opinions. I started sticking up for myself and for my own beliefs. I started questioning everything I was taught. My religion, my sexuality, my gender expression, my beliefs, the (cultural) norms, everything. I started asking, "Why am I doing this and who am I doing it for?" If the answer wasn't for myself then, I would tell myself that I couldn't expect that of myself because they weren't my own expectations. I started to wonder why everyone else wasn't asking the same questions and was hit with the reality that most people conform to the norm. They follow

> what is "expected" or what is "normal." Society teaches us that these expectations are the only norm when in reality they are not. Normal is subjective to every individual.
>
> Since coming to these realizations, I started to love myself for the way I am. I started accepting my own norms and my own reality. I stopped listening to everyone else's opinion and started valuing my own more. I also started preaching this to my family and friends. I try my hardest to remind them that being different is okay. I try to remind them that the expectations that are taught in society and culturally are sometimes not aligned with our life and that it's okay to stray away from normalcy. Coming out to my parents was extremely hard for me, coming from a Hispanic background. My family told me that I wasn't normal and that my life wouldn't be normal or like the rest of theirs. My family wasn't wrong, my life is different, but for all the right reasons. I get to love freely, I get to be me unapologetically. Being myself in my family has been by far my favorite role as a leader. I was the first in my family to come out and although I hated that because I had no one to relate to, it gave me the reality I needed to be faced with. My family still loves me and I hope that one day they realize that my life will still be a good one. All I've cared about is being true to myself and I hope that that is the message I offer to others in my family. Coming out was hard, but it made me question what was normal. It allowed me to be a leader to my younger family members. It allowed me to be a role model for those in my family that wanted to stray from the norms. It has warmed my heart to know that I am now someone my family can confide in because I know I wish I had someone to confide in all those years back. Owning my label as a queer individual allowed me to accept my own truth and to accept my role as a leader.

In Stephanie's opening sentence, she expresses that she has a deeply internalized sense of self as a leader, however, her relationship to what this means and how to embody her leader identity has shifted over time. Similar to Katherine, Stephanie begins her narrative by describing how she aligns with the dominant narrative of leadership. She refers to herself as bossy and recalls how her cousins would listen to what she said. However, Stephanie also reveals that she felt different and outside "the norm." This feeling of being different corresponds with descriptions of imposter syndrome and the fear of being found out as someone who deviates from the norm. She elaborates that she didn't fit into the stereotypical high achieving student or the "good girl" archetype of enjoying domestic chores such as cooking and cleaning like her other cousins. Instead, she sought out to discover her talents, although she remained unfulfilled as her interests ebbed and flowed. It was through her own identity development and reflecting upon different aspects of her identities (e.g., religion, sexuality, gender expression) that Stephanie began to question what was considered normal. In reflecting upon her identities, power, privilege, and oppression, Stephanie was engaging in critical perspectives in leadership and social justice. She recognized that trying to live under the crushing weight of her family's standards and society's expectations was preventing her from living an authentic life and contributing to feelings associated with imposter syndrome.

Stephanie's narrative is heartwarming as she described how her life has changed since she started questioning the dominant narratives of gender and leadership. By checking in with herself and reflecting upon the questions—"Why am I doing this?" and "Who am I doing it for?"—she was able to embrace her own values and expectations. She noted, "If the answer wasn't for myself then, I would tell myself that I couldn't expect that of myself because they weren't my own expectations." Ultimately, releasing herself from the obligations of society's expectations changed the way she felt about being different and about normalcy. Her feelings of imposter syndrome lessened as she developed a deeper and more authentic sense of self. As a result, Stephanie shared a crucible moment where she came out to her family. She articulated that now she loves herself, values her own opinion, and gets to be her true, authentic self, unapologetically. Stephanie recognized that these are essential components of leadership. She views herself as a leader within her family and prides herself on being a role model that her younger cousins can count on for support.

Nicollette: "Inclusive Leadership/Not Weaknesses, But Rather Strengths"

Finally we turn to Nicollette, whose narrative highlights how mentors (especially those with similar identities) can be instrumental in building one's own efficacy for leadership. Nicollette identifies as a female, Asian American/Hispanic/Caucasian, middle-class, able-bodied, atheist, American, first-generation college student.

> To everyone else, it may have seemed like any ordinary day. However, to me, that cold February day in 2016 was far from.
>
> I am a fifth generation Japanese American on my mother's side. Because I am fifth generation, I have experienced much disconnect from my culture and my ancestry. Being an active member of the Japanese American community as well as the larger Asian American community is how I am able to bridge that disconnect. February 18, 2016, was a day of great significance to me as I would be volunteering for the first time at the Annual Day of Remembrance. This day holds great significance in the Japanese American community as it commemorates the day on which President Franklin D. Roosevelt signed

Executive Order 9066, an order that enabled the U.S. military to incarcerate over 120,000 Japanese Americans men, women, and children.

With my plaid red dress and my hair braided tightly, I walked ecstatically and confidently into the museum where the event would be held. I joined the crowd of gathering volunteers, excitedly waiting to be appointed a job. However, as I stood and looked around, I noticed that every other volunteer was considerably older than me, and most of them were male. Standing at the back of the group, I could neither hear nor see the person delegating roles. As the minutes passed, I began to doubt myself. I could feel the imposter syndrome manifesting itself. I thought to myself, "Why am I here?"; "What did I possibly think I could bring to this team?"; "I have no experience compared to these other volunteers." As jobs continued to be delegated, I patiently waited with my hands tightly linked together for my name to be called. When this did not happen, I became increasingly tense, beads of sweat forming on my forehead. I truly began to fear that my assistance was neither wanted nor needed.

As hot tears welled in my eyes and my throat tightened, I began to turn around—giving up. Then suddenly, I heard a woman's voice say loud and clear. Looking at me directly she said, "My name is Janice Ogawa. Are you Nicollette?" I nodded carefully. "You will be on guest check-in. Will you please put this nametag on?" In a sense of disbelief, I put on the nametag and walked over to the check-in table. I wondered why, unlike the other volunteers around me, she had paid attention to my presence. After some long contemplation, I came to the realization that Janice did not call upon me because she pitied me for my age. She treated me the same way that she had treated every other volunteer: with respect and maturity. She made me feel included and she reminded me that I do have important and unique skills to bring to the table, that I am just as valuable to the community as anyone else. This moment was instrumental in forming my definition of leadership, which is that leadership is about effectively utilizing teamwork, having strong organizational skills, creating inclusive environments, giving everyone the space for their voice to be heard, and understanding that the unique identities of people are not weaknesses, but rather strengths.

Janice plays an incredibly important role in the Japanese American community. Her tenacity and confidence are incredibly inspiring to me, and something that I continue to learn from. As a young multiethnic, multiracial woman from a lower socioeconomic background, I recognize that I do not match the typical image of a leader. While I expect that my unique intersectionality of identities will bring challenges, like Janice, I will not let those challenges interfere with how I lead. I will use my identities as strengths, I will use my identities to empower other minority groups, and I will use my identities to re-illustrate the image of what leadership should look like.

Looking back, I notice a sort of irony of that day. On February 18, 1942, President Franklin D. Roosevelt, the person who is supposed to represent

> exactly what it means to be an effective and compassionate leader, did the complete opposite by signing Executive Order 9066. This truth has allowed me to come to the realization that leadership is not defined by a person's position of power, but rather by one's ability to lead inclusively, set an inspiring vision, and motivate people. No matter a person's position, no matter a person's identity, everyone has the ability to be a good leader.

Nicollette's narrative described a very particular memory from a very specific date. She wrote about feeling excited and confident when she entered the museum to volunteer for the Annual Day of Remembrance (commemorating the day that President Roosevelt signed an executive order permitting Japanese internment during WWII). However, these positive feelings turned into self-doubt when she noticed that she did not fit the demographic of the other volunteers (primarily older men). Beyond the negative questions and thoughts that raced through her mind, she vividly recalled the physical manifestations of her discomfort (e.g., tense, beads of sweat, hot tears, throat tightening). More broadly, she reflected upon how her identities as a young, multiethnic, multiracial woman from a lower social class background do not correspond with the "typical" image (or dominant narrative and identities) of a leader.

When Janice, another woman volunteer, assigned Nicollette a job and provided her with a way to contribute, Nicollette was able to overcome her feelings of being an imposter. Although their interaction was brief, Nicollette engaged in important meaning-making regarding leadership based on her observations and reflections from that day. Not only was Nicollette able to identify the leadership behaviors and values that Janice embodied, she also returned to them as a source of inspiration and continued learning. The latter half of the narrative revealed her clearly articulated perception of inclusive leadership and the qualities and characteristics of leaders she now understands and values. She concluded her narrative by juxtaposing President Roosevelt, the positional leader of the country during World War II who allowed the internment of Japanese Americans, with Janice, her leadership role model and how Janice advanced the socially just beliefs she now holds regarding leadership.

WEAVING THE NARRATIVES

Although each narrative is unique in both the context and the intersecting social identities of the women, there are some commonalities worth exploring. The first among them is that all three women expressed a sense and awareness of being "outside the norm" or what they understood to be the idealized, societal standard. Stephanie described herself as feeling different from her family, particularly her cousins, with regard to their interests and talents and the cultural expectations associated with her Hispanic background. Whereas Katherine became more aware of different types of (gendered) leadership styles and expectations. Lastly, Nicollette discussed how the different social identities (i.e., older men) of the other volunteers caused her to doubt her place and potential contribution to the Annual Day of Remembrance event.

Mentorship experiences were another common theme throughout the three narratives. We know from existing literature that women are more likely to engage in leadership opportunities when someone else encourages them or invites them to participate (Rupert, 2019; see Chapter 7 for more information about the significance of role models for college women). Therefore, it is not surprising that mentorship was also a part of their narratives regarding imposter syndrome. What we hope is that women have positive experiences with mentorship, such as how Nicollette described her admiration of and relationship with Janice. Existing literature supports that having leaders "who look like you" (i.e., leaders who share similar social identities) can be a powerful, supportive force in leadership development (Arminio et al., 2000). What we talk about less (but often remember more vividly) are the negative experiences we have with someone we look up to, such as a coach, advisor, boss, or teacher. Katherine recalled with detail the damaging and long-lasting effects of having her high school student government teacher call her a "bad leader." Stephanie recognizes the importance of mentorship because of her lack of mentorship during her formative years. She reflects on how her experience could have been different had she had that level of support and uses that as a motivation to serve in this role for her younger cousins.

Lastly, in an effort to focus on actually overcoming imposter syndrome, rather than just describing it, it is important to note the key transition that occurred across all three narratives. Each woman described the shift from recognizing imposter syndrome as self-doubt to associating imposter syndrome as the result of internalizing others' (and society's) expectations of them. This shift in association created pathways for agency where they could engage in critical perspectives and reject, instead of internalizing, society's standards. Similarly, this shift seems to coincide with their evolving conceptualizations of what leadership means. As they solidified their beliefs and thoughts about leadership, particularly in ways that are more justice-oriented, it also shaped their perceptions of who leaders are. As a result, it opens space for women and other people with marginalized identities to be included as role models for leadership. Having a more expansive perspective on who can be and who is a leader serves as a helpful mechanism for overcoming imposter syndrome in leadership and building leadership self-efficacy (refer to Chapter 10 for more information on conceptualizations of leadership; refer to Chapter 12 for more information on leadership identity).

While there are many similarities across the three narratives in this chapter, it is also important to note that there are also key features which make each one distinct. The most central distinction is that each woman who authored a narrative in this book is unique. Oftentimes in research on women, the focus is on their gender identity (and expression). This can mask key differences in women's narratives as it fails to consider how their unique combination of social identities intersect to influence the ways in which they perceive and navigate the world. In addition to the various social identities that they hold, each woman described their unique pathways and experiences regarding leadership. For some, such as Katherine, leadership development opportunities were plentiful and accessible through clubs and organizations at school. For others, like Stephanie, leadership development was mostly situated within her family context. For Nicollette and others, leadership development was tied to service and volunteer opportunities within their broader community. Despite these multiple pathways, the three women in this chapter still described, and in some cases named, imposter syndrome. We can learn a lot from their narratives regarding their different responses and reflective meaning-making in order to overcome their feelings of imposter syndrome.

APPLYING THE NARRATIVES

There is power in naming trends in phenomena like imposter syndrome so that people do not feel isolated in their experiences. In a previous role, I coordinated and facilitated a women in leadership cohort. One of my favorite aspects of this program was witnessing the "lightbulb" moment that would appear on students' faces when they learned about a concept or were introduced to a new language that described their feelings or experiences. It helped them realize some of their particular challenges were not unique to them or a result of an individual flaw. However, I also worry about how ubiquitous imposter syndrome has become and how embedded it is within the dominant narrative of women in leadership. Inevitably, in every woman in a leadership cohort, students raised imposter syndrome as a topic they wanted to explore. Yet, Tulshyan and Burey (2021) critique the over- (and mis-) use of imposter syndrome in their article, "Stop Telling Women They Have Imposter Syndrome." One must consider, "Are we perpetuating imposter syndrome when we assume that most women experience imposter syndrome?" In focusing on imposter syndrome as an individual deficit and building interventions and leadership development programs that address it, are we creating a self-fulfilling prophecy where women might internalize temporary feelings of discomfort and nervousness as imposter syndrome?

We lift up these three narratives as examples of how using feminist narrative methods and critical perspectives in leadership can reveal agency for women leaders and counter feelings of imposter syndrome. When shifting the focus from individual deficits to critiques of societal expectations and systemic oppression, college women become leaders who challenge and change the gendered associations with leadership within our cis-, hetero-patriarchal society. Instead of focusing on ways to adapt and navigate through oppressive structures, college women can embrace more expansive views and inclusive practices of leadership. Building women's leadership self-efficacy begets more women leaders who can serve as role models for other aspiring women leaders and make space to appreciate their contributions in creating a more just and equitable society. The next chapter will build upon these narratives of overcoming imposter syndrome to discuss further how college women build their identity, capacity, and efficacy for leadership.

REFERENCES

Arminio, J. L., Carter, S., Jones, S. E., Kruger, K., Lucas, N., Washington, J., Young, N., & Scott, A. (2000). Leadership experiences of students of color. *NASPA Journal, 37*(3), 496–510. https://doi.org/10.2202/1949-6605.1112

Ashford, S. J., & DeRue, D. S. (2012). Developing as a leader: The power of mindful engagement. *Organizational Dynamics, 41*(2), 146–154. https://doi.org/10.1016/j.orgdyn.2012.01.008

Bandura, A. (1997). *Self-efficacy: The exercise of control.* Harper Collins.

Barnes, A. C., Olson, T. H., & Reynolds, D. J. (2018). Teaching power as an inconvenient but imperative dimension of critical leadership development. *New Directions for Student Leadership, 2018*(159), 77–90. https://doi.org/10.1002/yd.20299

Bloom, L. (1998). *Under the sign of hope: Feminist methodology and narrative interpretation.* State University of New York Press.

Calizo, L. H., Cilente, K., & Komives, S. R. (2007). A look at gender and the multi-institutional study of leadership. *Concepts and Connections, 15*(2), 7–9. https://drive.google.com/drive/folders/1hpGbCtm4HWZGUKqycNPpDlYokZKQNbTp

Clance, P. R., & Imes, S. A. (1978). The imposter phenomenon in high achieving women: Dynamics and therapeutic intervention. *Psychotherapy: Theory, Research and Practice, 15*(3), 241–247. https://doi.org/10.1037/h0086006

Devies, B., & Guthrie, K. L. (2022). What mission statements say: Signaling the priority of leadership development. *Journal of Higher Education Policy and Leadership Studies, 3*(1), 91–107. https://doi.org/10.52547/johepal.3.1.91

Dugan, J. P. (2017). *Leadership theory: Cultivating critical perspectives.* Jossey-Bass.

Dugan, J. P., & Humbles, A. D. (2018). A paradigm shift in leadership education: Integrating critical perspectives into leadership development. *New Directions for Student Leadership, 2018*(159), 9–26. https://doi.org/10.1002/yd.20294

Dugan, J. P., & Komives, S. R. (2007). *Developing leadership capacity in college students: Findings from a national study. A report from the multi-institutional study of leadership.* National Clearinghouse for Leadership Programs.

Dwyer, L. P. (2019). Leadership self-efficacy: Review and leader development implications. *Journal of Management Development, 38*(8), 637–650. https://doi.org/10.1108/JMD-03-2019-0073

Eagly, A. H., & Carli, L. L. (2007). *Through the labyrinth: The truth about how women become leaders.* Harvard Business School Press.

Guthrie, K. L., & Chunoo, V. S. (Eds.). (2018). *Changing the narrative: Socially just leadership education.* Information Age Publishing.

Haber-Curran, P., Miguel, R., Shankman, M. L., & Allen, S. (2018). College women's leadership self-efficacy: An examination through the framework of emotionally intelligent leadership. *NASPA Journal About Women in Higher Education, 11*(3), 297–312. https://doi.org/10.1080/19407882.2018.1441032

Howes, S. D. (2016). "You're kind of just conditioned": Women and female college students' defiance of dominant social messages in the development of leader self-efficacy [Doctoral dissertation, Loyola University Chicago]. https://ecommons.luc.edu/cgi/viewcontent.cgi?article=3134&context=luc_diss

Hoyt, C. L. (2005). The role of leadership efficacy and stereotype activation in women's identification with leadership. *Journal of Leadership and Organizational Studies 11*(4), 2–14. https://doi.org/10.1177/107179190501100401

Lockwood, P. (2006). "Someone like me can be successful": Do college students need same-gender role models? *Psychology of Women Quarterly, 30,* 36–46. https://doi.org/10.1111/j.1471-6402.2006.00260.x

McCormick, M. J., Tanguma, J., & Lopez-Forment, A. S. (2002). Extending self-efficacy theory to leadership: A review and empirical test. *Journal of Leadership Education, 1*(2), 34–49. https://doi.org/10.12806/V1/I2/TF1

Osteen, L., Guthrie, K. L., & Bertrand Jones, T. (2016). Leading to transgress: Critical considerations for transforming leadership learning. *New Directions for Student Leadership, 2016*(152), 95–106. https://doi.org/10.1002/yd.20212

Owen, J. E. (2020). *We are the leaders we've been waiting for: Women and leadership development in college.* Routledge.

Pedler, M. (2011). Leadership, risk and the imposter syndrome. *Action Learning: Research and Practice, 8*(2), 89–91. https://doi.org/10.1080/14767333.2011.581016

Rupert, K. A. (2019). Shattering the collegiate glass ceiling: Understanding the experiences of women student government presidents [Unpublished dissertation]. University of Maryland, College Park.

Tulshyan, R., & Burey, J. A. (2021, February 11). Stop telling women they have imposter syndrome. *Harvard Business Review.* https://hbr.org/2021/02/stop-telling-women-they-have-imposter-syndrome#:~:text=Imposter%20syndrome%20is%20loosely%20defined,they're%20deserving%20of%20accolades

CHAPTER 9

BLOOMING WHERE WE ARE PLANTED

Growth in Leadership Development

Brittany Devies

I (Brittany) vividly remember as a young girl being told I could never be president or play football because I was a woman. I remember being told to play in a sandbox at school rather than the basketball court. I was often told where to exist and what I should be doing. This also translated into how and where I should lead.

From a young age, I loved the idea of human development and growth, it is what called me to become an educator. I love being able to reflect on our past, to see how much we have grown, and to look to the future to see possibilities. I have always loved the possibility of growth, but not the reality of it. The reality for many women, including myself, is that it is measured, determined, and projected onto us by others. It is being told you will never be president because of your gender identity. It is being told you are too quiet, too small, too weak. My desire to be an educator was to be a part of crafting a version of leadership that celebrated, advocated for, and championed

> how *all* women lead and worked tirelessly to ensure they had access to leadership. I wanted to make spaces for growth, for leadership capacity and efficacy development, the spaces I wish I had had access to as a young girl.

In the narratives in this chapter, I celebrate how four women defined growth and emergence for themselves as people and leaders. Growth is not always linear or easy, but these women share stories that remind us all that we hold the agency and authorship for our growth as leaders.

APPROACHING THE NARRATIVES

Growth is often connected to the concept of leadership capacity and leadership efficacy. Leadership capacity can be defined as the doing of leadership (Owen et al., 2021). However, leadership efficacy is the attitudes, beliefs, messages, and assessments about one's ability to succeed in the leadership process (Bandura, 1997; Dugan et al., 2013). Devies (2023) studied how undergraduate women develop leadership capacity and efficacy and the critical connections between them. Even though research has found that women in college have higher capacity to engage in the leadership process, they often have lower leadership efficacy which can result in women opting out of leadership experiences because they do not believe they are capable of leading (Dugan, 2017; Dugan & Komives, 2007; Dugan & Komives, 2010). Misalignment of women's leadership capacity and efficacy development could be a result of many things, including gender socialization, perfectionism, and imposter syndrome (Owen, 2020). For more on imposter syndrome, see Chapter 8.

Leadership Efficacy Development

Efficacy can be defined as "one's internal belief in the likelihood that they will be successful when engaging in leadership" (Bandura, 1997, p. 6). Efficacy "contributes to increased motivation to enact leadership behaviors" (Dugan et al., 2013, p. 16) and is a significant predictor of socially responsible leadership capacity (Dugan & Komives, 2010).

The Multi-Institutional Study for Leadership (MSL) found evidence that college "men reported more self-confidence in their leadership abilities than women" (Dugan & Komives, 2007, p. 13). Additionally, the MSL found women scored higher on seven of the eight capacities for socially responsible leadership compared to men; however, women scored significantly lower in their leadership efficacy (Dugan & Komives, 2010). It is critical to note that even if women have the capacity to lead, women are less likely to actually engage in the leadership process if they have a low efficacy (Dugan, 2017).

Growth Versus Fixed Mindset

Guthrie et al. (2021) noted, "Dominant narratives about minoritized identities are often framed from a deficit perspective, perpetuating the harmful notion that those with minoritized identities are lacking in some important aspect and therefore not fit for leadership" (p. 40). Minoritized identities, such as those identifying as women and Women of Color, have historically and systemically been projected to have fixed mindsets about their capacity to lead. Fixed and growth mindset terminology come from Carol Dweck's (2006) work in psychology about human capacity and people's belief in their ability to grow. Guthrie et al. (2021) noted that in leadership, holding a fixed mindset can create leaders who "believe their basic abilities, their intelligence, their talents, are just fixed traits" (p. 71). Holding a fixed mindset around leadership can translate to believing one has a maximum or stagnant threshold to lead or that certain people are "born" to lead. A growth mindset allows an individual to believe they can always develop, evolve, learn, and grow as a person and leader; this happens through accepting feedback, overcoming obstacles, and embracing challenges (Dweck, 2006). Leaders with a growth mindset around their capacity and efficacy to lead believe leadership is a practice that can be learned and that they can continue to grow and develop as a leader (Guthrie et al., 2021).

Domains of Leadership Development

Dugan (2017) wrote about the four domains of leadership development: leadership capacity, leadership efficacy, leadership enactment, and leadership motivation. Leadership capacity is "the knowledge, skills, and attitudes associated with the ability to engage in leadership" (Dugan et al., 2013, p. 6). Leadership efficacy "contributes to increased motivation to enact leadership behaviors, gains in leadership capacity as well as performance, and the ability to reject negative external feedback including stereotype threat" (Dugan et al., 2013, p. 16). Leadership enactment is putting one's leadership capacity into practice in the leadership process (Dugan, 2017). Finally, leadership motivation bridges leadership capacity and leadership enactment, focusing on what affects leaders' effort and persistence to lead. These four domains are essential tools for analysis when considering the following narratives about growth in leadership development. In this chapter, I employed feminist narrative analysis (Bloom, 1998) to consider the theory of fixed/growth mindset and the leadership efficacy domain of leadership development for the narrative authors.

EXPLORING THE NARRATIVES

Below are four narratives from women about their growth as leaders throughout their lives. In these narratives, we see stories of women finding a growth mindset about their ability to lead and developing their leadership capacity and efficacy. Jessie, Kat, Deya, and Mollie shared moments from their lives where their understanding of leadership and their leader identities grew and evolved.

Jessie: "Am I Too Feminine?"

First, we hear from a college woman named Jessie, who was 20 years old at the time of writing her narrative. She explored her growth through lessons learned alongside her mother and their different mindsets around gender expression and leadership.

> Growing up I was always told I was most like my mother. We looked the same, acted the same, and had the same outlook on life. She was very black and white with how she believed success was formed. Her life revolved around the premises of structure, a very rigid formula. This formula was the one that worked for her father so as she adapted it, she pushed it on to me. I saw how hard she worked at her job, so I worked just as hard at school. The same followed if we would go on runs together, therefore I would do the same with the sport I was playing. She made sure to drill in my head that no matter if boys were competing, I was capable of the same if not better.
>
> As I got older this stigma stuck in my head that you must be a pusher to achieve your goals. To achieve your goals would make everyone want to follow you, and in turn you would become the "leader." While working at my first job I realized these ideologies come to reality. Whenever I or any of the girls I worked with had to lift anything heavy, there was always a man around the corner offering to help. Thanks to my mother, I would never agree even if my 15-year-old self could hardly hold up whatever item I was carrying. As for the other girls, they would happily let someone else do the work for

them. This irritated me as I believed they were giving up their power to these men and therefore giving up their position as a leader.

Time after time I was taught to believe the best way for women to excel was to conform to masculine standards of leadership: power, strength, and so on. My mom was a hard worker and a feminist, but she was missing the entire point. She hated women who only care about their appearance. It was almost as if you embraced femininity at all you would be giving in to the negative stereotypes of women. This perspective didn't last long with me as I fell in love with fashion. I taught my mom those feminine things are fun to do and just because we do them doesn't make us weaker in comparison to men.

Somewhere down the line my mother and I learned very important stances on feminism from each other. She taught me that I was capable of doing anything a man can do, and all the same I taught her how to embrace her femininity through hobbies like fashion and make-up. I began to understand that I don't have to be the "man" to prove myself. It is okay to just be a woman and the hobbies you choose or sports you play do not make you any less of one.

Within this narrative, Jessie explores the beauty of learning to not only challenge her own understandings on gender performance and expression, but how to lead in educating those who were influential in our growth journeys. She leans into the complexity of challenging socialization while also affirming her own identity as a woman and a leader. In this narrative, it appears her mother holds a more fixed mindset on gender expression and femininity whereas Jessie holds a growth mindset, which she uses to challenge the dominant narrative around gender expression and femininity. While the narrative focuses primarily on gender expression and appearance as the dominant narratives being challenged, there is certainly evidence of leadership from Jessie. In using her growth mindset, Jessie is engaging in leadership motivation and enactment when leading her mother through having her own reckoning with her socialization around gender, leadership, and what it means to be a woman (Dugan, 2017). For more on familial relationships, see Chapter 6.

Kat: "Someone to Guide Me"

The next narrative in this chapter comes in the form of a poem, which also explores a relationship with her mother; one that is complicated and nuanced. The author, Kat, is a cisgender woman who is bisexual and of Bolivian and Salvadoran descent. Kat also identifies as a first-generation college student from a low-income household.

BETTER FOR HER
Katherine
When I was younger,
I experience trauma
I felt so alone.

Mother, where were you?
I called you but no answer
You abandoned me.

At that time, it's hard to know,
all that you don't as a kid
But it still hurts me.

I trusted you, Mom
the illusions of safety,
Maybe I'm no one.

Who do I turn to?
I'm waiting for a leader,
I need a hero.

BETTER FOR HER
Katherine
You called me a slut?
What does giving consent mean?
Why don't you love me?

I need a hero
What is a feminist, mom?
What would *you* know about that?

How do I move on?
Can I be a feminist?
Are you a **bad feminist**?

Next stop high school, oh Lord
Me and you don't get along,
Who will lead me now?

I need a hero,
I'm waiting for a leader
Someone to guide me.

Blooming Where We Are Planted ▪ 153

Kat beautifully illustrates how, as leaders, we often learn to grow despite familial influence, especially when familial connections may cause pain and not be the models we need in our journeys (see Chapter 5 for discussions of gender violence and Chapter 6 for more on family and leadership). After experiencing trauma, Kat was waiting for a hero in the form of her mother and had to turn elsewhere in her development in the abandonment she felt. Often, familial members are attributed to early development and socialization (Harro, 2013), but Kat's poem about her mother is a reminder that those familial relationships can cause unexpected growth out of necessity.

In multiple stanzas, we gain insight to Kat's understanding of the leader role. She emphasized, "I need a hero, I'm waiting for a leader, someone to guide me." Kat's chorus offers dual definitions of a leader. On the one hand, she perpetuates the trope of leader as synonymous with being a hero. This makes sense as Kat wrestles with childhood trauma and expectations of an adult who should be the hero who protected her from harm. Expanding her view, in her third line, she clarifies her need for a leader as a desire for guidance to navigate the significant trauma she's experienced.

We see Kat's growth as a leader and as a woman in her grappling with her relationship with her mother in her poem. Kat writes, "You called me a slut" and "What does giving consent mean?"—questioning her mother's reinforcement of gender-based stereotypes in response to violence. Kat was looking for her mom to be the leader, to guide her in her development, but by the end, we see her mother was not able to fill that role for her. She needed to be her own leader. Kat's leadership efficacy (Bandura, 1997; Dugan et al., 2013) was being developed, not from the encouragement of a loved one like her mother, but rather from a lack of a role model and the driving need to believe in herself despite the modeling from others (for more on role models and leadership, see Chapter 7). Her motivation to lead still existed even though she was not able to learn it from her mother (Dugan, 2017).

Deya: "The Blind Leading the Blind"

The third narrative in this chapter comes from Deya, a Latina college woman who identifies as blind. She explores a formative experience as a leader attending the Washington Seminar for The National Federation of the Blind.

> The biggest moment that defined leadership for me was in Washington DC in 2020. I'd gone the year before, and it opened my eyes to social justice. However, 2020 was when I saw myself differently.
> I received a scholarship from The National Federation of the Blind to

> attend Washington Seminar, a week in DC when blind people from across the country come together and go to congress about issues affecting them. The second time I went, I went with my best friend. I was excited to share the experience with her and show her my newfound love for social justice. I wanted to show her the way, be her leader in the crazy world I could barely understand myself.
>
> In 2019, I had gone with a teacher that I'd grown up with. She was always there when I needed help or felt lost. Now I was on my own. Everyone I was with now had little to no vision. It scared me because I've never gone anywhere so big without vision assistance. But these people did it all the time, and somehow I trusted them. It was the best decision I'd made.
>
> We went to dinner Tuesday night at a restaurant deep in the middle of the city. We had to take the metro from our hotel to the restaurant. The metro gives me so much anxiety to this day. It's loud and overwhelming, with trains coming on two different levels in all directions. If it was overwhelming when I had a sighted guide, I was dreading doing it without one. But my visually impaired and blind guides figured out exactly where we needed to go and which trains we needed. I was impressed. Watching them do this was so different from hearing about it. Before long, we had traveled all the way to our restaurant and met up with some friends. Even ordering the food was a different experience. We couldn't just ask each other to read the menu. We had to be creative. But even that was cool to watch. On the way back to the hotel, it was a similar experience. However I was expecting our leaders to keep their serious demeanor. Not what actually happened, which was a loud exciting trip home.
>
> This night helps me define leadership to this day. I had people leading that wouldn't traditionally be considered leaders. There's that saying, "The blind leading the blind," right? But truly there's no better leader in that moment I could have asked for.

Deya explored how developmental and formative experiences can be crucible moments as she continued to understand her leader identity. From this trip experience, Deya's growth is evident in her expansion of leadership capacity, efficacy, motivation, and enactment (Dugan, 2017). Her leadership capacity developed in the "tangible" examples of how she was able to do leadership, like her ordering at the restaurant or traveling to the seminar without visual assistance. Her leadership efficacy grew in her belief that she is able to be a leader in these spaces, even without the support she had previously had, like a sighted guide. It is clear Deya's leadership motivation continued to blossom throughout the trip; we see her passion and excitement regarding the need for advocacy and the role of The National Federation of the Blind. Finally, her leadership enactment can be clearly seen throughout, but especially the ending of her narrative. Deya wrote,

This night helps me define leadership to this day. I had people leading that wouldn't traditionally be considered leaders. There's that saying "the blind leading the blind," right? But truly there's no better leader in that moment I could have asked for.

The phrase, "the blind leading the blind" is grounded in an ableist, oppressive socialization that someone who is blind cannot lead, let alone lead others who are also blind. Deya reclaims this phrase, stepping into her leadership efficacy and enactment by asserting the blind *can* and *do* lead the blind. It is also a beautiful statement of reclaiming her own leadership identity, capacity, and efficacy, especially when systemic oppression has historically led to ableist understandings of who can lead (for more on systemic oppression, see Chapter 4). She exhibits her growth in the experience by noting the advocacy they achieved on this trip was the best enactment of leadership for which she could have asked.

Mollie: "Choose What Feels Best to Us"

The final narrative in this chapter comes from a leadership studies alumnae and future therapist, Mollie. Mollie reflects on her evolving understanding of leadership over her lifetime and especially since her time in college nearly a decade ago.

> My definition of leadership began to emerge as a Sophomore in high school. I did not know it yet but I had already begun paving my own path. It was a natural decision for me and a series of continuous actions that just felt intuitive even though I felt completely out of tune with what a high school experience is "supposed" to be like. I studied a lot. I was a cheerleader and a member of a few clubs. Boys who were a year or two above me asked me to go to dances with them but I did not want to be a part of the drinking or smoking scene that usually happens with the older kids, nor did I want to have sex (there was a lot of pressure to go to hotel rooms or after parties after the dance) and I didn't feel like explaining myself on any of those so I just said no. I was all about my future.
>
> I was really serious about getting myself into a good school and looking forward to a career to take care of myself. I believe I began thinking way ahead of high school years because my parents got divorced when I was in the third grade. With this, there were so many things I did not have control over. I promised myself I would do whatever it took to care for myself and create a beautiful life! Now, I know that having this fearful and resentful outlook on my childhood took me away from some exposures in high school that could have spiced up my world, but I didn't see it that way at the time.

> Both of my parents are actually great people! They just got married in very little time after meeting one another and didn't really know each other at all. I share these pieces of my upbringing because they shape how I've made most of my decisions, especially the jobs I took post college in social work and now as a health coach. It took many books and recovery from an eating disorder that nearly took me out of an incredible future to understand that how we feed our minds and the environment we surround ourselves with is so crucial for our physical, psychological, spiritual and emotional health. And we need to keep that growth mindset to stay happy.
>
> As a young girl, I saw through my mom, it's so important to develop yourself and get to know yourself first before getting involved romantically with someone. I believe we all have gifts to share with the world and it takes daily moments of solitude to feel those inclinations and be able to act on them and grow them in the world. Along with my early career-oriented mind, I worked for years on understanding "my knowing" as Glennon Doyle (2020) phrases it in her book *Untamed*. I think this is a *huge* part of leadership. According to Doyle, the knowing is being able to make decisions for yourself beyond logic, in the way of being able to "sink" and go from the wisdom of your gut (Doyle, 2020, p. 105).
>
> All in all, if I would have started to read more self-development books, like *Untamed*, in my high school years, I would have learned that I could have more fun going to dances and I didn't have to work so hard. I would have realized, possibly, that the universe has my back even when I decide to take a break, because we all need them. And I probably could have stated my boundaries with the boys asking me to dances and I'm sure it all would have worked out just fine. To me, now as a woman, I believe that leadership is moving with faith with each next right step. It's also being open to different ways of thinking and doing things. Lastly, leadership may both look like the quiet actions that lead up to big things over time while also those crazy moves we are being guided to take that are meant to get us out of our comfort zones and show us that we can trust ourselves. The beauty of leadership is that it can have so many different meanings and we all get to choose what feels best to us.

Mollie focused specifically on the longevity of growth as a woman and leader—it does not happen in one moment. As a young girl, she thought she had to restrict her actions in order to avoid missteps and concerns she might face in a gender inequitable world. She knew her priorities for education and feared being pulled into quintessential adolescent experiences because it might disrupt her path. Mollie's reflection showed us how knowing self is an act of leadership. She also teaches us leadership is a lifelong, developmental process (Guthrie & Jenkins, 2018). From an alumnae perspective, it is a long and nonlinear road to grow as a leader and often comes from a multitude of people, places, and experiences. It can also look like relinquishing control to consider the fluid nature of development. Mollie writes about leadership as the "quiet actions" that lead to bigger things over time, developing smaller pieces of a whole. Her growth mindset is apparent in this narrative, especially as she ends her writing. She notes, "Leadership is moving with faith towards the next step." She has grown to understand that leadership is a complex process that evolves over time. The complexity of leadership is also its beauty.

WEAVING THE NARRATIVES

These four narratives share powerful stories of growth in leadership identity and leadership development. First and foremost, the narrative authors evidence the importance of embodying a growth mindset, for both ourselves and others. Jessie shared how she challenged her mother to have a growth mindset around gender expression while Deya talked about some of her own growth mindset moments on her trip navigating Washington DC with other blind and vision impaired individuals. Mollie wrote on growth mindset in understanding the complexity of leadership while Kat wrote about her growth in her understanding of her own leadership and her mother's leadership.

Additionally, these stories show how having a growth mindset can influence one's leadership capacity and efficacy development. In many of these stories, including Jessie's, Deya's, and Kat's stories, we see how observing the leadership of others was influential in their development both in positive and negative ways. Leadership observation is "the social, cultural, and observational aspects of leadership learning" (Guthrie & Jenkins, 2018, p. 65). In using this constructivist approach grounded in evaluation and meaning making of other's leadership performance (Guthrie & Jenkins, 2018), these narrative authors identified their own growth as a result. Mitra et al. (2010) evaluated leadership observation as a developmental practice with medical students and found that the practice of leadership observation enhanced the students' skills while also resulting in a significant sense of personal development. Devies (2022) wrote about how important actively observing leadership and making meaning of what we observe can be for leadership learning. In Jessie's, Deya's, and Kat's narratives, we can see how their reflection on these observable moments led to their own growth as a leader.

We see each of the narrative authors provide evidence of themselves moving through Dugan's (2017) domains of leadership development. Jessie writes about her leadership motivation and leadership enactment to lead when reckoning with both her and her mother's socialization around womanhood and gender expression. Kat is building her leadership efficacy, even without the encouragement of her mother while also evidencing through her pain her motivations to lead. Deya writes brilliantly about her increased leadership capacity and efficacy to lead as a result of her trip, both having chances to develop new, hands-on skills while also feeling more confident in her ability to lead. By the end of her story, we also see an increased motivation to lead in the future. Finally, Mollie's narrative demonstrates how leadership capacity and efficacy can develop over time and how reflection on our past and present selves is a practice of growth as a leader.

It is important to note that while these narrative authors have similarities in the importance of growth, they have distinct contexts, life experiences, and relationships with others that challenge them to grow. I often think of influential people in my own life challenging me to grow because of their modeling exceptional behaviors; however, Jessie and Kat evidence how growth can come from observing leadership practices and behaviors we do *not* want to emulate. Both experiences have different values, and both can lead to a stronger development of leadership identity, capacity, and efficacy. Moving forward, it is important to know the effect a growth mindset has on ourselves and others; as leadership educators, we can continue to be empowering influences in the leadership development of our students.

APPLYING THE NARRATIVES

As noted earlier, observation of the leadership process can lead to important growth and development. Devies (2022) discussed how leadership educators can use leadership observation in practice; she noted the utility in observing power dynamics in leadership, using observation pedagogy to connect real life observations to course content, and practicing observation to increase engagement in learning spaces. Additionally, observation of leadership can be used to amplify student experiences. Devies (2022) noted, "Educators should give students agency to pull relevant and contemporary examples from their lives, their observations of leadership" (p. 105).

Building upon the need to make space for lived experiences in learning spaces, Owen et al. (2021) emphasized leadership educators need to develop leadership learning spaces where women can increase their efficacy, especially given that research shows college women have significantly lower leadership efficacy than men (Dugan, 2017; Dugan & Komives, 2007; Dugan & Komives, 2010). Using the narratives above and the way we see the domains of leadership development (Dugan, 2017) operationalized within them, I hope that leadership educators create developmental opportunities for women to increase their leadership capacity, efficacy, motivation, and enactment in the future. Leadership developmental spaces often focus on increasing the skills of leadership capacity, but it is also critical to make space for leadership efficacy development to help operationalize the growth moments the narratives above highlight so brilliantly.

REFERENCES

Bandura, A. (1997). *Self-efficacy: The exercise of control.* W. H. Freeman & Company.
Bloom, L. (1998). *Under the sign of hope: Feminist methodology and narrative interpretation.* State University of New York Press.
Devies, B. (2022). Making the world your classroom: Observation as a pedagogical tool for leadership learning. In K. L. Guthrie & K. L. Priest (Eds.), *Navigating complexities in leadership: Moving towards critical hope* (pp. 99–108). Information Age Publishing.
Devies, B. (2023). *Undergraduate women's leadership capacity and efficacy development.* Florida State University [Unpublished dissertation]. Florida State University. https://www.proquest.com/openview/90057574738f0baf3d8fd1839e6bd7f6/1?pq-origsite=gscholar&cbl=18750&diss=y
Doyle, G. (2020). *Untamed.* The Dial Press.
Dugan, J. P. (2017). *Leadership theory: Cultivating critical perspectives.* Jossey-Bass.
Dugan, J. P., Kodama, C., Correia, B., & Associates. (2013). *Multi-institutional study of leadership insight report: Leadership program delivery.* National Clearinghouse for Leadership Programs. https://static1.squarespace.com/static/5873de271e5b6c645d5b5ac3/t/5894dbc5f5e2314d79d7e184/1486150604939/2014-02-06-mls-full-report-optimized.pdf
Dugan, J. P., & Komives, S. R. (2007). *Developing leadership capacity in college students: Findings from a national study.* National Clearinghouse for Leadership Programs. https://www.researchgate.net/publication/237536892_Developing_Leadership_Capacity_In_College_Students_Findings_From_a_National_Study
Dugan, J. P., & Komives, S. R. (2010). Influences on college students' capacities for socially responsible leadership. *Journal of College Student Development, 51*(5), 525–549. https://doi.org/10.1353/csd.2010.0009
Dweck, C. (2006). *Mindset: The new psychology of success.* Random House.
Guthrie, K. L., Beatty, C. C., & Wiborg, E. (2021). *Engaging in the leadership process: Identity, capacity, and efficacy for college students.* Information Age Publishing.
Guthrie, K. L., & Jenkins, D. M. (2018). *The role of leadership educators: Transforming learning.* Information Age Publishing.
Harro, B. (2013). The cycle of socialization. In M. Adams, W. J. Blumfield, R. Castaneda, H. W. Hackman, M. L. Peters, & X. Zuniga (Eds.), *Readings for diversity and social justice* (3rd ed., pp. 45–52). Routledge.
Mitra, A. M., Hsieh, Y., & Buswick, T. (2010). Learning how to look: Developing leadership through intentional observation. *Journal of Business Strategy, 31*(4), 77–84. https://doi.org/10.1108/02756661011055212
Owen, J. E. (2020). *We are the leaders we've been waiting for: Women and leadership development in college.* Stylus.
Owen, J. E., Devies, B., & Reynolds, D. J. (2021). Going beyond 'add women then stir': Fostering feminist leadership. In K. L. Guthrie & V. S. Chunoo (Eds.), *Shifting the mindset: Socially just leadership education* (pp. 89–99). Information Age Publishing.

CHAPTER 10

WHAT LEADERSHIP *ISN'T*

Conceptualizing Leadership Through Reflection

Rebecca Shetty

Often leadership scholars and educators describe leadership as a process (Day & Harrison, 2007; Northouse, 2016). In addition, leadership learning and capacity have been described as a process (Komives et al., 2011). This chapter explores a nuanced aspect of the leadership process—the conceptualization of leadership, a process all its own. Through analyzing the narratives of Skye, Mio, and Alea, I explore how reflection, reflective behaviors, and reflective experiences contribute to the conceptualization of leadership as a concept and dismantle oppressive views of leadership. It is through the act of reflection that individuals can experience cognitive dissonance and create new knowledge contributing to our understanding of inclusive leadership learning. My own leadership journey is filled with reflection and the ongoing evolution of my personal conceptualization of leadership.

> "EVERYONE, SHUT UP!!" I raged at the top of my lungs. One moment I was leading a group of 50 peers, the next I had completely lost their trust. My leadership journey has been far from perfect. From a young age, I (Becka) felt like a leader. I am not sure I fully understood what leadership meant, but I certainly associated leadership with power and prestige, with positions and roles. As early as elementary school, I was chosen for leadership positions (ex: safety patrol, the lead in the class play) and I was often given, selected, or chosen for roles throughout my entire childhood and upbringing (officer roles within organizations, president of organizations, peer leadership programs, etc.). Unlike many women, I do not recall experiencing overt sexism or discrimination for any of my identities in these roles, though perhaps I was simply oblivious.
>
> Because my experience with leadership consisted of positions and roles, I also bought into the leadership myth that a leader has the loudest voice in the room. In my first year of college, I had been selected for a prestigious role in my sorority. I had been selected by 50 of my peers to serve in this role. I thought this meant my position among my peers was solidified. During a circumstance of tension and frustration, I hostilely screamed at the very top of my lungs at a room of 50 of my peers to garner control. Instead of earning their respect or trust, I broke it. I was not trusted by that group again. I learned a very hard lesson about the role of values-alignment, staying humble, and seeking consensus as means for motivation and inspiration as opposed to using force, a loud voice, or my own righteousness.
>
> I currently lead a team of four women. We have taken on the challenge of rebuilding our department from almost nothing. They don't need me to yell at them, to provide harsh critique, or to disparage their work. They need to see me working just as hard as they are, admitting when I've made a mistake or don't know the answer to a question. They need to see themselves as valuable to the team, as leaders. We are all leaders on our team; each in our own way. Leadership is about a collective journey towards creating more just spaces—small workplace microcosms and large societal macrocosms.

Like the narratives explored in this chapter, it took tremendous time, reflection, and trial and error to begin understanding what leadership is, how to practice effective leadership strategies, and to understand that leadership is a relationship among and between people. Just as my conceptualization of leadership continues to evolve, the narratives of the women in this chapter demonstrate their own evolution and understanding of leadership at this moment in time. For the women in this chapter, their journey is just beginning. To analyze their stories, I use Kolb's (1984) cycle of experiential learning as a means to understand the ways in which these women reframe their thinking about leadership and conceptualize leadership for themselves, shifting away from traditionally patriarchal, sexist, or outdated ways of thinking of leadership.

As I read and reread the narratives of these women, I think of how these young women are shaped by the world and are shaping the world concurrently. Reading their words, words of beauty, pain, inspiration, empowerment—they make me want to reach through the page, to take their hands, to hug them. I want to tell them the ways they are thinking about leadership are normal, to be encouraged, to be explored. I want to tell them to remain humble enough to keep learning. I want to tell them that I believe in a future of women leaders, a future where things are better than they are now. So much of understanding leadership and who we are as individual leaders comes through growth and reflection. As written in the previous chapter, growth is paramount to the leadership process. I know it has been for me.

I feel a sense of belonging as I read these narratives. I relate so much to their experiences, their longing, particularly when it comes to seeing examples of how to be and how not to be a leader. I am still a work in progress; my leadership journey is not over, and neither is theirs.

APPROACHING THE NARRATIVES

This chapter uses the framework and method of feminisms and counter-storytelling respectively to center the voices of women, voices that disrupt and counteract dominant narratives of leadership (Bamburg & Andrews, 2004). See Chapter 3 for more detail on these methodological approaches. Through the narrative analysis in this chapter, we see how counter-stories teeming with reflection lead to the creation of new knowledge regarding leadership and its possibilities. Through the narrative authors' critical inquiry, we see women pushing the boundaries of leadership beyond existing definitions, which are often rooted in patriarchy, sexism, racism, xenophobia, and other systemic oppression. They themselves are creating the future of leadership, creating new ways of thinking, and dreaming of enacting leadership according to their own principles. How individuals come to conceptualize leadership is a complicated process but an important one to understand.

Conceptualizing Leadership

The leadership identity development process will be discussed further at length in Chapter 12; however, I want to note the role "conceptualizing leadership" plays in leader identity development. Varying leadership and leader identity development models refer to the way individuals conceptualize leadership during the identity development process (Day & Harrison;

2007; Komives et al., 2005; McKenzie, 2018; Shetty, 2020). "Conceptualization" tends to refer to growth, development, and changed ways of thinking, particularly referring to the way individuals think about themselves as leaders, understand leadership behaviors and practices, or think about leadership as a broad, ever-evolving concept. The process of conceptualization is what makes it possible for an individual to move towards considering "leader" as part of their identity, integrated into their existing, intersectional being. With the importance of conceptualization being recognized, we can turn to how conceptualization occurs.

Reflection in Leadership Learning

Guthrie and Bertrand Jones (2012) wrote, "Reflection has been predominantly conceptualized as the key process through which human beings extract knowledge from their experiences" (p. 56). Reflection is essential to learning as we experience cognitive dissonance and reframe what we know based on new experiences. Reflection is also essential to the leadership learning process, specifically. According to Volpe White et al. (2019) reflection contributes to self-awareness, identity development, and more effective relationship-building. Volpe White et al. (2019) also argue that reflection and leadership go hand-in-hand for the purpose of creating social change; they write, "Leadership needs reflection for students to develop cognitive complexity and respond to adaptive challenges; reflection needs leadership as an action-oriented discipline that empowers and enables learners to develop individually and in community to create positive change" (p. 23). Reflection is not simply a learning tool but one that can be used for challenging dominant discourse.

Kolb's Cycle of Experiential Learning

This chapter focuses on the role of reflection in the leadership learning process, and "reflection" provides the scaffolding for analyzing the narratives to come. To explore the concepts of reflection and conceptualization from a learning perspective, I turn to Kolb's (1984) cycle of experiential learning as my theoretical framework. When outlining the foundations for Kolb's work on experiential learning theory, Kolb and Kolb (2017) described reflection as necessary for meaning making and for guiding future life experiences. The learning cycle is dependent on the duality of concrete, actionable experiences *and* abstract, reflective thinking.

Kolb's (1984) cycle of experiential learning has four key phases: (a) concrete experience (learning by encounter), (b) reflective observation (learning by reflecting), (c) abstract conceptualization (learning by thinking), and (d) active experimentation (learning by doing; Guthrie & Bertrand Jones, 2012). Kolb and Kolb (2017) argued that an individual learns best when engaging with all four phases. In the model, it should be noted that conceptualization comes after reflection; reflective observation leads into abstract conceptualization. Guthrie and Bertrand Jones (2012) described reflective observation as making careful observations, identifying relationships, withholding judgment, and cultivating new perspectives. They describe abstract conceptualization as "logically analyzing ideas," planning in some way to act, or actually taking action to learn more about a particular topic.

For learning to occur, experience must be interrupted at some point to allow for reflective thinking. Through reflection, an individual can work their way towards conceptualization and can form new perspectives based on their experiences. Eventually, the hope is that an individual will take their new conceptual understanding of a topic and move towards active experimentation to determine how their newfound ideas or beliefs fare in real-world experiences. This then begins the learning cycle anew. In the case of leadership, this is just one way that leadership continues to be a process of learning, ever evolving for an individual as they experience, reflect, conceptualize, and act. In the case of this chapter, reflection is used as a learning and developmental tool that allows the narrative authors to shatter old ways of thinking, to break down socialized norms of leadership, and to create and co-create new knowledge of leadership that better serves themselves, their communities, and society.

EXPLORING THE NARRATIVES

Through discrimination, pain, imposter syndrome, or through combatting these and other challenges, the narratives below describe new understandings of leadership based on the narrator's personal reflection and experiences. Each woman comes to conceptualize leadership in their own way.

Skye: "Leadership Radiated All Around Me"

Skye's narrative mirrors my own experiences in so many ways, particularly having a strong mother figure who taught me independence, strength, yet also a mistrust for others. Like Skye, I also learned vulnerability and a different way of leading through reflection and new conceptualizations of leadership. Skye, a culturally Christian, bisexual, first year college student with Native American and Hispanic heritage wrote:

> I have always known a singular definition of leadership.
> An only child raised by a single mother.
> A leader who stood tall and mighty at the top of a pedestal.
> Someone who didn't need to ask others for help, self-sufficient and strong.
> Always holding their head high, as a beacon of hope for everyone else
> Over time, my definition of leadership expanded
> A leader who encouraged all and asked for help.
> Someone who does need the help of others and isn't afraid to ask
> For admitting failure and needing help does not show weakness.
> We all need leaders in our life who support us and keep us afloat.
> I came to understand my definition of leadership, as I came to understand my purpose in life.
> Many nights grew long and spirits flew low.
> And I came to understand my purpose through feeling purposeless.
> Rationalizing the irrational until the sun comes up.
> And on that day, hope and leadership radiated all around me.
> You showed me I wasn't alone. That I didn't have to lead singularly.
> You taught me how to ask for help and admit when I could no longer pay the wages of the world
> My definition of leadership expanded and grew.
> Cultivating a passion of hoping for a better future.
> Wishing to pass the hope onto future generations like you did.

In Skye's narrative, several critical factors influence her conceptualization of leadership. Overall, the changes in her perspective seem to occur due to reflection. We know the importance of reflection in the leadership process, and this narrative affirms this as a means of conceptualizing leadership. Skye described "rationalizing the irrational until the sun comes up," time spent in thought. Skye has clearly used her own time and interactions with others to think about what being a leader means to her and to formulate her own, independent understanding of leadership.

First, we see a shift in Skye's conceptualization of leadership from being an independent, self-sustaining endeavor to one that requires vulnerability, asking for help, and admitting failure. For some, growing up may result in learning the most trusted adults in our life are fallible. Skye had known one type of leadership, an example provided by her mother. While she did not wholly disparage that relationship, she clearly found there is more to leadership than she originally thought. Age and authority do not necessarily predicate leadership expertise.

The turning point for Skye seemed to be this point of feeling "low" to the point of hopelessness before rising again towards understanding, confidence, and expectation. Skye's stance of openness in her line "hope and leadership radiated all around me" so powerfully roots the rest of her reflection and was the primary inspiration for the title of this book. Not only did her own commitment to leadership grow, but it grew so much that she potentially reached a stage of generativity (Komives et al., 2005) in her desire to "pass the hope onto future generations." This is significant in the leadership identity journey.

Finally, while it is not clear who "you" is in the second half of the poem, it appears as though another mentor or teacher significantly influenced her understanding of leadership. As we've seen throughout the narratives in this book, and from what we know from existing leadership identity research and literature, family, mentors, and peers all significantly shape how we view leadership and how we view ourselves as leaders (Komives et al., 2005; McKenzie, 2018; Shetty, 2020). Please see Chapter 7 on role models related to leadership. It is unsurprising that another person, in addition to her mother, had a striking influence on Skye's conceptualization of leadership. This particular person seemed to provide support or scaffolding, allowing Skye to be vulnerable in asking for help, and showed that leadership is not an individual process or exercise.

Skye also acknowledges "the wages of the world" she could no longer pay. Whether these wages are expectations, norms, or ways of being, Skye recognizes that there are standards in this world that are exhausting to her. Through her narrative, Skye combats any notions of leadership that have not come from her own, deep reflection. By establishing her own expectations, norms, and ways of being, Skye is able to act upon her conceptualizations through active experimentation and seems to have found hope and a future in her newfound beliefs. Leadership can be how Skye chooses to define it.

Mio: "A Light in My Head Went Off"

Like Skye, Mio also felt like she was taught the "wrong" ways to conceptualize leadership. Through engaging with new peers, discussing leadership, and reflecting on leadership, Mio comes to a new understanding of leadership, and she is able to articulate her understanding well. Mio identifies as a female Asian American student and, at the time of this writing, was a member of a women and leadership program at her university that was primarily composed of Women of Color. Mio writes:

> I was always quiet in high school, and only in senior year did I start to get out of my shell more. I was always told in band that I "didn't look like a drum major," or "was too quiet to be a leader," and that, along with being Asian

amongst a white-dominated group, quickly shut me off to even dream about becoming a leader, let alone what good leadership was.

I've always been told leadership is about leading, about motivating others to follow whatever you say, and growing up in a marching band setting, my views of leadership was that the more powerful role you held in a group, the louder your voice was. That was completely wrong.

I got to college and finally understood what leadership was about when I got to my first class for leadership studies. Having a group of ladies from such diverse backgrounds, all with so many different experiences, helped me understand what leadership was really about. As a Japanese American, and one of maybe five asians at my high school, and pretty much being the only asian girl in a predominantly white band, I always felt like my voice wasn't heard, and even as a member of the leadership team, my role didn't feel "important" enough. I felt like I was being shut down, and all of my ideas to make the band better would be ignored by people who were in roles higher than me. Getting to talk about leadership with other girls who've felt the same way as me showed me what leadership was. It was like something clicked and a light in my head went off; it was the first time that I saw every single person that was talking in the group have a voice, and genuine opinion about the topic. It was the first ever time I saw the teacher hearing each individual and actually caring, and everybody else in the class was also open to hearing everybody else's thoughts as well. I've learned so much, and I just wish I knew about true leadership sooner. Part of me was scared to go into a leadership class because I'd heard the same thing year after year in band—"a good leader is good at leading" and pretty much just that. I think I've been able to grow as a leader even within these first few weeks of college; I've felt like I've been exposed to so many new experiences and stories, and I've learned that it's so important to hear everybody's stories and not invalidate or ignore anybody's voice.

Leadership isn't holding power over others; it's about using that role for the better. Not to shut others' opinions or ideas, but to do the exact opposite. Listening to the people you're leading and representing them as a leader is what real leadership is. It's hard to always see good leadership because politics and leaders in big groups tend to become corrupted and toxic but coming to college and getting to be part of the leadership scholars program has helped me understand that leadership is about understanding each person in the room.

It's been eye opening hearing about other's stories of feeling like their voices weren't heard, and as someone who is part of a minority group, it felt so validating to finally be able to voice my opinions and ideas and feel heard. A person can be quiet and not always fit in with the crowd, but that doesn't mean that they can't be an excellent leader; a leader doesn't have to follow the herd, and I've learned that being Asian American and a woman doesn't have to interfere with being a great leader for others.

Through Mio's narrative, we see a clear path of transformation as she conceptualizes leadership for herself. Mio traveled from self-doubt and misunderstandings of leadership to an experience with peers that provided empowerment and support to being able to define leadership in a new way. Mio's reflective journey seems to be active, ongoing, and involves the engagement of other people including peers and the instructor of her leadership course. This educational environment provided the context and opportunity for Mio to pause, reflect, and reconsider her past perspectives. Her academic experience included peers, with whom Mio found a likeness and empowerment. This was an opportunity to see leadership in action through her teacher and classmates who demonstrated active listening, care, and vested interest in Mio's thoughts and opinions (Jackson et al., 2022; Palmer & Maramba, 2015).

As we saw in Chapter 8, imposter syndrome can plague young women as they attempt to understand or to practice leadership. We see this theme here as Mio described the discrimination she experienced as a young, Asian woman who did not look or sound the part of a leader as described by others. Like me, she was taught that being a leader meant having a loud voice. As an introvert with a quieter voice, it is possible Mio felt fearful or unable to assume formal leadership roles. Oftentimes extroverts are seen as the more capable or likely leaders, though we know introverts can also bring effective talents to their leadership style (Farrell, 2017). A 2017 study by Spark et al. showed that introverts are less likely to emerge as leaders because they fear the possible negative feelings that may come upon assuming a leadership role. Fear and misconceptions about leadership contributed to Mio's self-doubt because she did not seem to fit the mold of what it meant to be a leader according to her community.

Mio also aptly described the role her peers in a college leadership class played in providing validation and support. Mio reflected with other women who had similar experiences. In addition, being in a group with these women showed her leadership in action, in which each group member was valued and heard for their ideas and opinions. It was this group that allowed Mio to have a pivotal moment that reshaped her beliefs and understanding of leadership. Her narrative describes the way in which she dismantles notions of leadership that were socialized per her experience in high school and in band. Through reflection and co-creation of new knowledge, Mio conceptualizes leadership in a way that appreciates individuals' social identities, listening to the varying voices within a group, and understanding group members as part of the leadership process.

Alea: "Trying to Make Sense of the World We Live In"

While the previous narratives described reflective behaviors and reflective moments, Alea's narrative, itself, is a reflective behavior and moment.

Her reflection itself is also a form of resistance—calling out double standards and reclaiming the word "bossy" as a plausible leadership descriptor. Through her narrative, I see her making meaning of the identities she holds and the experiences she has had. She processed through what her identities and experiences mean to her and where she has traveled on her leadership journey because of them. Alea, a biracial, cisgender, heterosexual woman, wrote:

> Leadership has always come naturally to me—whether it's because I had great role models to look up to or because I'm a Leo is actually the question. Ever since I was very young, I was the leader of the group. It started when I would play with my friends and try to direct what was going on. I then became captain of my soccer team and always the leader in a group project. One word followed me around like a fly, always there and hard to escape: bossy. It may seem like a benign word, but I take offense to that word because I would be assertive and confident if I were a man. But women, on the other hand, are domineering and demanding. This double standard is the one thing that hasn't been able to escape me, no matter my astrological sign. Though I have been a leader my whole life, it doesn't mean it was always easy.
>
> While I have had many leadership positions, interestingly enough, most of them have not been positions where I was leading men. I was a section leader in my all-female choir, a vice president of a club that consisted of all women, and currently, I serve on the executive council of my sorority. Though gender is a social construct and no longer widely considered binary, the lack of men's presence in my leadership experience has allowed me to develop as a leader without the misogyny that often comes with that growth. Men are not the only ones who practice sexism, but they happen, rightfully so, to dominate that narrative. I have been very privileged in that regard. When it comes to my privilege and gender, I'm a cisgender woman and free to express my gender identity without fear of being retaliated against. Not all women or women presenting people have privilege. As a leader, I have tried to make sure I am as inclusive as possible by implementing policies that take my gender privilege into account. For instance, this year, during my sorority's recruitment, our name tags will have each member's preferred pronouns. Having pronouns on our nametags shows our members that we care enough about you as a human being to allow you to express yourself however you feel most comfortable. As a leader, I always put people before the task or goal; that way, the people under your leadership don't feel overruled, and my privilege doesn't run amuck.
>
> The intersectionality of race, gender, and leadership has long proceeded my leadership journey. Being a black woman has definitely shaped my leadership experience because my skin color is one of the first things people

see when they look at me. Race has felt most important when it comes to my leadership role in my sorority. I am membership vice president of a Panhellenic sorority, which means that I oversee a whole lot of white women. I can say with almost certainty that I am the first black woman to serve in that role. While I am proud and excited to be the first, I'm also sad that this organization has taken decades to put a black woman in this role. I still have advantages over other black women regarding my light skin color. I am also half white and half black; combining that with my caramel-colored skin can give me a more "palatable" appearance than women darker than me. Colorism is huge in leadership and representation in general and will never end if it isn't acknowledged or addressed. My responsibility is to make sure my chapter creates more opportunities for all Women of Color to serve in all leadership positions. The responsibility doesn't stop when I leave my sorority; it is a burden I will happily carry the rest of my life, unlike the one where I am expected to cook for my family, but that is for a different essay.

Where I am in life now, I think the word bossy is a compliment. I am bossy; I know what I like and won't settle for less than I deserve. Finally, in the words of the great Roxanne Gay, "I am just one woman trying to make sense of the world we live in. I'm raising my voice to show all the ways we have room to want more, to do better" (Gay, 2014, p. xiv).

Alea's narrative strikes me differently than the other two narratives in this chapter—not simply because of Alea's perceived confidence as a leader but in the experiences she described. In this reflection, Alea is clear in identifying the concrete experiences she has had as a person and as a leader—being soccer captain, an officer in her sorority, and in leadership roles in other organizations. Upon describing these specific experiences, we then see her reflective observation and abstract conceptualization through this narrative. Through these experiences, she has learned various lessons and has developed her own opinions about what it does and does not mean to be a leader. According to Owen (2020), women—particularly Women of Color—tend to experience sexism related to leadership. Women may experience the double standard of "being called bitchy for being assertive, while men exhibiting the same behavior are rewarded for showing initiative" (p. 120). While it can be easy for women to experience internalized oppression (Owen, 2020), Alea has clearly developed the confidence in understanding that her assertiveness as a woman is acceptable and that perhaps being "bossy" is a form of leadership. When she shares, "I think the word bossy is a compliment. I am bossy; I know what I like and won't settle for less than I deserve," we see an emerging definition of leadership built by herself, untainted by the opinions of others or by societal norms.

In Alea's case, she spent time reflecting specifically on her gender and racial identities that have shaped her experiences with leadership. She faced a dichotomy of feeling strong and capable of leadership while also recognizing the discrimination she has and could face as a Black, biracial woman. Because of this, Alea's abstract reflection led her to conceptualizing leadership as something that is inclusive and generative, filled with the responsibility of giving back and empowering others.

Within this narrative, I do not see a clear endpoint of development or a specific "ah-ha" moment. Alea is still in the process of developing, which is appropriate given the iterative and process-oriented nature of leadership itself. She recognizes ways that she can influence those around her, and I see her leaning more towards active experimentation in the way she discussed creating opportunities for other Women of Color in her sorority. It seems that she has even taken some risks through previous experimentation through adding pronouns to name tags during sorority recruitment. Alea's narrative helps us see all stages of Kolb's (1984) cycle of experiential learning. Alea establishes new conceptualizations of leadership unhindered by "experts" and developed through her own thoughtful reflection about her experiences and how she hopes to shape the world.

WEAVING THE NARRATIVES

From exploring Skye's, Mio's and Alea's narratives, we see similarity in the ways they came to discover their own understanding and conceptualization of leadership. There are three, primary shared themes among these narratives. First, these narratives demonstrate that leadership learning can take place by understanding what leadership is not. Particularly in the cases of Skye and Mio, they learned what leadership is by experiencing poor examples of leadership. They were provided examples and experiences that were, in many ways, painful (see Chapters 4 and 5 for more on systemic oppression and harm). Skye realized that leadership was more than strength, fortitude, and independence. Mio learned that leadership is open to people of all identities and is not simply for the most outspoken person in the room. In Alea's narrative, we see her immediately reject terminology that would tear down women in leadership. She faced the double standard women face in a patriarchal society and refused to feed into that narrative. She immediately recognized what leadership is not.

Second, reflection is central to each narrative as a means of conceptualizing leadership. Each woman has drawn upon life experiences to approach the reflective observation and abstract conceptualization stages within Kolb's (1984) cycle. The exercise of providing a written reflection on leadership allowed each woman to highlight their different beliefs of leadership and how those beliefs developed or have changed over time. Their descriptions of leadership are everything from poetic to messy to concise to more stream-of-consciousness. Regardless of how each woman described their current understanding of leadership and how that came to be, this exercise demonstrated that each woman had clear views they could express at that moment in time. These women have actively created new knowledge for the world to read on what it means to lead.

Finally, within these narratives, specifically reflecting on gender and race seems to be an integral piece of the leadership journey. Reflecting on their gender and racial identities led to overcoming feelings of helplessness and results in feelings of confidence and empowerment, particularly when processed in community with others (Lardier et al., 2022; Ospina & Su, 2009). These women realized that being a woman is powerful, that women are worthy of leadership. As Women of Color, they described feeling hopeful, strong, and capable. By finding mentors, peers, teachers, or other women to lead and be led by, they were able to find others who made them feel worthy of their own thoughts, opinions, and leadership.

While these narratives share many similarities, a couple of noticeable differences are worth mentioning. First, while Skye and Mio seemed tentative at first, not fully understanding their power as leaders, Alea began her narrative with a statement describing that she has always felt like a leader. From these narratives we see that understanding leadership and feeling confident as a leader may come at different stages of the leadership and conceptualization journeys; some face terrible imposter syndrome, others feel like leaders immediately. In addition, what most greatly influences our understanding of leadership varies person to person. In Skye's case, there seemed to be a mentor that really transformed her way of thinking. In Mio's case, it was a teacher and her peers in a leadership class that revolutionized her beliefs about leadership. In Alea's case, specific experiences, and the women she found herself surrounded by in those experiences, all contributed to her confidence.

APPLYING THE NARRATIVES

Through the analysis of Skye's, Mio's, and Alea's narratives, several important implications come to mind for consideration. First, it is important to remind ourselves that individuals move at their own pace when it comes to their understanding of leadership. Many individuals begin their journey with a lot of baggage, good and bad, when it comes to their understanding of leadership. While some women, like Alea, may have had very positive experiences through their lives, some women may and will have to unlearn years of discrimination, oppression, and bad examples of leadership. My hope is that women like these come to recognize themselves as knowledge-bearers that can actively contribute to reshaping how society views leadership and who can serve in a leadership capacity.

Second, for those who may teach leadership (through both curricular and cocurricular programs), educators should consider implementing intentional reflective pedagogy associated with leadership programs and development opportunities. To this point, Guthrie and Bertrand Jones (2012) wrote, "It is important to identify what learning objectives the experience will meet and connect that learning with reflection questions and activities that will produce the most meaning making for students" (p. 58). We see from these narratives the importance of reflection in developing an understanding of leadership; as educators we have the opportunity and privilege to create reflective experiences that can help students progress in their conceptualization of leadership. In addition, educators can create women-only spaces where women-identifying individuals can join in reflection, conceptualization, and action as they journey together towards better understanding leadership as a concept and themselves as leaders. In these spaces, my hope would be that each participant is considered an expert and that we reevaluate who can contribute new conceptualizations of leadership. If we are all experts of our own experiences, how does this type of expertise lend itself to the creation of new knowledge overflowing with diversity of thought, youthful optimism, and more inclusive ways of leading? The possibilities are both endless and exciting.

Next, each of these women described the role other women played in their personal growth and understanding of leadership as a concept. May we all consider how we can serve as mentors and advocates for rising generations of women leaders or help these women identify alternate mentors.

Finally, by recognizing what leadership is not, these women were freed from the constraints and burdens of societal expectations and allowed them to think and dream without hindrance. In their reflection, thinking, dreaming, and conceptualizing, they were able to weave together a new narrative of leadership for themselves. What they choose to believe about leadership, how they choose to act, who they choose to uplift and empower—all these choices are up to them. They are the experts of their own leadership; they are the driving force behind their own leadership. They possess a power within to serve as creators and co-creators of knowledge that inform their own leadership practice. Through their narratives, we can all learn more about what it means to lead, how to lead across differences, and how to reevaluate who is a student and who is a teacher when it comes to leadership learning.

CONCLUSION

This chapter explored how three young women have conceptualized leadership and how reflection was paramount to that process. We see the strength and challenges young women face as they learn, at its most basic, how to define leadership for themselves. Women may face an uphill battle as they combat myths about leadership or as they overcome imposter syndrome and discrimination. Developing a leader identity includes how a person conceptualizes themselves as a "leader" and how they interweave "leader" with their already existing identities such as race, class, or gender (Komives et al., 2011; McKenzie, 2018). Conceptualizing leadership is paramount as part of the leadership identity development journey, and it is the role of leadership educators to create spaces in which women can develop their leadership identity through thoughtful and intentional reflection. The following chapters will address narratives that discuss authenticity as a function of leadership as well as leadership identity specifically.

REFERENCES

Bamburg, M. G., & Andrews, M. (Eds.). (2004). *Considering counter-narratives: Narrating, resisting, and making sense*. John Benjamins Publishing Company.

Day, D. V., & Harrison, M. M. (2007). A multi-level, identity-based research approach to leadership development. *Human Resources Management, 17*(4), 360–373. https://doi.org/10.1016/j.hrmr.2007.08.007

Farrell, M. (2017). Leadership reflections: Extrovert and introvert leaders. *Journal of Library Administration, 57*(4), 436–443. https://doi.org/10.1080/01930826.2017.1300455

Gay, R. (2014). *Bad feminist*. Corsair.

Guthrie, K. L., & Bertrand Jones, T. (2012). Teaching and learning: Using experiential learning and reflection for leadership education. *New Directions for Student Services, 2012*(140), 53–63. https://doi.org/10.1002/ss.20031

Jackson, A., Colson-Fearon, B., & Versey, H. S. (2022). Managing intersectional invisibility and hypervisibility during the transition to college among first-generation women of color. *Psychology of Women Quarterly, 46*(3), 354–371. https://doi.org/10.1177/03616843221106087

Kolb, D. A. (1984). *Experiential learning: Experience as the source of learning and development*. Prentice-Hall.

Kolb, A. Y., & Kolb. D. A. (2017). Experiential learning theory as a guide for experiential educators in higher education. *Experiential Learning & Teaching in Higher Education, 1*(1), 7–44. https://nsuworks.nova.edu/elthe/vol1/iss1/7

Komives, S. R., Dugan, J. P., Owen, J. E., Slack, C., & Wagner, W. (2011). *Handbook for student leadership program* (2nd ed.). National Clearinghouse for Leadership Programs.

Komives, S. R., Owen, J. E., Longerbeam, S. D., Mainella, F. C., & Osteen, L. (2005). Developing a leadership identity: A grounded theory. *Journal of College Student Development, 46(6)*, 593–611. https://doi.org/10.1353/csd.2005.0061

Lardier, D. T., Opara, I., & Roach, E. (2022). A latent profile analysis of psychological sense of community and ethnic identity among racial–ethnic minority young adults from the southwestern United States. *Journal of Community Psychology, 50(2)*, 857–875. https://doi.org/10.1002/jcop.22686

McKenzie, B. L. (2018). Am I a leader? Female students leadership identity development. *Journal of Leadership Education, 17(2)*, 1–18. https://doi.org/10.12806/V17/I2/R1

Northouse, P. G. (2016). *Leadership: Theory and practice* (7th ed.). SAGE.

Ospina, S., & Su, C. (2009). Weaving color lines: Race, ethnicity, and the work of leadership in social change organizations. *Leadership, 5(2)*, 131–170. https://doi.org/10.1177/1742715009102927

Owen, J. (2020). *We are the leaders we've been waiting for: Women and leadership development in college.* Routledge.

Palmer, R. T., & Maramba, D. C. (2015). The impact of social capital on the access, adjustment, and success of Southeast Asian American college students. *Journal of College Student Development 56(1)*, 45–60. https://doi.org/10.1353/csd.2015.0007

Shetty, R. L. (2020). *The leadership identity development of Black women in college: A grounded theory* [Unpublished doctoral dissertation]. University of Georgia. https://esploro.libs.uga.edu/esploro/outputs/doctoral/The-Leader-Identity-of-Black-Women/9949365960702959

Spark, A., Stansmore, T., & O'Connor, P. (2017). The failure of introverts to emerge as leaders: The role of forecasted affect. *Personality and Individual Differences, 121(15)*, 84–88. https://doi.org/10.1016/j.paid.2017.09.026

Volpe White, J., Guthrie, K. L., & Torres, M. (2019). *Thinking to transform: Reflection in leadership learning.* Information Age Publishing.

PART II

EXPLORING THE NARRATIVES—ENACTMENT

Art by Imani

I want to be the Sun.

Having attracted others to my core being—my core values.
To release a heat of healing and growth.

I want to have boundaries for both me and my planets
for us to build a great system together.

Able to reach beyond itself.

—Imani, Chapter 11, p. 182

CHAPTER 11

LEADERSHIP LOOKS LIKE...ME

**Julie Henriquez Aldana
Lauren Contreras**

We should all feel like we are able to show up as our true selves in the places and spaces we encounter. As Women of Color working in higher education, we have seen how living authentically can impact the students we work with. We can and desire to show them how they can lead just as they are, with all of their identities. However, to lead authentically is not as simple as knowing who you are and acting in accordance with your values (Ngunjiri & Hernandez, 2017). To be an authentic leader, we must also consider our context and relationships to others (Jones, 2016; Jones et al., 2012; Jourian, 2014; Liu et al., 2016; Ngunjiri & Hernandez, 2017). For those who are historically marginalized in society, including women, Women of Color, and LGBTQ+ women, being authentic, and thereby being an authentic leader, can be difficult as identities, context, and relationships with others are fluid and complex. While we hope we can show up every day as ourselves, we are aware that in our society women, Women of Color, and LGBTQ+ women cannot always show up how we would like due to

Rooted and Radiant, pages 179–194
Copyright © 2024 by Information Age Publishing
www.infoagepub.com
All rights of reproduction in any form reserved.

systemic racism, xenophobia, sexism, genderism, heteronormativity, ableism, and other forms of discrimination. The narratives of the students in this chapter demonstrate how Imani, Sam, and Melanie are on a journey to embrace authenticity despite context and relationships that encouraged them to suppress their identities. They show us the importance of supporting women, Women of Color, and LGBTQ+ women so that they can show up as authentic leaders in all contexts.

> I'll never forget the moment my queer TA shared how he would rather be shunned for sharing his identity if it meant that another LGBTQ person was helped in the process by seeing someone like themselves. My (Lauren) first introduction to leadership was in high school. I was very involved in my church youth group and would even attend national youth conferences. I was also just beginning to understand my identity as a queer person. While no one ever said anything to me explicitly, I knew being these two identities, a youth group leader and queer, at the same time was not acceptable to those in the church. This led me to hide a very significant part of who I was becoming and who I am today. Leading authentically as a queer person in this situation would have presented many challenges and likely backlash from people within the church. As religious communities and society, in general, have become more accepting, I have also grown in my acceptance of myself and my pride in my queer identity. Still, there were times within my role as a higher education practitioner when I was not sure if I should share my queer identity with students. I had the fear that I may not be accepted or that students would not connect with me. Now, and remembering the impact of my TA, as I enter the first year on tenure-track, I introduce myself to my students as a proud queer Latina. These identities are important to me, and they impact the ways I teach, mentor, research, write, and lead. I hope by sharing my identities I can show others that it is okay to live and lead as their authentic selves.

APPROACHING THE NARRATIVES

To adequately address the experiences of systemic oppression facing Black women, Kimberlé Crenshaw (1989) developed the theoretical framework of intersectionality, which argues that Women of Color experience interlocking systems of oppression, including racism and sexism, that compound to further oppress, marginalize, and cause harm. An understanding of intersectionality allows for the experiences of Women of Color to be centered and better understood. See Chapter 3 for a more detailed discussion of intersectionality as a theoretical framework. Much of the early research on authentic leadership did not use an intersectional approach to understand how Women of Color develop and enact authentic leadership (Avolio & Gardner, 2005). However, more recent work has shown how taking an intersectional approach can better illuminate the experiences of Black women (Ngunjiri & Hernandez, 2017) and queer Student Leaders of Color (Miller & Vaccaro, 2016) who enact authentic leadership. This chapter also draws from intersectionality to understand how women from historically marginalized backgrounds developed and enacted authentic leadership. The women featured in this chapter experienced multiple overlapping forms of systemic oppression based on their race, ethnicity, immigration status, gender, and sexuality that has impacted how they understand authenticity and ultimately how they act as authentic leaders.

EXPLORING THE NARRATIVES

Authentic leadership is often described as simply knowing oneself and does not regard context, relationships, or identities of leaders (Avolio & Gardner, 2005). This chapter challenges this notion by sharing how contexts and identities do matter for Women of Color seeking to lead authentically. As such, our chapter draws from a counter-storytelling methodology. Counter-stories are told by those on the margins of society to challenge the majoritarian, deficit-based stories told about People of Color, to create new and richer stories about People of Color, and to transform established belief systems (Delgado, 1989; Solórzano & Yosso, 2002). Chapter 3 provides more information on counter-storytelling methodology. By openly sharing their identities and unique experiences, the narratives shared in this chapter are counter-stories to the dominant narrative about what it means to lead authentically as historically marginalized women.

Imani: "Inspirational Suns"

In the following narrative, Imani, who identifies as Black, queer, and femme. She also identifies as neurodiverse and navigates the world with ADHD. Imani shared how she understands and embodies authentic leadership.

> Spoken Word
>
> Time—Time is constant
> Knowledge is too,

> The only difference is one comes in a stream guiding us, every moment.
> The other—like the big bang changes the course of wisdom whenever we scream Eureka!
>
> Strong women are the sun, gravitating worlds, and planets close to her.
> The core of her being, attracting only those worthy to habitat her inner circle and live.
> Many times, others who get too close are burned or don't reach her warmth and freeze.
>
> Authentic leaders have stages, cycles of life, whatever you may call it.
> This cycle, to the stages of the Sun, brings many that can be close.
> This closeness lets someone flourish in its presence to go on and bloom incredible things.
>
> I want to be the Sun.
> Having attracted others to my core being—my core values. To release a heat of healing and growth.
> I want to have boundaries for both me and my planets for us to build a great system together.
> Able to reach beyond itself.
>
> As the sun, as a leader, as a femme, I see the connection between everything and anything.
> The ugly and the beautiful.
> As one who has seen Suns set and rise into the world we live and bring great change,
> I desire to be that garden in bloom after years of gardening, after years of setting suns.
>
> Authenticity—to be one's true inner form in front of millions of stars.
> To the Universe
> Is to be a sun—
> In the middle of a system
> Crossing other systems
> Bounding the universe as it endlessly expands.
>
> A strong femme—an authentic leader—the fiery sun—my future self.
>
> Inspirational Suns

Traditionally, Black women leaders have had to embrace their multiple identities, and define for themselves what it means to be an authentic leader (Winkle-Wagner et al., 2019). Furthermore, Black women in higher education are subject to negative stereotypes, microaggressions, and lower expectations from faculty and peers (Leath & Chavous, 2018). Over time these experiences can lead to mental and emotional exhaustion (Corbin et al., 2018). Imani is a Black, young femme whose definition of leadership embodies joy, confidence, strength, connectedness, and is fueled by positive energy. She conceptualizes a leader as a bright light that guides and inspires others to shine from within. She aspires to draw others in and connect with them through shared core values, through a collectivistic approach that draws strength from community and group belonging. These characteristics draw on the traditional conception of authentic leadership as values-based (Shamir & Eilam, 2005). Authentic leaders demonstrate confidence, optimism, hope and resilience, and consistency between their words and deeds (Luthans & Avolio, 2003, as cited in Avolio & Gardner, 2005). However, many theorists have neglected to acknowledge the influence of context on authentic leadership, which according to Jones et al. (2012) and Jourian (2014) plays an integral part in how leaders are able to lead authentically. Imani's narrative illustrates the role of context in defining leadership, as she saw "the connection between everything and anything," she appreciates the interconnectedness of people, context, values, self-awareness, and influence in leading authentically (Ngunjiri & Hernandez, 2017). Imani wrote the following which directly highlights this:

> Authenticity—to be one's true inner form in front of millions of stars.
> To the Universe
> Is to be a sun—
> In the middle of a system
> Crossing other systems
> Bounding the universe as it endlessly expands.

It is also important to note that Imani has also recognized the importance of setting boundaries as a leader. Setting boundaries and prioritizing and managing time are often espoused as "critical leadership skills" (Rhode, 2017, p. 28); however, women, and particularly Women of Color, often struggle to engage in boundary-setting. In embracing and redefining leadership as joy, confidence, and strength, Imani counters the stereotypes that have been assigned to her as a young, neurodiverse, Femme of Color.

Melanie: "Capable of Anything"

The next leadership narrative is from Melanie who identifies as a straight, Latina female. In her narrative, Melanie shared about her identity as an undocumented immigrant from El Salvador. In contrast to how Imani described her leadership as bright as the sun, Melanie's story illustrates the hardship of hiding one's identity and how it affects one's ability to develop a positive self-concept.

> My family moved here from El Salvador in 2008. Growing up, my parents did their best to shield me from the realities of having that as part of my identity, so I did not become aware of it until I entered middle school. It started off by seeing myself get rejected for opportunities because of my status, seeing my parents be harassed by higher authority figures, and even feeling unsafe in my school environment in the wake of the 2016 presidential election. When applying for a scholarship for high school, I was rejected after being told the chances of me making it to college were too low for them to invest in my education. As I got older and understood the severity of that comment, I internalized this mindset, and it took a toll on my confidence in my abilities.
>
> Although it took a lot of work, I started feeling more comfortable and happier with that part of my identity, but I was still restricted and scared of fully opening myself up. A group I had been open about it with was my Latina affinity group, and for our affinity day event, they asked me to participate in a documentary they were planning to make. It focused on the members' lives outside of school, including their families, and a large aspect of it was being undocumented. At first it was kind of intimidating because this was a documentary that everyone in my high school was going to watch. Either way, I decided to do it because I decided I had enough of hiding and it was an important topic to discuss; I would be honored to be part of that. I filmed my part, and then I had to wait for it, none of us watched it until the actual event day. The questions asked about my journey here to the United States, what the experience was like for my parents and me, and what I was hoping to teach my peers about being undocumented in the United States. I was excited but also scared, this was a large group watching me in a vulnerable state and sharing an intimate part of my identity, and there were so many different reactions I could receive.
>
> Watching the film was bittersweet. On the one hand I felt free and accomplished, on the other, I feared how my peers would react. But to my surprise, everyone was extremely impressed by the film and my group members. But the effect of what had just happened did not hit me until I attempted to make a comment for my peers, in which I just started crying. I felt terrified, upset, confused, but most of all I felt free. In that moment, I had finally confronted my biggest fear, and to my surprise, was met with nothing but love and appreciation from both classmates and teachers. It felt like a weight had been lifted off my shoulders that I had not even realized had been there for so long.
>
> That was when I most felt like a leader. I came to understand that being a leader does not always have to mean being bold or upfront. Sometimes it

> means having the courage to be able to speak for yourself and take care of your well-being. It is still astounding to me that it took me so long to have the bravery to confront this fear of mine because I feared what others would say. Even if I do not exactly always consider myself a leader, that day I did lead, and I will always remember the impact it had on me. In my toughest moments, I will try to remember that day to remind myself that I am capable of anything, and even if I can't do it quite yet, I will grow to that goal.

For many years, Melanie's immigrant status was weaponized against her, which forced her to hide and repress parts of her identity out of fear for her safety and ability to pursue opportunities. Jones (2016) found leaders who hold marginalized identities may silence themselves because they are negotiating their own identities and managing other's perceptions of them. Gaytan et al. (2007) contended that undocumented students often hide salient parts of their identity because of uncertainty around their safety. They may fear the constant threat of deportation, which increases their levels of anxiety, stress, and depressive symptoms. Melanie felt the pain and shame of being "othered" by her community. Previous research on undocumented students found, out of a survival instinct, they chose to be silent rather than face hostility from others (Chang et al., 2017). Melanie shared how a particular incident impacted her self-concept:

> When applying for a scholarship for high school, I was rejected after being told the chances of me making it to college were too low for them to invest in my education. As I got older and understood the severity of that comment, I internalized this mindset, and it took a toll on my confidence in my abilities.

Salient experiences like these contributed to Melanie's identity development and self-awareness. Jones (2012) emphasized that leadership organizations can often be places that contribute to marginalizing and silencing. This is why it is important to have organizations that support marginalized identities and that tend to the intersectionality of identities. DeAngelo et al. (2016) found when undocumented students were part of groups with other undocumented students, they "were able to provide social support networks, and buffer the repercussions associated with one's legal status" (p. 223). Similarly, when Melanie met other students who shared her identity and heard their stories, she felt supported and was able to find her voice and the courage to accept and speak her truth. In sharing her true story, she found support and liberation from the burden of hiding. In sharing narratives, undocumented students disrupt their imagined identity and inscribe power (DeAngelo et al., 2016). Through sharing her experiences, Melanie began to recognize her worth, power, and leadership ability; her perspective on her leadership potential shifted as she "came to understand that being a leader does not always have to mean being bold or upfront." She disrupted the ways others marginalized her and defined for herself her leader identity (DeAngelo et al., 2016). Her courage and bravery, demonstrated by her participation in the documentary brought her to liberation. When she was able to present her whole, authentic self, Melanie embodied her definition of a leader: "Sometimes it means having the courage to be able to speak for yourself and take care of your well-being."

Sam: "Growth and Development with Confidence and Pride"

In her narrative, Sam, who identifies as Hispanic (White and Mexican), genderqueer/nonconforming, and Lesbian, recognized that by holding these identities, she will experience systemic oppression. Similar to Melanie, Sam was driven by societal expectations and the environment around her to shield her identity as a Mexican American lesbian.

> There are many things you learn about yourself while being locked in a car in an empty Steak 'n Shake parking lot.
>
> While I sat in my shiny Mercedes-Benz prison ("It's a hand-me-down from my mom, we aren't rich!"), I had come to this earth-shattering realization that I was in fact a Mexican-American lesbian surrounded by a group of disapproving, very straight, very White Mormon men. Where I grew up, it was very easy to fall prey to the cult of "anti-identity" politics. The people in power constantly reassure you that there are absolutely no differences between people, everyone has equal opportunity, "I don't see color," "I accept you just not *your* lifestyle." Lulling you into a sense of security and assurance while ripping the rug from under your feet. In our free America, everyone will treat you as their equal (until they don't). The people who have placed themselves above you will never truly understand the experiences of the people they have put beneath them, if they care to try at all.
>
> I hold a tested theory that every minority comes to a (dread-inducing, pit-in-your-stomach, "oh shit") point in their life where they realize they are different. To this point, I had the privilege of hiding my identities as much or as little as I wanted. Unless I stood side by side with my family, I could easily go throughout my day as your average White girl. Even my name was infallible ("Samantha Smith," 10th most popular baby girl name of 2003 + ambiguously European surname = shining pinnacle of American mediocrity). Just as easily, I could gesture to any man on the street, make a vaguely heterosexual comment for the audience, and move about my day. This was unsustainable. I was beginning to gain leadership roles in my school, my friendships were

becoming more serious, I was preparing for the process of applying to college, and I was growing up. I could not expect to be taken seriously if I did not have the courage to live authentically. When you purposely suppress your identities, it is easy to ignore how much influence they hold over you. It's a fairly serious trade-off you commit to as a kid: unrestricted access to the model suburban lifestyle for the low, low price of your entire identity.

When you do finally take the step into self-actualization, you are bound to face some roadblocks. The people who previously reassured you of your identities will turn on you for breaking their conformity (e.g., "You really don't have to shove it down our throats"). You may find yourself reconsidering which parts of your family are still safe to be around (save getting one free consultation with your local conversion therapist). You may find yourself locked in your closest friend's car at midnight being lectured about your sins against humanity (or, my personal favorite, "One-way ticket to hell").

I do not intend for this paper to come across as the typical "I only cared until it affected me" narrative. I was incredibly, unnervingly aware of how discrimination affected my family and friends: those experiences were what led to my (albeit, cowardly) hiding in the first place. I often consider my life if I simply continued living incognito. Would my life be easier? Would I be able to seriously live with myself? How unfair was it to everyone else who had no way to just "hide" themselves? I know now that my advocacy comes from someplace deeply personal and connected to me. Progress is impossible if we are all working overtime to appeal to societal expectations. So, I am, against my better judgment, grateful for the flamboyant demonstration of bigotry that broke me out of my shell. I hope to continue my journey of growth and development with confidence and pride.

In addition to recognizing the systemic oppression she faces due to her identities, Sam also understands the privilege she holds in being able to hide the parts of her identity that did not conform to others' expectations of who she should be based on her name and physical appearance. "Passing" allowed her to protect herself from the disapproval of others. However, as she progressed through her leadership journey, she started to recognize the value of being authentic as a leader, rather than hiding core aspects of herself to fit in. Through leadership roles, she gained a deeper understanding of herself, her values, and how to be genuine and to honor all her identities. She found the courage to challenge what she had been socialized to believe about success and acknowledged the cost she had paid for conformity: "It's a fairly serious trade-off you commit to as a kid: unrestricted access to the model suburban lifestyle for the low, low price of your entire identity."

Sam's narrative demonstrates the conflict young leaders grapple with as they lead in spaces where they feel marginalized. They must choose between being authentic or carrying the burden of conforming to be seen as an effective leader (Jones, 2016; Jones et al., 2012; Liu et al., 2015, 2016). Due to stereotypes and discrimination, leaders with marginalized identities make decisions about how much of themselves to reveal. This does not mean Sam was inauthentic in her leadership, she was only trying to protect herself from harm (Jones, 2016). Sam found comfort in conforming when she was younger, but as she developed and embraced her identity, she realized she was no longer willing to trade authenticity for comfort. She started to challenge her context and the value of relationships that she worked to maintain by hiding her genuine identity. The tension between societal expectations and the need to be herself drove Sam to reflect and to define her values and who she wanted to be as a leader. In that exploration, she found the courage to present herself authentically and to be a proud and confident leader.

WEAVING THE NARRATIVES

Through their stories, Imani, Melanie, and Sam illustrated their processes of identity exploration and development and how their identity informs their definition of leadership. Each of them demonstrated how they learned to embrace authenticity over suppressing their identities and conforming to society's espoused values. Each of their stories highlights liberation, pride, confidence, growth, and hope, all of which are characteristics of authentic leadership (Avolio & Gardner, 2005). They also recognized that as leaders they contribute to a larger whole where both leaders and followers can thrive collectively. This relational focus is often not considered when analyzing authentic leadership models (Jourian, 2014).

The three narratives also convey the negative effects of authentic leadership on individuals: the pain, disconnect, and disapproval from those holding dominant identities, and the constant feelings of marginalization they experience. Melanie acknowledged the unseen toll of emotional labor that women, and especially Women of Color, have to endure when she reflected on the aftermath of sharing her story—"A weight had been lifted off my shoulders that I had not even realized had been there for so long."

Some of the key criticisms of authentic leadership theory are that it mostly centers around the leader and their characteristics, it assumes a positive relationship between the leader and follower(s), and it neglects to consider the context in which leadership is enacted (Avolio & Garner, 2005; Eagly, 2005; Jones, 2016; Liu et al, 2016). Ngunjiri and Hernandez (2017) argued for a more complex exploration and understanding of authentic leadership:

> Authenticity is complex, because it has to be enacted within specific contexts, in relationship with other actors—such as peers, students/followers, other leaders within hierarchical organizational structures—and therefore, being

authentic leaders cannot simply be a matter of knowing oneself and acting true to that self-knowledge. The role of others and the context in which relationships are enacted are critical elements of the equation. Together, they contribute to perhaps a more fluid definition of authentic leadership. (p. 397)

Similarly, Liu et al. (2016) contended that "the capacity for leaders to influence their authentic leadership narratives is shaped by power dynamics including gender and cultural norms" (p. 714). Thus, context and power dynamics are very influential in the experience of authentic leaders.

These elements of the theory are especially salient when we consider leaders from historically marginalized groups. Even self-awareness, one of the core elements of authentic leadership, is often difficult to develop because "self-awareness for us is complex, fluid, and context dependent given the racialized subtexts that accompany interactions in the United States" (Ngunjiri & Hernandez, 2017, p. 398). Leaders who hold marginalized identities often experience microaggressions and struggle to embrace and share all aspects of their identity in spaces that, by design, reject and oppress them. This struggle is magnified when gender intersects with other identities like immigrant status and race. Hernandez et al. (2015) wrote, "When gender intersects with other social identities, along with diverse organizational or social contexts, what it means to be a leader becomes rife with complications" (p. 96). Jones et al. (2012) described how leaders have to make "moment-to-moment negotiations and decisions about managing who we are, given the context" (p. 711). Imani, Melanie, and Sam were engaging in code-switching, "the temporary 'switching on' or adjustment of behaviors to optimize the comfort of others in exchange for a desired outcome" (McCluney et al., 2021), as they made decisions about sharing their identities in different contexts. Navigating these complications requires that leaders expend more effort to be seen as competent and effective, and often, like Sam shared, they choose to hide those aspects of their identity to be able to exist "safely" in contexts where they lead.

Imani's, Melanie's, and Sam's narratives share an interesting thread: their definition of leadership has become analogous with their identity expression. Imani's narrative captured the bold, energetic, and connected aspects of leadership, which are all characteristics that reflect in her identity. Melanie, on the other hand, highlighted the more abstract or subtle aspects of leadership—being a quiet leader, finding her voice and using it to influence others, and having courage to liberate herself from the burden of hiding her identity. She embodies these characteristics in how she presents herself to others. Lastly, Sam focused her definition of leadership on growth, developing confidence, having pride in who you are, and being brave enough to disrupt and counter societal expectations. This influenced how she approached her leadership development and her identity exploration and celebration.

Although there are many similarities and shared experiences among the narratives, there are also distinct differences in how each woman approached their authentic leadership journey. Each woman's identity has been shaped by the environments in which they have been raised, which influences how they approach authenticity. Imani chose to claim the joy and positive influence she can have as a leader, countering the stereotypes of anger and animosity that are often attributed to Black women. Melanie remained true to her introverted nature by finding strength and courage in using her story to inspire others and to show how she will no longer be silenced because she is an undocumented student. She embraced her inner power and how she can use it to advocate for herself and to lead her peers. Sam spent her childhood and young adulthood in a falsely "accepting" community, which drove her to often hide herself to fit in and conform to her environment. She recognized that conforming was not sustainable as she developed her identity. This constant suppression of parts of herself really cemented Sam's aspiration to be authentic and unapologetically present her true self to everyone.

APPLYING THE NARRATIVES

I (Julie) did not consider myself a leader when I was younger. I was not charismatic, assertive, nor did I command a room as I pictured a leader would in my mind. When I thought of a leader, I immediately thought of the great inspirational leaders we learn about in history class. As an AfroLatina, I easily thought of men as leaders, as I was socially conditioned to believe. My quiet, bookish, thoughtful and disciplined nature made me a follower, not a leader.

Like Melanie, I am also an immigrant, stamped as a nonresident alien from the day I arrived in the United States to attend college. Alien. Someone who didn't belong, who was allowed into a space not designed for my success. I lived in the background, supporting those whom I recognized as leaders, working hard to ensure that they were successful. Even when I was placed in a leadership role as a resident assistant, I felt like I was playing a part that was not meant for me. However, I worked hard, served my community, and was promoted to higher leadership roles. I still felt like I was not suited for leadership because I did not fit the image of a leader I created in my head.

My definition of leadership shifted as I progressed through my graduate program, and studied leadership more deeply. I had to challenge the idealized concepts of leadership I held and read about, and recognized that leadership is more than charisma, more than power. A leader can be a

> woman who does not see herself as anything special, but who works hard, who can inspire and be a catalyst to help others achieve their potential. I value my power as a leader, and embrace the responsibility I have to utilize my positionality to open doors for other leaders who may not see themselves in that light.

As leadership educators and practitioners, we can reflect on Imani's, Melanie's, and Sam's narratives and parse out the common themes in their journey toward defining leadership and leading authentically. Each narrative highlights the importance of identity exploration and self-awareness through understanding and defining leadership. They reinforce that students' understanding of leadership can evolve as their identity develops. This means that we cannot limit how students make meaning and define leadership, each student will develop their own understanding and by doing so, will likely embody and recognize the characteristics of leaders within themselves.

First, as we work with students, one recommendation is to provide and facilitate opportunities for identity exploration early on in the leadership education process. Self-awareness plays a key role in authentic leadership, thus giving students opportunities to explore and understand their identities will allow them to know themselves as they define and enact leadership. Chapter 12 takes a deeper look at leadership identity and provides more context, implications, and recommendations related to leadership identity development.

Second, we must be transparent with our student leaders, particularly those who hold intersecting marginalized identities, and openly discuss the challenges they will potentially face as leaders. Offering support through providing spaces where students can have difficult conversations and process their challenges within a supportive community is very important. Ngunjiri and Hernandez (2017) encouraged forming small groups to help students develop as authentic leaders:

> Authentic leadership is dependent upon relational authenticity. Supportive communities would be spaces for authentic relationships to thrive. Smaller groups for specific minority groups can help provide support to those on the margins, while mixed culture groups can become spaces for cultural bridge building. (p. 403)

Imani, Melanie, and Sam all reflected on how the support and encouragement they received through structured leadership and affinity programs helped them grow and embrace their identity and leadership style. Therefore, the programs and interventions that educators develop and manage are valuable to students as they seek to understand themselves and to become authentic leaders. Furthermore, educators should create more leadership and affinity groups focused on the leadership learning and development of Women of Color and LBGTQ+ students. These groups may allow them to further develop their leadership identity in a supportive environment that can serve as a counterspace to the unwelcoming, harmful spaces in which they may become leaders.

Strong leadership is necessary to overcome the racial, social, economic, political, and environmental challenges our students will continue to face. We believe that these leaders must be trustworthy, transparent, and courageous in order to connect with and mobilize their followers. They will need to connect and work across differences. Jones (2016) underscored the importance of understanding identities in the development of the skills they will need to do this, particularly their own identities. Therefore, developing leaders who are self-aware, authentic, and who understand the context in which they are leading will be our challenge as educators. By investing in our students, particularly our students who hold historically marginalized identities, we are contributing to their growth, development, and their ability to be the leaders we will need in the future. If you are interested in learning more about the themes discussed in this chapter, we recommend Chapters 4, 5, 6, 10, and 12 specifically, as they provide a deeper perspective on some of the themes covered in this chapter.

REFERENCES

Avolio, B. J., & Gardner, W. L. (2005). Authentic leadership development: Getting to the root of positive forms of leadership. *The Leadership Quarterly, 16*(3), 315–338. https://doi.org/10.1016/j.leaqua.2005.03.001

Chang, A., Torrez, M. A., Ferguson, K. N., & Sagar, A. (2017). Figured worlds and American dreams: An exploration of agency and identity among Latinx undocumented students. *The Urban Review, 49*(2), 189–216. https://doi.org/10.1007/s11256-017-0397-x

Corbin, N. A., Smith, W. A., & Garcia, J. R. (2018). Trapped between justified anger and being the strong Black woman: Black college women coping with racial battle fatigue at historically and predominantly White institutions. *International Journal of Qualitative Studies in Education, 31*(7), 626–643. https://doi.org/10.1080/09518398.2018.1468045

Crenshaw, K. (1989). Demarginalizing the intersection of race and sex: A Black feminist critique of antidiscrimination doctrine, feminist theory and antiracist politics. *University of Chicago Legal Forum, 1989*(1), 139–167. http://chicagounbound.uchicago.edu/uclf/vol1989/iss1/8

DeAngelo, L., Schuster, M. T., & Stebleton, M. J. (2016). California dreamers: Activism, identity, and empowerment among undocumented college students. *Journal of Diversity in Higher Education, 9*(3), 216–230. https://doi.org/10.1037/dhe0000023

Delgado, R. (1989). Storytelling for oppositionists and others: A plea for narrative. *Michigan Law Review, 87*(8), 2411–2441. https://doi.org/10.2307/1289308

Eagly, A. H. (2005). Achieving relational authenticity in leadership: Does gender matter? *The Leadership Quarterly, 16*(3), 459–474. https://doi.org/10.1016/j.leaqua.2005.03.007

Gaytan, F. X., Carhill, A., & Suarez-Orozco, C. (2007). Understanding and responding to the needs of newcomer immigrant youth and families. *The Prevention Researcher, 14*(4), 10–13. https://eric.ed.gov/?id=EJ793963

Hernandez, K.-A. C., Ngunjiri, F. W., & Chang, H. (2015). Exploiting the margins in higher education: A collaborative autoethnography of three foreign-born female faculty of color. *International Journal of Qualitative Studies in Education, 28*(5), 533–551. https://doi.org/10.1080/09518398.2014.933910

Jones, S. R. (2016). Authenticity in leadership: Intersectionality of identities. *New Directions for Student Leadership, 2016*(152), 23–34. https://doi.org/10.1002/yd.20206

Jones, S. R., Kim, Y. C., & Skendall, K. C. (2012). (Re-)framing authenticity: Considering multiple social identities using autoethnographic and intersectional approaches. *The Journal of Higher Education, 83*(5), 698–724. https://doi.org/10.1353/jhe.2012.0029

Jourian, T. J. (2014). Trans*forming authentic leadership: A conceptual framework. *Journal of Critical Thought and Praxis, 2*(2), 113–125. https://doi.org/10.31274/jctp-180810-78

Leath, S., & Chavous, T. (2018). Black women's experiences of campus racial climate and stigma at predominantly White institutions: Insights from a comparative and within-group approach for STEM and non-STEM majors. *The Journal of Negro Education, 87*(2), 125–139. https://doi.org/10.7709/jnegroeducation.87.2.0125

Liu, H., Cutcher, L., & Grant, D. (2015). Doing authenticity: The gendered construction of authentic leadership. *Gender, Work and Organization, 22*(3), 237–255. https://doi.org/10.1111/gwao.12073

Liu, H., Cutcher, L., & Grant, D. (2016). Authentic leadership in context: An analysis of banking CEO narratives during the global financial crisis. *Human Relations, 70*(6), 694–724. https://doi.org/10.1177/0018726716672920

Luthans, F., & Avolio, B. J. (2003). Authentic leadership development. In K. S. Cameron, J. E. Dutton, & R. E. Quinn (Eds.), *Positive organizational scholarship: Foundations of a new discipline* (pp. 241–261). Barrett-Koehler Publishers.

McCluney, C. L., Durkee, M. I., Smith, R. E., Robotham, K. J., & Lee, S. S.-L. (2021). To be, or not to be . . . Black: The effects of racial codeswitching on perceived professionalism in the workplace. *Journal of Experimental Social Psychology, 97* (2021), 1–12. https://doi.org/10.1016/j.jesp.2021.104199

Miller, R. A., & Vaccaro, A. (2016). Queer student leaders of color: Leadership as authentic, collaborative, culturally competent. *Journal of Student Affairs Research and Practice, 53*(1), 39–50. https://doi.org/10.1080/19496591.2016.1087858

Ngunjiri, F. W., & Hernandez, K.-A. C. (2017). Problematizing authentic leadership: A collaborative autoethnography of immigrant women of color leaders in higher education. *Advances in Developing Human Resources, 19*(4), 393–406. https://doi.org/10.1177/1523422317728735

Rhode, D. (2017). *Women and Leadership*. Oxford University Press.
Shamir, B., & Eilam, G. (2005). "What's your story?" A life-stories approach to authentic leadership development. *The Leadership Quarterly*, *16*(3), 395–417. https://doi.org/10.1016/j.leaqua.2005.03.005
Solórzano, D. G., & Yosso, T. J. (2002). Critical race methodology: Counter-storytelling as an analytical framework for education research. *Qualitative Inquiry*, *8*(1), 23–44. https://doi.org/10.1177/107780040200800103
Winkle-Wagner, R., Kelly, B. T., Luedke, C. L., & Reavis, T. B. (2019). Authentically me: Examining expectations that are placed upon Black women in college. *American Educational Research Journal*, *56*(2), 407–443. https://doi.org/10.3102/0002831218798326

CHAPTER 12

NAVIGATING SHIFTING TIDES

The Development of Feminist Leadership Identities

Julie E. Owen
Adrian L. Bitton

There is an ancient Indian proverb that cautions us "before we can see properly, we must shed tears to clear the way." Such is the nature of socialization—as people interact in social systems and face challenges, they evolve in what they believe about themselves, in how they value others, and in how they see the world. The preceding chapter centers the role of authenticity in feminist leadership. Central to authenticity is how one's multiple and often intersecting identities change over time. Similarly, leadership identity also develops and deepens in complexity as people confront challenging circumstances, experience different forms of leadership, and evolve their own leadership efficacy, capacity, and identity. This chapter applies Harro's (2013a, 2013b) cycles of socialization and liberation, the leadership identity development grounded theory and model (Komives et al., 2006; Komives et al., 2005), and Jones and Abes's (2013) intersectional model of multiple dimensions of identity (I-MMDI) to three narratives from college women gathered as part of a feminist narrative analysis process (Bloom, 1998).

The narratives included in this chapter invite questions of how one develops an identity as a feminist capable of leadership. As authors, we offer brief reflections on our own evolutions on these fronts before we delve into making meaning of student narratives.

> The first time I (Julie) took the Myers-Briggs Type Indicator in college, my results came back as "ENTJ: natural leader." I equated the very idea of leadership with top-down, authoritarian, patriarchal control. When I reflect on my youth, I can now recognize that I was surrounded by examples of certain kinds of leadership. My father was a captain in the U.S. Navy and as such was afforded respect and influence due to his position as a high-ranking officer. He would be frustrated when his power did not carry over to the home front, where my mother (who jokingly called herself the admiral) and his children did not obey his every order or when we had the nerve to talk back. My mother was equally formidable as a high achieving type A personality who rose to the top level of everything she set her mind to doing—an ace at tennis and golf, a prize winning photographer, a master gardener, a legendary teacher. As White, Anglo-Saxon protestants (WASPs) from New England we also had access to all the social, academic, and economic capital that comes with those privileged identities. I can now see how my family history conformed to many hegemonic and implicit assumptions about leadership in the United States, and how I benefited and continue to benefit from this alignment.
>
> It took me many years, including deep dives into feminist and critical theories, to see the limitations and inequity of this approach to leadership. Numerous mentors, friends, and students took time to help me broaden my view of the world. I began to question and unlearn my ingrained assumptions to arrive at a leadership identity that aligns more closely with the values and beliefs I hold as an adult. I now have a much more inclusive leadership identity. I am committed to using my voice to advocate for positive social change leading to more equitable leadership for all, and to consider how identities and social power shape practice. I will never completely shed the privileges afforded to me by my upbringing and identities, but I consciously work to find ways to elevate unheard voices, to disrupt and share power, and to dismantle narrow and normative views of leadership.

APPROACHING THE NARRATIVES

In addition to recognizing how our own positionalities influence our analysis of the narratives, we utilized the theoretical frames of Harro's (2013a, 2013b) cycles of socialization and liberation and the leadership identity development theory and model (Komives et al., 2006; Komives et al., 2005) to move beyond the individual-level focus of each narrative in order to highlight systemic-level influences across all three narratives.

Harro's (2013a) cycle of socialization describes how people are each born into a set of social identities—gender, class, religion, sexual orientation, race, culture, ability status, among others—which predispose us to "unequal roles in the dynamic system of oppression" (p. 45). Individuals are then subject to powerful forces to embody (or to enact) the roles assigned to us within this unequal system. Harro (2013a) describes how socialization is pervasive, consistent, circular, self-perpetuating, and often invisible or unconscious and unnamed. Individuals are socialized first by parental figures, relatives, and teachers, and later by our larger culture and institutions. These forces are often difficult to recognize and counteract as there are enforcements ingrained within our society to maintain the system. People who challenge the existing power structure are often labeled as troublemakers, experience discrimination or violence, are institutionalized, imprisoned, or even killed. The reward for not making waves is that one is left alone to continue operating as usual, but then the cycle continues. People often internalize the messages of oppressive systems so that the system itself does not have to do any work; people start to believe stereotypes about groups with which they identify and experience helplessness and hopelessness. The cycle of socialization is further complicated when we consider intersectionality. Intersectionality refers to the effects of interlocking systems of power, privilege, and oppression and how these forces shape lives and multiple social identities (Collins & Bilge, 2016; Crenshaw, 1991). It offers nuance so that when we consider the women's narratives, we are not erasing the differences in women's experiences and presenting them as a monolith, rather, we are creating more space to consider how the experiences of Women of Color differ from White women (or how women from a working-class background experience the world differently than women from an upper or upper-middle class background, etc.).

Understanding that our world is socially constructed and recognizing how the cycle of socialization works within our society allows us to also imagine a different, more just future. Harro (2013b) offers ways that individuals can start to disrupt the cycle of socialization through behaviors like raising consciousness, education, questioning, reframing, interrupting, and taking action. Harro's (2013b) cycle of liberation depicts seven stages of change based on patterns common to successful critical transformation and liberation efforts. Though working to end oppression is sadly never completely achievable, there is agency and critical hope in being able to name and to address the systemic structures and forces that contribute to oppression (Owen, 2020).

As women's leadership identities evolve in complexity, they are better equipped to resist dominant and gendered messages of leadership and to use their agency to further their own and others' liberation. Recognizing the transformative potential of a society that values women in leadership, we turned to the leadership identity development (LID) model as an additional theoretical lens. LID is a framework for understanding how individuals develop the identity of being collaborative, relational leaders interdependently engaging in leadership as a shared process. The model includes six stages (awareness, exploration/engagement, leader identified, leadership differentiated, generativity, and integration/synthesis) which address the process by which people become comfortable with nonhierarchical leadership and move from thinking of leadership as only positional, to considering that leadership can happen anywhere (Komives et al., 2006; Komives et al., 2005). Leadership identity development occurs across one's lifespan. For many students, college serves as a transition from adolescence to emerging adulthood (Arnett, 2000), making it a pivotal setting for leadership identity development.

Jones and Bitton (2021) brought together aspects of leadership development and socialization when applying Jones and Abes's (2013) intersectional model of multiple dimensions of identity (I-MMDI) to leadership learning. They described sites of intersection as "the location where social identities intersect with dominant narratives of leadership and other systems of inequality (the -isms)" (Jones & Bitton, 2021, p. 170). The authors suggested how higher education, curricular and co-curricular leadership programs, and student organizations can also serve as sites of intersection where leadership identity development is possible. Depending upon the content and experiences within these sites of intersection, college women can either be encouraged to develop their leadership identity or to continue to internalize the dominant narrative that perpetuates the myth that the identity of woman and the role of leader are mutually exclusive. It is here Jones and Bitton (2021) explored the possibility of a leadership meaning-making filter:

> The expansion and contraction of the leadership meaning-making filter reflects evolving conceptualizations of leadership. Moreover, it is situated between the micro- and macrolevels of context, thereby allowing power to flow in both directions. Just as the dominant narrative of leadership exerts pressure on the individual, individuals also have agency to resist contextual forces to advance more socially just societies, whereby leadership experiences and conversations take on new meaning. This explains why people exposed to the same context/institutional culture (e.g., higher education institution, co-curricular leadership program, class) have different conceptualizations and experiences with leadership. (p. 171)

The narratives explored in this chapter reflect how these women were socialized around both leadership and their identities as women. As the women's leadership identities develop, their leadership meaning-making filter contracts, letting fewer of the dominant narratives about leadership pass easily through the filter. In turn, the women are activated and engage more fully in the cycle of liberation.

EXPLORING THE NARRATIVES

It is intriguing to note that central to the cycle of liberation is a core set of values, including self-love, self-esteem, balance, joy, support, security, and spirituality. Harro (2013a) suggests that liberatory leadership requires nurturing authenticity, integrity, and wholeness in one's self and others. Note how the women in the ensuing narratives become increasingly aware of the forces of socialization around them and how these shape their gender and leadership journeys. Then look for evidence of how these women are spreading hope and inspiration and are seeking and claiming liberation. We see this first in Andrea's narrative.

Andrea: "Leadership as an Aspiration, an Influence, and a Motivation"

We begin our narrative exploration with Andrea, a Latina first-generation college student, who was a third-year student when she wrote her story.

> My definition of leadership currently relates to leadership as an aspiration, an influence, and a motivation. Not something or someone physical per se but something that many can look up to in order to reach a common idea or goal. I believe that leadership is a communal thing that should be seen and practiced by all not just one person while the rest follow. Ironically, this used to be my definition about leadership when I began my freshman year of college. My influencers back then were the common concept that I saw when leadership was brought up. I would see this in the group dynamics at school, where a group leader would always be assigned. Then there is the family dynamics that I saw in the Mexican culture that I grew up around. These dynamics are very rooted in machismo which refers to sexism and the whole idea of the woman following the man in the family whether they are the father, the older brother, or the husband. So, my leadership idea and definition were defined by the idea that I had to follow the man and only the man could be a leader. When I began to learn more about leadership in the perspective of a woman and the perspective of empowerment is when I realized that the machista dynamic was not as severe in my own household

> as it was around me and I feel that this had to do with the fact that my father was one of two boys in a nine children household raised by a single mother so all he has to look up to is women and then he ended up having three daughters and one boy so he is mostly surrounded by women. I feel that this is why although I was raised with some machista ideas like the man of the house and that the man is the breadwinner. I was also raised by my parents to be independent and self-sufficient so that I will never have to depend on a man. I am just astounded that I realized this only after taking leadership courses that although aspects of my upbringing were a bit sexist there were others that were progressive and that all had to do with the way my father was brought up and how he treated my mother. Now that I think about it, growing up my parents were perceived as the weird couple because they worked together to raise their children. My father takes my mother's opinions very seriously when he is trying to make important decisions and so does my mother. They equally help raise us and implement the independent woman concept on their daughters as well.

Andrea's narrative illuminates aspects of Harro's (2013a) cycle of socialization. She discussed the power of group dynamics at school, the role of her family, and her Mexican cultural heritage in influencing her beliefs about both leadership and feminism (for more information on the role of family, see Chapter 6). She discussed how witnessing acts of *machismo* in her household, where women were deferential to men, reinforced ideas that only men could be leaders and her role was to follow. The genderization of domestic labor is evident where women do most of the household chores, and the men of the family are to be respected and obeyed. These beliefs are typical of LID Stage 3—leader-identified—thinking where hierarchy and dominance are associated with leadership (Komives et al., 2006; Komives et al., 2005).

As Andrea is exposed to differing views of leadership in her college experiences, she is able to evaluate her own socialization with more objectivity. She realized that while some aspects of her cultural identity promote patriarchy and hierarchy, her immediate family unit is actually filled with powerful women. She described her father as the product of seven sisters and a strong single-mother and realized that he fostered a more egalitarian household than she originally thought. Yes, her father was the primary earner, but her mother's and sisters' views were highly valued. She was raised to be an independent and self-sufficient woman. Andrea began to explore a LID Stage 4, or differentiated, approach to leadership where she saw more interplay between leaders and collaborators and acknowledged their mutual influence. She saw that people of any gender are capable of making a difference, and are capable of leadership. She saw that she can transgress some of the machismo elements of the way she was socialized and move towards more liberatory views of gender and leadership.

Renuka: "Seeing Me"

Like Andrea, Renuka recognizes and eventually resists the forces of socialization that surround her. Renuka self identifies as an Asian American, cisgender, heterosexual woman with origins in the Indian subcontinent, raised in a highly conservative, middle-class household. It is also important to note that Renuka is a nontraditional aged college student, which shapes the way she makes meaning of her own leadership identity development journey. Renuka's narrative was initially accompanied by a photo of Indira Gandhi sitting side-by-side with President Richard Nixon.

> There she was on TV again. I would wait patiently for the evening news to watch her speak. What else could an 11-year-old girl from a lower middle-class family in Mumbai, India, do to step out of the social boundaries that were imposed on her. When I watched the then prime minister Indira Gandhi on tele, I was inspired. I wanted hair like hers, wanted to be able to speak like her—confidently, slowly, in an unperturbed, assertive manner. Indira had crossed all societal boundaries and yet found a way to maintain her unique identity. Her outward appearance of wearing a saree when meeting with international leaders and negotiating deals, wars . . . had me thinking, it's possible. It is possible to be like the kelp forest underwater. Anchored in your roots but amenable to the ever-changing tides. Experience life in ways that did not seem possible in that moment. I would cringe when my mum turned off the television and asked me to do my homework. "Get back to your studies—if not, you are not going to pass the exam," she would say.
>
> While it was hard for me to imagine what life could be back then, I knew I wanted to do more than what others thought was possible for me. I grew up to be a "kind rebel." And yes, that might seem like an oxymoron at the outset. But being a kind rebel has helped me break through the tribulations of life while maintaining the core of my values. I call it my AIR—accountability, integrity, and respect. This identity that I created for myself was born from the memory of those days watching Indira Gandhi.
>
> Leadership has been defined by several scholars and I am grateful to be in class learning about these definitions and gaining a deeper understanding of how humans propel other humans towards positive intent. My own definition of leadership is anchored in leading oneself first. As outlined in the book *We Are the Leaders We've Been Waiting For* (Owen 2020)—the principles of contemporary leadership adapted from Komives et al. (2013)—"Leaders are made, not born and you do not have to have followers to be a leader."

> I believe when I can lead myself to go beyond what others think is possible (social boundaries), I would naturally inspire others to find their own path that they desire. As such I can call myself a leader, a seeker, and a feminist.
>
> There is much more to be done. I think my leadership journey is just getting started. I could have many blind-spots to confront, much more work to do to expand my horizon and be more inclusive.

Similar to Andrea's narrative, Renuka reflected on the power of strong female leaders as role models to create new possibilities and pathways. She too recognized how the forces of socialization shaped her experience as a young girl from a lower middle-class family in Mumbai, India. As Harro (2013a) described, gender, race, religion, social class, and culture combine to shape expectations, roles, values, and even aspirations. Renuka's youthful views of leadership are examples of LID Stages 1 and 2—awareness and exploration. In the awareness stage, the power of external images of leadership are especially important to shaping views of leadership. Seeing Indira Gandhi, a confident and powerful woman dressed in a sari, working effectively with world leaders to address pressing social issues, inspired Renuka's views of both feminism and leadership. Only later is she able to articulate the difficult balancing act of staying anchored to one's own culture while also being able to counteract the forces of socialization that work so hard to promote the status quo. Her powerful metaphor of being like the kelp forest navigating shifting tides, while still firmly anchored to her roots, connects with the theorizing of the I-MMDI model. As she navigated the tides, she experienced the expansion and contraction of the leadership meaning-making filters, as described by Jones and Bitton (2021).

As Renuka explored and tried on her own feminist leadership, she developed a working philosophy that reflects elements of Harro's (2013b) cycle of liberation. She described the essentiality of maintaining her core values—AIR—in her leadership and social change efforts. She imagined critically transforming people and communities in her integrated approach to leadership. As an adult, Renuka articulated an approach to leadership that approximates LID Stage 5 or 6 (Komives et al., 2006; Komives et al., 2005). She valued generativity (Stage 5) in that she is committed to developing leadership in others and is passionate about working in community to create social change. She evidenced integration and synthesis (Stage 6) in that she viewed her leadership identity as an integral part of her being. She is humble and committed to continuous growth and development.

Jocelyn: "More of a Leader"

Similarly to Renuka, Jocelyn experienced a shift in her own perception of self as leader. Jocelyn self identifies as a Latina woman from a Salvadoran household who is a first-generation college student.

> Identifying as a Latina woman has placed me in a struggle with the concept of leadership my whole life. My Salvadoran culture is rooted in machismo, the idea that men are more powerful than women and that they should take charge of everything within their families and households. They are in fact seen as leaders, and it is almost as if they are born with and entitled to that position in society. I grew up with both of my parents working, my father has always worked in construction and my mother as a cook. Although they both worked long hours, the person who cooked all meals was always my mother, and the person who cleaned the house was also my mother. While my father got time to relax after work my mother never did. My father's leisure time after work has always involved drinking. His drinking was tolerable when I was younger, but as time went on his drinking habits became worse and soon all my memories with my father became memories of dealing with his aggressive drunk behavior. Growing up in a household with such toxic masculinity made me feel small and silenced. I have always been a reserved person; I was the quiet kid growing up in school and at home. Always afraid to speak up. Had I grown up in an environment where my voice was not constantly being ignored I might have been less afraid to speak up. My parents divorced when I was a senior in high school, after my mother could no longer handle my father's aggressive alcoholic behavior. Their separation brought tranquility into my life, I no longer had to deal with living in a toxic household, I was no longer afraid.
>
> Growing up and not having the best role models for leadership, made my definition of leadership limited. The leaders I learned about in school were all men, with similar characteristics, the typical heroes of history. I did not grow up with the perception of a good leader being a woman, much less a Latina. Because of how boxed my definition of a leader was, I was always intimidated by the idea of leadership and felt as though I could never be one. As I got older and started to realize that leadership is not constructed on gender, race or ethnicity. I also realized that good leadership skills are not something you are born with. Although growing up I did not learn about or know many strong Latina leaders does not mean that I should restrict myself and my capabilities simply because of my identities. I can be part of the change and I have the power to lead and become a good leader instead of waiting for a specific role model to inspire me.

> When thinking about my journey with leadership and how it intersects with different aspects of my identity, I have come to realize that I am a leader and have been a leader. Being the oldest daughter in my family, I have had responsibilities such as taking care of my younger sister ever since I was 8 years old. In most Hispanic households the oldest daughter often takes on the role of a second mom to younger siblings. I have always been her role model and continue to be an example for her every day. I am also the first generation in my family to graduate from high school and attend college. I am paying for my education and have managed to handle working two jobs while being a full-time student. I may not be the best leader, and my leadership skills are still developing as time goes on. However, I'm still more of a leader than I give myself credit for.

In Jocelyn's narrative, we saw another example of the socializing cultural force of machismo in action. This time, however, it was exacerbated by substance abuse. Jocelyn described Salvadoran machismo where men are entitled to leadership and power simply for being born a male. In Jocelyn's family both parents had to work outside the home to support the family, so paid work was not a gendered experience as it was in Andrea's Mexican household. Yet, the majority of the unpaid domestic labor still fell on Jocelyn's mother. Jocelyn articulated the effects of these early examples of toxic masculinity on her views of feminism and leadership. She described feeling "small and silenced." Her reaction to seeing only men elevated as archetypes of leadership was to feel intimidated by the very concept. The core of Harro's (2013a) cycle of socialization is fear, ignorance, confusion, and insecurity. The pervasiveness and consistency of the messages in Jocelyn's young life become self-perpetuating. These invisible, unconscious, and unnamed systemic forces resulted in Jocelyn believing the stereotypes she is surrounded by and sadly causes feelings of hopelessness. She adopted LID Stage 3 leader-identified approaches but took a silenced or non-participative approach to that stage (Komives et al., 2009). Both her efficacy and capacity for leadership were diminished.

For Jocelyn, life changed when her parents divorced during her senior year of high school. She immersed herself in college courses about the social construction of gender, race, and leadership. She realized that she did not need identity-specific role models to become an effective feminist leader. Similar to Andrea, Jocelyn described how her views of her own experiences and capabilities shifted upon reflection (see Chapter 10 for more information on how reflection can be used as a framework for leadership learning and development). She was able to see how aspects of her prior experiences, such as being the eldest, and her self-sufficiency actually prepared her for feminist leadership. She journeyed through phases of the cycle of liberation called "waking up" and "getting ready" (Harro, 2013b). Through introspection, education, and consciousness raising she found empowerment. She dismantled some of the internalized oppressive forces that told her she was not capable of leadership. She gained tools and inspiration for her future feminist leadership efforts and crystallized into a powerful force for change.

WEAVING THE NARRATIVES

There are numerous overlapping themes among the three narratives featured in this chapter. Each narrative author struggled to reconcile narrow, historical, cultural conceptions of gender roles with a strong desire and commitment to maintain their cultural identity while leading. This is evidenced by Renuka's poetic wish to be like the underwater kelp forest that is firmly anchored in place yet still able to bend and adapt to shifting tides. A second common theme among the narratives is the life-changing power of representation. Each author found powerful role models who showed them that a path to feminist leadership was possible (see Chapter 7 for more information about the importance of role models). For Andrea it was seeing the egalitarian nature of her parents' partnership, for Renuka it was watching Indira Gandhi on the television, and for Jocelyn, powerfully, it was finding her own self-efficacy for leadership.

A third common theme among the narratives is finding voice. Each of the authors reflected on feeling or actively being silenced. Though they didn't name it directly, each of them found liberation through education. Andrea mentioned insights gleaned from critical reflections in a women and leadership course. Renuka discussed actively working to expand her horizons and to reveal and address blind spots and limitations. Jocelyn described the perils of education that only features men as historical and current leaders. Later she credited learning about the social construction of gender, race, and leadership, along with the compelling idea that leadership can be learned, as empowering her own feminist leadership identity. Finally, each of the narrative authors found ways to interrupt the cycle of socialization. Rather than submitting to the status quo, they shifted their own consciousness and aspirations for change.

Each narrative is also unique from the others. For Andrea, family served as a buffer of cultural messages about women and leadership whereas for Jocelyn family was the source of many of those messages. For Renuka, culturally anchored role models encouraged her personal aspirations for leadership whereas Jocelyn's lack of role models inspired her to find leadership within and to serve as a role model for others. Each of the narratives suggested differences in how the authors defined and approached leadership, and in the evolution of their LID. Andrea initially defined leadership as a hierarchical affair, but exposure to shared leadership in her family, education, and community invited Andrea to explore a LID Stage 4, or differentiated, approach to leadership where she saw more interplay between leaders and collaborators and acknowledged their mutual influence, regardless of gender. Reunka evolved her own personal set of leadership values—accountability, integrity, and respect. She exhibited an integrated approach to leadership that approximates LID Stage 5 or 6 in her commitments to generativity and synthesis (Komives et al., 2006; Komives et al., 2005). For Jocelyn, leadership felt linked to responsibility, self-sufficiency, and her evolving efficacy for leadership. She was clearly in transition from a leader-identified (LID Stage 3) to leadership differentiated (LID Stage 4) approach to leadership.

APPLYING THE NARRATIVES

> Above all else, my (Adrian's) mother emphasized the value of an education. She instilled in me that notion that education was THE pathway to upward mobility and that no one would ever be able to take away my knowledge or my love of learning. For the first part of my life, I grew up as the only child of a single mother. We were a team and with my mother's encouragement, I grew stronger and more confident that we could overcome any obstacle in our way.
>
> This is in sharp contrast to the messages of women and leadership that I was exposed to as a child. Disney princesses and children's story books often contained a narrative of a woman or girl as a damsel in distress in need of saving from a man. As I think back, I struggle to recall women leaders, real (e.g., politicians, religious leaders, etc.) or imagined (e.g., superheroes, dolls, etc.), who served as role models for leadership. I did not realize the harmful effect this had on me until I was an undergraduate student taking a course on gender and leadership. As a White person, I have been socialized to think of myself as an individual and not a representative of my race. Moreover, as a Jewish person, I was taught that we, as Jews, are unique and special (i.e., the Chosen ones). Although my race is a majoritized identity and my religion is a minoritized identity, both reinforced the dominant narrative of heroic leadership and built my efficacy as a leader.
>
> My mother and I certainly had many challenges, particularly financial stability, however, my basic needs were always met. What we lacked in traditional "resources," was replaced with lessons in resourcefulness, creativity, passion, hard work, and resilience. These messages have shaped the trajectory of my life and sustained me as I work toward my doctorate degree. As I reflect back on these formative years, I recognize how much my mother encouraged me to form and voice my opinions, live in alignment with my

> values and on my own terms, and how her approach to parenting has, in turn, influenced my efficacy and interest in leadership. I also now realize that a lot of these messages about being an individual are also tied to the particular social identities I hold. Still to this day, I wonder how my leadership journey would unfold or look differently had I not received these contrasting messages of who was a leader and which identities get mapped onto our collective psyche of our society's representation of a leader.

Through all the narratives in this chapter, we see evidence of early socialization affecting thoughts, feelings, and beliefs about leadership and who can serve as a leader. The powerful narratives of the three feminist leaders featured in this chapter invite a series of questions for leadership educators: "How do women navigate multiple social identities given hegemonic views of leadership?"; "How can women avoid internalizing the social constructions of systemic sexist and patriarchal environments?"; and "Where can women look for examples of inclusive leadership?" (adapted from Owen et al., 2017). The intersections of women's multiple identities can affect their leadership journeys profoundly.

The narratives in this chapter show us how identity, capacity, and efficacy intertwine to shape leadership learning. The LID model (Komives et al., 2006; Komives et al., 2005) reminds us that leadership identity must be addressed in intersectional and developmentally sequenced ways. Harro's (2013b) cycle of liberation suggests that leadership capacity should expand beyond individual cognitive domains to also address intersubjectivity, critical reflexivity, sociopolitical competence, collective action, and agency. Leadership learning needs to emphasize not only individual self-efficacy but also collective efficacy to educate women to take action through groups and to organize with unified effort. Feminist leadership learning requires going beyond individual learning to also interrogate and disrupt organizational, institutional, and systemic dynamics (Owen et al., 2017). A core element of the cycle of socialization (Harro, 2013a) is to critically transform institutions and create new culture—essentially, to create change. Thus, the next chapter in this volume delves more deeply into women's leadership enactment.

REFERENCES

Arnett, J. (2000). Emerging adulthood: A theory of development from the late teens through the twenties. *American Psychologist*, 55(5), 469–480. http://doi.org/10.1037/0003-066X.55.5.469

Bloom, L. (1998). *Under the sign of hope: Feminist methodology and narrative interpretation*. State University of New York Press.

Collins, P. H., & Bilge, S. (2016). *Intersectionality*. Polity Press.
Crenshaw, K. (1991). Mapping the margins: Intersectionality, identity politics, and violence against women of color. *Stanford Law Review, 43*(6), 1241–1299. http://doi.org/10.2307/1229039
Harro, B. (2013a). The cycle of socialization. In M. Adams, W. J. Blumenfeld, R. Castaneda, H. W. Hackman, M. L. Peters, & X. Zuniga (Eds.), *Readings for diversity of social justice* (3rd ed.; pp. 45–52). Routledge.
Harro, B. (2013b). The cycle of liberation. In M. Adams, W. J. Blumenfeld, R. Castaneda, H. W. Hackman, M. L. Peters, & X. Zuniga (Eds.), *Readings for diversity of social justice* (3rd ed.; pp. 618–625). Routledge.
Jones, S. R., & Abes, E. S. (2013). *Identity development of college students: Advancing frameworks for multiple dimensions of identity*. Jossey-Bass.
Jones, S. R., & Bitton, A. L. (2021). Applying the lens of intersectionality to leadership learning. In K. L. Guthrie & V. S. Chunoo (Eds.), *Shifting the mindset: Socially just leadership education* (pp. 163–174). Information Age Publishing.
Komives, S. R., Longerbeam, S. D., Mainella, F. C., Osteen, L., & Owen, J. E. (2009). Leadership identity development: Challenges in applying a developmental model. *Journal of Leadership Education, 8*(1), 11–47. https://doi.org/10.12806/V8/I1/TF2
Komives, S. R., Longerbeam, S. D., Owen, J. E., Mainella, F. C., & Osteen, L. (2006). A leadership identity development model: Applications from a grounded theory. *Journal of College Student Development, 47*(4), 401–418. https://doi.org/10.1353/csd.2006.0048
Komives, S. R., Lucas, N., & McMahon, T. R. (2013). *Exploring leadership: For college students who want to make a difference* (3rd ed.). Jossey-Bass.
Komives, S. R., Owen, J. E., Longerbeam, S. D., Mainella, F. C., & Osteen, L. (2005). Developing a leadership identity: A grounded theory. *Journal of College Student Development, 46*(6), 593–611. https://doi.org/10.1353/csd.2005.0061
Owen, J. E. (2020). *We are the leaders we've been waiting for: Women and leadership development in college*. Routledge.
Owen, J. E., Hassell-Goodman, S., & Yamanaka, A. (2017). Culturally relevant leadership learning: Identity, capacity, and efficacy. *Journal of Leadership Studies, 11*(3), 48–54. https://doi.org/10.1002/jls.21545

CHAPTER 13

TAKING UP YOUR LEADERSHIP

Women's Courage, Strength, and Persistence in Enacting Leadership

Paige Haber-Curran

> *We will all, at some point, encounter hurdles to gaining access and entry, moving up and conquering self-doubt; but on the other side is the capacity to own opportunity and tell our own story.*
>
> —Stacey Abrams

As a doctoral student, I was introduced to the idea of *taking up your leadership*. It is a concept that involves moving into your role, whether characterized by formal or informal authority, and enacting leadership (Hayden & Molenkamp, 2002). I resonated with the idea that we all have the capacity to engage in leadership, and at times we may need the courage to do so.

> As a young girl, I (Paige) didn't seem to have any problems with taking up my leadership; I was eager, competent, and liked to take action. Yet, as I

> grew into my teenage, young adult, and adult self, I found greater challenges in taking up my leadership; internal voices and external systems made me acutely aware of the modifier of "women's" leadership. The modifier signified to me that something was different; the concept of leadership was not developed with women in mind. I received feedback that I was "too much" and began to hold back and second-guess myself in ways I never had before.
>
> If and how I took up my leadership varied considerably based on context. A moment in my doctoral journey in which I consciously and courageously took up my leadership happened in a group setting with fellow classmates (and faculty members) in a team teaching assistant community. I was struggling to find my place in the group, questioning my worth and value, particularly since I was significantly younger than most everyone in the group. As I saw dynamics emerge instigated by an older member in the group that were targeted at me and another group member, I realized how this woman's actions were negatively affecting the group's progress and my feeling of agency. I confronted her in front of the group and pushed back on the behaviors I found to be destructive and harmful, and the assumptions she was making to guide her behaviors. I didn't hold back. In a way, my younger less-filtered-self came through and took over. The situation rattled me and shook me up—and it also ignited me and made me feel powerful and as if I acted with purpose. It helped me recognize the power of my voice and simultaneously my responsibility to others, the group, and the process to step up when I felt the need to do so, even when—and perhaps particularly when—it was scary to do so.
>
> Now, in my continued journey as a scholar of women's leadership, and as a woman who has influence, I experience a multitude of feelings—often simultaneously—in professional and personal realms—strong, challenged, frustrated, powerful. Recognizing each of these feelings serve a purpose, I seek to harness them as I continue to move forward and take up my leadership.

In connection with the concepts of authenticity and leadership identity covered in the two preceding chapters, this chapter will examine, through the narratives of three women, the concept of taking up one's leadership. Through their stories, we can see the challenges and power that come from taking up one's leadership, as so acutely stated in Stacey Abram's quote that begins this chapter.

APPROACHING THE NARRATIVES

This chapter uses intersectionality (Crenshaw, 1989) as a theoretical framework for understanding the narrative authors' stories. An intersectional frame brings value to the study of women's leadership, specifically, because:

(a) intersectionality exposes the hierarchical discourse in women's leadership studies; (b) intersectionality foregrounds the complexities of women leaders' identities; and (c) intersectionality explicates the multifariousness of women leaders' experiences. (Ngunjiri et al., 2017, p. 251)

The three contributions of intersectionality to the study of women's leadership provide a theoretical framework specifically relevant to the concept of taking up one's leadership. This framework allows for a focus on women's individual identities and the larger systemic dynamics affecting their leadership experiences and their connection to leadership as a concept. For more information on intersectionality (Crenshaw, 1989) see Chapter 3.

In literature, the concepts of taking up one's leadership and/or enacting leadership are conceptualized in a number of different ways. In the emotionally intelligent leadership model, the capacity of *initiative* is described as taking action and capitalizing on opportunities, which involves having motivation, commitment, and focus to engage (Shankman et al., 2015). Research on professional women and leadership across numerous sectors revealed the theme of *engaging* as a key element to successful leadership for women (Barsch et al., 2009). According to Barch et al. (2009), "engaging" is characterized by taking ownership of one's life and of opportunities, facing one's fears, taking risks, and using voice. Similarly, a study focused on how graduate student women take on authority roles found that women's ability to find and use their voice, which was connected to their ability to own their power, was central to their capacity for taking up their authority (Sulpizio, 2010).

Bell and Nkomo's (2003) groundbreaking study of the experiences of Black and White women leaders in business speaks to the challenges and barriers of the larger context and systems affecting women's ability to use their voices and to take up their leadership. The research also highlights the persistence the women in the study demonstrated as they took up their leadership. Their research highlights the value of using intersectionality as a lens to understand women's leadership experiences; the intersection of race, gender, and social class, and the organizational and systemic barriers faced by the women in the study, were particularly salient for the Black participants. Although the data used in Bell and Nkomo's (2003) research is over 20 years old, recent scholarship on women and leadership speaks to the continued importance of intersectionality as a framework for examining women and leadership (Owen, 2020).

This chapter expands on the theme of taking up one's leadership using counter-storytelling methods. Counter-storytelling brings forward the voices and stories of those who have been historically marginalized and disrupts dominant perspectives and narratives that further perpetuate systemic inequities (Bamberg & Andrews, 2004). Recently, counter-narratives have been skillfully used by leadership scholars in conjunction with an intersectional frame, centering the thoughts, experiences, and feelings of individuals who have been historically marginalized in the conversation and scholarship on leadership (Dugan, 2017; Owen, 2020; Torres, 2019; Turman, 2017). In the context of this study, counter-storytelling allows for elevating and examining the experiences, perspectives, thoughts, and feelings of Women of Color who take up their leadership, centering their stories and considering their identities, experiences, and interactions with the larger systems in which they live and lead.

EXPLORING THE NARRATIVES

Three Women of Color share their stories of taking up their leadership through leadership narratives that focus on coming to understand the concept of leadership. At the time of data collection, the first two women, Jasmin and JoAnne, were undergraduate students enrolled in a women and leadership program with a leadership studies minor, and the third, Cathy, completed her degree approximately 10 years prior and took a women and leadership course while in college. What ties their narratives together is not their roles or their contexts; rather, it is their motivation, drive, and actions while navigating the various systemic barriers and hurdles they face. Stacey Abrams' quote that begins this chapter speaks to the challenges and courage of taking up one's leadership and alludes to the power that comes from doing so. The narratives shared by the three women highlighted in this chapter illuminate their journeys of taking up their leadership.

Jasmin: "Through Darkness, Emerges the Brightest Star"

In this first narrative, Jasmin shares a story of taking up her leadership from her childhood. Jasmin describes herself as a heterosexual female with Thai, Japanese, Russian, Chinese, German, Dutch, American, and Native American (primarily Thai and Japanese) heritage. She is a first-generation, low-income student and identifies as Buddhist (primarily). She has U.S. and Thai dual citizenship.

> 七転び八起き (Nanakorobi Yaoki). "Fall down seven times, stand up eight." Ever since I heard that quote, I've always been captivated by it. In my eyes, giving up was never an option, but why now—in this moment—am I doubting my own resilience?

As the winter of 2015 approached Denver, Colorado, my 12-year-old self—wearing, what seemed like, the thinnest jacket I could find—was on the corner of Welton and 16th Street. A Mason jar grasped tightly in one hand and, in the other hand, a white, slightly-bent, 24 inch by 32 inch cardboard sign with the words "Save My Mama" plastered across it. Smiles galore, yet my mind was occupied with the different narratives fighting each other within my own consciousness. For the past 7 years, I've dealt with the grief that made every moment with my mother feel as though we were marching towards her inevitable demise. I've gone through restless nights of feeling resentful at the fact that my mother's health was taken from her at such a young age. But at this moment I was dealing with something entirely different—self-confliction. A few months back, I decided to take on the most daunting leadership role I've ever had, in which I created and managed my mother's tongue cancer fundraiser. Despite putting my utmost persistence into this project and knowing how important this was to my mother; my mind wasn't immune to negative thoughts. As I stood in front of bustling crowds of people fundraising for my mother, I was completely divided. *One side of myself cried out for me to give into the ease of surrendering* and the **other carried the courage and strength of a true trailblazer**.

It's too cold out here to be doing this.
Shush! Mama's relying on us, and it isn't even that cold.

I've been standing out here for hours, and all we are getting are dollar bills.
We just have to stay optimistic; we never know who might want to help.

My legs are hurting, let's just take a break.
We never know who could pass by while we're away, let's just stay.

Oh my god! This isn't what a 7th grader should be doing.
And Mama shouldn't have to deal with cancer, we have no right to complain.

Come on, let's go, I'm tired of falling behind in biology.
School can wait, our family needs us now.

Those Asians are looking at me and aren't helping; they're probably embarrassed for me.
Who cares what they have to say or what they're thinking, we're here doing our best.

I hate it when people smoke in 16th street mall, it's making me sick
I know it's hard, but don't worry about them. They'll go away soon.

Look at those kids having fun with their family, that's what I should be doing.
We aren't in the same position as those kids, this is what we want to be doing.

I look so poor in front of these people.
We shouldn't feel the need to hide the fact that we—mostly Mama—are struggling.

> **If society wasn't so fucking greedy and universal healthcare was offered, I wouldn't even have to do this.**
> *I know it's frustrating, but after we take care of Mama, we will focus on making a difference for the future and the world.*
>
> **But what if we aren't doing enough?**
> *We're doing this for the sole purpose of supporting Mama. We're doing what's right.*
>
> **Why do I feel so hopeless?**
> *Like I always say: when there's life, there's hope.*
>
> **Can we really save Mama from cancer?**
> *Every day we come out here, we help Mama. Financially or mentally, she knows we're here for her every step of the way.*
>
> **Then why do I feel like this, why do I complain so much?**
> *It's natural to feel tired, frustrated, and even scared. We are all under so much stress, but we'll get through this.*
>
> **I'm scared.**
> *Don't be. Trust me, we are doing enough. Mama knows we love her. On top of that, we are so powerful. We won't let these struggles deter our resilience.*
>
> **You promise?**
> *I promise.*
>
> "Sometimes leadership isn't about how we lead others, rather the strongest leaders are those developed through leading our own personal narratives."
> —Jasmin (2021)

Jasmin's narrative is not what one might initially think of as a leadership experience recounted by a college student, yet for Jasmin, this is the moment she identified as pivotal in coming to understand leadership. She writes about the two different *sides* of herself as she takes on the daunting task of trying to help save her mother. While one side wishes to surrender and has doubt, the other shows courage, strength, power, and resilience. These sides start out conflicting and even a bit combative, yet at the end, demonstrate empathy and coming together.

Jasmin's narrative provides depth in understanding the challenges of taking up one's leadership and in persevering through difficult and even unimaginable personal challenges. Her narrative brings further understanding to what it means to be courageous, battling her own feelings of fear, exhaustion, and hopelessness. The adversity she faces reflects systemic challenges that not only led her to be in the situation that she recounts, but also are evident throughout the back-and-forth thoughts—inequities in wealth distribution, lack of universal healthcare, individualistic American culture, and insufficient social supports.

JoAnne: "Identity + Leadership"

In this second narrative, JoAnne shares her story of taking up her leadership in a college student leadership context. JoAnne identifies as a Japanese Chinese American female. She grew up in Denver, Colorado and was President of the Asian Student Alliance at the University of Denver.

> "President: JoAnne M.," the words shone on my phone's screen. Mouth agape, I was overcome with shock and disbelief that out of all candidates, the University of Denver's Asian Student Alliance had chosen *me* as president! Scared that the group chat message was an illusion bound to disappear, I bolted down the stairs to screech the results of the executive board's elections to my parents.
>
> As a Japanese Chinese American born to a third-generation Japanese American father and a Singaporean immigrant mother, I was raised to take pride in my cultural heritage and appreciate my ethnic roots. Having lived in Denver for decades, my parents had established a reputation around town for being highly involved in the Asian American community. Growing up, my parents' involvement meant attending numerous functions and events related to these various Asian American organizations. Being immersed in such a cultural environment created a desire to advocate for Asian American issues. Inspired by my parents' hard work and dedication, I had decided early in high school that I would continue this legacy and contribute to my own community.
>
> White-dominated culture and society paints Asian Americans to be submissive followers rather than strong and independent leaders. While these stereotypes persisted throughout my high school career, I was determined to make a change as ASA's sophomore president. Immediately, I felt an intense pressure to live up to what I believed were this affinity organization's expectations. My inability to see myself as deserving of such a high position of power became a detrimental roadblock early on. This imposter syndrome was a challenge, especially when my personality did not encompass the outspoken characteristics typically seen in leaders. In contrast to mainstream media's White, masculine, and aggressive portrayals of leadership, my modest nature made it difficult to conform to such ideals.
>
> Fortunately, with the help of my peers and family, I realized that I brought a unique perspective that would guide my sophomore year as president. Being a multi-ethnic Female of Color, my background has inspired and influenced me to be inclusive and ensure that all issues pertaining to all Asian

> identities are represented in the advocacy space that ASA is expected to provide. Furthermore, experiences from my childhood where I was ostracized for not sticking to conventional gender norms have fueled my desire to lead without using my gender as a limiting factor. Instead, I draw strength from my female peers and better understand that with leadership seen as a male-dominated industry, I have the power to shake things up—a notion that gives me immense glee as I continue to lead my Asian American community within a white-dominated environment.

JoAnne's narrative describes the role of advocacy and the drive to contribute to her "own community" as motivations for taking up her leadership. Through her family and upbringing, JoAnne is deeply connected to her ethnic roots and the Asian American community in Denver, and this commitment is what drives her to seek out the role of ASA president as a sophomore. She feels a sense of responsibility to serve and advocate for the Asian American community, and she draws strength from this sense of responsibility.

JoAnne demonstrates a keen sense of self-awareness, naming her feelings of imposter syndrome and being acutely aware of her identities and how they shape her perspective. She also has awareness of the larger systems in place that can impact her role and her ability to take up her leadership. She recognized and named gendered and racial/ethnic expectations of how one takes up leadership and the male- and White-dominated context of leadership. JoAnne's awareness of self and of the larger context helps her intentionally take up her leadership despite these societal expectations in which she doesn't seamlessly fit; she sees she has "the power to shake things up."

Cathy: "On Leadership and Burnout in Academia"

In this third narrative, Cathy writes about taking up her leadership in the context of her career and the connection between professional and personal spheres. Cathy was an assistant professor of of political science at the time this book was written. During her undergraduate studies, she took a course on women and leadership, which played a key role in her decision to study women and politics.

> I'm still very much in the process of figuring out what "leadership" means to me as a teacher, researcher, and mentor. The concept, in my eyes, is malleable; it can take on different characteristics at different times by different people. For me, right now, leadership involves three main components:

compassion, honesty, and vulnerability. Are my actions rooted in *compassion* for others and for myself? Am I being *honest* about the institutional and societal barriers that limit opportunities for others? And finally, am I open to being *vulnerable* and to showing my full self—my insecure, struggling, failing, persevering self—to people who need to see it the most?

I am currently a tenure-track assistant professor, and today I received glowing evaluations on my annual review. The letter from my department chair reads, "Her tenured colleagues unanimously agreed that she either *exceeded* or *greatly exceeded* the standard set out in the evaluation plan." The pride I felt reading that was quickly stymied by the realization that serious sacrifices to my mental health and my free time are being rewarded.

I'm writing this narrative at 10:00 at night. I've been overbooking and overworking myself and the result is intense burnout. I spent the 3-day weekend grading assignments until 11:00 p.m. each night. My daughter's preschool has been shutting down due to COVID-19 exposures, and the time I have with her includes driving to get a PCR test and trying to work from home while she sings songs next to me. I'm never fully present in my work or home life. (Don't worry—I have a therapist!). But these realities are not just about me; I'm realizing now that despite any success that may come from it, my perpetuation of this culture of overwork is the opposite of leadership.

As a first-generation college student and a Latina in a male-dominated discipline and predominantly White institutions, I've worked hard to prove myself in settings that did not always feel welcoming to me. At the same time, my many privileges—including my class privilege—afforded me the resources to successfully navigate academic life. The many women mentors I've had along the way have also been pivotal in shaping my experiences. And as I begin to step into mentorship roles myself, I'm coming to reshape my own definition of leadership.

Being a leader, I'm learning, is not about providing tips and tricks for success; it's about compassion, honesty, and vulnerability. I absolutely adore my students, and it is from that place of love and compassion that I am re-evaluating how I do my work. Opening doors for students into a system that thrives on overwork is not leadership; it's exploitation. Going forward, I'm choosing to be open and vulnerable with students about the joys and hardships of this profession, I'm setting boundaries for myself and prioritizing my mental health, and I'm challenging the (often celebrated) norms that uphold barriers to academia and lead to burnout. This is easier said than done, perhaps, but that's how I hope to lead from now on.

Cathy's story of taking up her leadership is characterized by academic and career ambition and achievement, proving herself in a discipline and in environments with few others who share her same identities. Her achievement and reward is not without cost or sacrifice. She experiences burnout and feels like she is not able to be fully present with her work life or her home life as she navigates her role as a junior faculty member and as mother to a preschooler. As Cathy continues and moves forward and is reframing how she approaches her work, she is committed to being vulnerable, honest, and compassionate with her students in her role as a professor. She is aware of the barriers she has overcome to get to where she is, and recognizes much of what got her there is what may also lead to burnout and dissatisfaction, acknowledging the cost of her achievement and professional success. She is thoughtful about needing to shift the way that she takes up her roles; although she does not explicitly state it, I see in the closing of her narrative that just as she is seeking to do with her students, she is seeking to be vulnerable, honest, and compassionate with herself. This reflects a journey toward authenticity as she takes up her leadership (see Chapter 11 for more on the theme of authentic leadership).

Cathy is acutely aware of the larger systems in place affecting her career path, particularly as a Latina first-generation college student in male-dominated discipline who has studied and worked at predominately White institutions. Her presence alone challenges norms and disrupts dominant narratives of academia. Although she has been able to successfully navigate these systems, she recognizes the toll it has taken on her in doing so and she uses this awareness to intentionally seek to support and prepare students for what they may expect in the progression.

WEAVING THE NARRATIVES

The three narratives illuminate the theme of taking up one's leadership as told by three Women of Color—Jasmin, JoAnne, and Cathy. Each narrative describes distinctly different contexts and journeys—Jasmin's for a loved one, JoAnne's in a student organization, and Cathy's in her career. The themes within each are aligned in many ways, bringing further insight to the topic of taking up one's leadership. There are also themes distinct across the narratives. In this section I present themes from further analysis through weaving of the narratives.

Taking up One's Leadership Through Persistence, Drive, and Motivation

Evident across all three narratives is the persistence, drive, and motivation to continue forward. Although their journeys aren't without challenge, they take action and take up their leadership. Through this perseverance, consciously or not, JoAnne and Cathy are also paving ways for others to follow in their paths as women taking up their leadership in male-dominated realms. They both feel a greater purpose in taking up their leadership—for the larger Asian American community in JoAnne's case, and for helping prepare students for their future in Cathy's case.

Each narrative speaks to the barriers each woman faces in taking up her leadership. They experience internal barriers of self-doubt and aspects of imposter syndrome (see Chapter 8 for more on the theme of imposter syndrome) and also external barriers of the larger organizational and societal systems (e.g., inadequate social systems in Jasmin's; stereotypes of Asian Americans in JoAnne's; predominately White institutions in Cathy's). They see the impact of these larger systems on their enactment of leadership, recognizing how the systems perpetuate inequity in connection to their identities as Women of Color. As they see these inequities and seek to navigate them, each expresses a great deal of self-awareness and uses intentional self-talk to purposefully engage despite these challenges, and in Cathy's situation, refocus because of the challenges.

A final theme ties the narratives together—the role of family. Jasmin's story is about taking up her leadership for her family, specifically her mom. JoAnne speaks to the strong ties within her family and beyond her family with the larger Asian American community, which impacts her leadership. Cathy discusses the challenges with navigating her career and her family life, struggling to be present in both realms. See Chapter 6 for more on the theme of family.

Leadership for What?—Distinctions in Life Stage and Motivation

The focus of each women's narrative was quite distinct. As one considers the question—"Leadership for what?"—each story is different. This could be in part due to the life stage in which each of the narratives were situated and the motivations each woman shared. Jasmin at 12 years old is motivated by helping her mother and feels responsibility to do so, taking up her leadership in a very vulnerable and unconventional way. JoAnne is motivated by serving the larger Asian American community on her campus and more broadly, and she sees seeking out a leadership position in the ASA as a path to do so. She seeks out this role despite not fitting the perceived mold and societal expectations of who a leader is and how they should lead. Cathy, well into her professional career, is motivated by her inner drive to succeed in her field and by the compassion and sense of responsibility she feels for her students. In her journey, Cathy is aware of how her professional and personal realms are interconnected and gains greater motivation to show herself the same compassion and authenticity she so purposefully takes up for her students. Although these contexts, motivations, and life stages differ so greatly, each narrative highlights the inner strength and power each woman demonstrates as they take up their leadership.

APPLYING THE NARRATIVES

I present here implications that can be gleaned from this study presented as questions for us to consider as we support others in their leadership development and/or research leadership. The questions can also be reframed as one considers how they take up their leadership.

- How do we provide space for individuals to process the challenges and systems they may be navigating as they take up their leadership (as often we only see the actions of others and not the struggle behind the actions)?
- How do we help individuals name, navigate, and challenge imposter syndrome that may hold some back from taking up their leadership?
- How do we allow space in educational settings to honor and learn from leadership experiences and learning opportunities that take place outside of traditional campus life (where many may be taking up their leadership)?
- How do we help women understand their multiple, intersecting identities—and the ways in which this can encourage and challenge if and how one may take up their leadership?
- How does one balance navigating systems and disrupting systems as they seek to take up their leadership?
- Whose voices are missing in the exploration of taking up one's leadership?

As I reflect back on my connection to the theme of taking up my leadership that I shared at the beginning of the chapter and sit with the powerful narratives shared by Jasmin, JoAnne, and Cathy, I am affirmed in the value of intersectionality as a lens for this narrative study. I shared the impact of messages about leadership making me at times doubt myself and my ability to leadership because I was a woman. As a White woman with socioeconomic privilege, the messages and feedback I received were likely very different from what Jasmin, JoAnne, and Cathy experienced based on what they described in their narratives. Although I certainly faced challenges in some aspects of my identity and do not want to diminish my experiences and feelings, I operated (and continue to operate) in interlocking systems that benefit individuals who are White and individuals with socioeconomic privilege. This is something I am constantly aware of—and yet this awareness has grown even more through Jasmin, JoAnne, and Cathy's narratives.

Analyzing these narratives has made it exceedingly clear that there is considerable power in counter-storytelling. Without her story, one may see Jasmin as a thriving college student without knowing what incredible perseverance and courage she exhibited as a 12 year old fighting for her mom. Without her story, one may see JoAnne as someone who takes on a prominent leadership role as a sophomore without knowing her internal struggles with imposter syndrome and immense sense of responsibility and pride she feels in taking on this role to serve her community. Without her story, one may see Cathy's glowing comments and feedback on her annual review without knowing the daily struggle she experiences in feeling like she can't be present with her family or her work, and the strain and burnout weighing on her. Through their stories, the women disrupt dominant narratives of how one takes up their leadership. Their stories matter, and they provide depth in the examination of how women take up their leadership. I am inspired by and grateful for these narratives. Connecting back to Stacey Abrams' quote that begins the chapter, I end this chapter asking: "How can we take this new insight to empower women (those with whom we interact and ourselves) to own opportunity and to tell their story so that we all can learn from them, too?" The next chapter, which focuses on the impact of women and leadership programs, helps move the conversation to focus on how women-centered leadership learning opportunities can help facilitate women's leadership development.

REFERENCES

Bamburg, M. G., & Andrews, M. (Eds.). (2004). *Considering counter-narratives: Narrating, resisting, and making sense*. John Benjamins Publishing Company.

Barsch, J., & Cranston, S., & Lewis, G. (2009). *How remarkable women lead: The breakthrough model for work and life*. Crown Business.

Bell, E. L. J. E., & Nkomo, S. M. (2003). *Our separate ways: Black and White women and the struggle for professional identity*. Harvard Business Review Press.

Crenshaw, K. (1989). Demarginalizing the intersection of race and sex: A Black feminist critique of antidiscrimination doctrine, feminist theory, and antiracist politics. *University of Chicago Legal Forum, 1989*(1), 139–167. https://chicagounbound.uchicago.edu/uclf/vol1989/iss1/8

Dugan, J. P. (2017). *Leadership theory: Cultivating critical perspectives*. Jossey Bass.

Hayden, C., & Molenkamp, R. (2002). *The Tavistock primer II*. A. K. Rice Institute for the Study of Social Systems.

Ngunjiri, F. M., Almquist, J. M., Beebe, M., Elbert, C. D., Gardiner, R. A., & Shockness, M. (2017). Intersectional leadership praxis: Unpacking the experiences of women leaders at the nexus of roles and identities. In J. Storberg-Walker & P. Haber-Curran (Eds.), *Theorizing women and leadership: New insights and contributions from multiple perspectives* (pp. 249–263). Information Age Publishing.

Owen, J. E. (2020). *We are the leader we've been waiting for: Women and leadership development in college.* Routledge.

Shankman, M. L., Allen, S. J., & Haber-Curran, P. (2015). *Emotionally intelligent leadership: A guide for students.* Jossey-Bass.

Sulpizio, L. L. (2010). *Women and authority: Transitioning into a role of assigned authority as a graduate teaching assistant in a leadership class* [Unpublished doctoral dissertation]. University of San Diego.

Torres, M. (2019). *Ella creyó que podia, así que lo hizo: Exploring Latina leader identity development through testimonio.* [Doctoral dissertation, The Florida State University]. http://purl.flvc.org/fsu/fd/2019_Summer_Torres_fsu_0071E_15207

Turman, N. T. (2017). *Centering the margins: Elevating the voices of women of color to critically examine college student leadership* [Doctoral dissertation, Loyola University Chicago]. https://ecommons.luc.edu/luc_diss/2865

CHAPTER 14

THE TRANSFORMATIONAL POWER OF FEMINIST WOMEN'S LEADERSHIP EDUCATION

Sasha Taner

I (Sasha) was a student sitting in an introductory class on women, culture, and society when a visitor arrived, announcing that there was a new program about women and leadership for social change at the Institute for Women's Leadership (IWL). Just married and back in New Jersey after years of living and working abroad, I came to Rutgers to complete my undergraduate degree, to connect the dots surrounding some of the global issues I observed while abroad, such as forced displacement and refugee resettlement, and to gain advocacy tools to make a difference. I was considered a nontraditional student, having an associate degree from community college, and spending a good part of my twenties living and working abroad. I was seeking a place to belong and make meaning of what I'd learned abroad and hoped to learn in completing my degree.

> Joining the leadership scholars certificate program at the IWL transformed my life. It helped me grapple with and reflect on the intersections of my identity and upbringing to formulate my own understanding of leadership, power and privilege, and social change. In this program, I was able to connect my experiences such as being the eldest child of a single mother who raised three children by cleaning houses to broader trends of labor, politics, and gender. As a first-generation college student, I further grounded my abilities to persevere and succeed in my higher education endeavors through the mentorship and support of caring women faculty, staff and peers who were committed to our individual and collective growth as socially responsible leaders. As a PhD student in the Division of Global Affairs, I began a deep dive into the plight of transnational families, particularly first- and second-generation women in higher education. These academic pursuits, combined with my professional endeavors and lived experiences has shaped who I am as an educator and researcher.
>
> Two decades later, I now direct the program that I graduated from at the IWL. I seek to create generative spaces for students to connect the dots between their passions for social change and their identities, and to cultivate a diverse community in which to grow and build with others committed to social justice. These roles have afforded me the privilege of being part of the undergraduate experience of immigrant families in the United States, and in this work, I crafted this collection of narratives to better know, highlight and support this incredibly brilliant, inclusive, and visionary group of women leaders. These women's narratives, as well as my own, are the reason I do the work of developing women and leadership today.

The contributors of this book recognize there are important approaches to leadership that are often overlooked. A main critique of leadership education is that the predominant discourse around leadership is assigned to traditional, top–down positional forms of power hierarchies embedded within corporate and government business models. In a program with a feminist leadership studies perspective, the curriculum embraces a wide scope of conceptualizing leadership while also paying close attention to the intersections of gender and other identity formations in relation to power, systemically, institutionally, and individually. This chapter highlights narratives of alumni who graduated from a 2-year, interdisciplinary certificate program in women's leadership for social change, to deepen an understanding of the power and importance of a feminist orientation toward leadership education, specifically focusing on 1.5 and 2nd generation immigrant women's experiences in post-secondary education.

APPROACHING THE NARRATIVES

South Asian activist-scholar Srilatha Batliwala believes wherever we are situated in our lives, we can advance a feminist agenda. In her seminal work entitled "Feminist Leadership for Social Transformation: Clearing the Conceptual Cloud," Batliwala (2010) outlines transformational feminist leadership as a concept that embraces an inclusive model of leadership. For her, a definition of leadership must be one where an individual embraces

> a feminist perspective and vision of social justice, individually and collectively, transforming [oneself] to use their power, resources, and skills in non-oppressive inclusive structures and processes to mobilize others, especially other women, around a shared agenda, of social cultural, economic, and political transformation for equality and the realization of human rights for all. (p. 29)

Batliwala builds on leading global scholar and activist, Peggy Antrobus' (2000, 2002) work, who outlined the underpinnings of a transformational feminist leadership theory almost 20 years ago in her scholarship on gender justice, that is, leadership that commits to social action. The organizational context of Antrobus' work is DAWN (Development Alternatives with Women for a New era), a global, feminist, nongovernmental organization that has been touted as the organizational example of operationalizing feminist values of sharing power, particularly within authority and decision-making structures, to achieve a shared vision of social, legal, political, economic, and cultural equality.

In the United States, a leader in the field of women's history, Mary S. Hartman, founded the Institute for Women's Leadership (IWL, 2023) consortium in 1991 at Rutgers, the State University of New Jersey. Alongside other prominent women scholars in their fields, Hartman's mission, previously outlined on IWL's website, was centered around promoting women in leadership. Hartman (1999) identified an important need to center women's voices through research and data collection and to ensure women's focused research informed all communities and forums where decisions were made. She reminded us of the importance of creating the conditions in which these needs can be met—in all settings where women are present.

Batliwala, Antrobus, and Hartman had an eye toward the transformative possibilities of empowering women who are emboldened to create change. This idea translates well into women and leadership programming by building diverse women's capacities and confidence to be leaders in their communities. All humans can practice feminist leadership. At IWL, we practice leadership with a reflexive and intersectional lens and with an understanding of the associated privileges and interlocking oppressions that are embedded within an imperialist, White supremacist heteropatriarchy (hooks, 2014).

Charlotte Bunch (1990) is a global rights activist who initially coined the phrase "Women's rights are human rights" (p. 496). Bunch is the founder of the Center for Women's Global Leadership at Rutgers University. A professor in the Leadership Scholars Certificate Program, Bunch (2002) reminds her students,

> Who gets support and who gets honored or killed for their leadership depends on a society's values, prejudices, hierarchies, and structures. If we want more democratic and inclusive leadership in our society, we must look at whether and how various leaders are recognized and supported and seek to make changes in those structures and values. (p. 16)

Bunch (2002) argues that women's leadership development programs can address this:

> We don't make women into leaders, but we can provide opportunities to enhance and support women's leadership and to make it more visible and more viable. We can work to change the climate of the society toward greater acceptance of women's leadership so that women leaders are taken more seriously and have more opportunities to be heard and exercise power. (pp. 16–17)

Mary Trigg's (2010) book on the leadership scholars program—*Leading the Way: Young Women's Activism for Social Change*—highlights 21 narratives of alumni of the leadership scholars certificate program with a 24-year history, a notable anthology in the field of young women's leadership. This book inspired the research and writing of our current text. One of the unique components of this undergraduate women's leadership program is that its curriculum is set within the Department of Women's, Gender, and Sexuality Studies. As the program founder, Trigg (2010) points out that the program "draws on the rich scholarship in women's studies to train women to reimagine leadership, to accelerate their own leadership, and to prepare them to make a difference in the world" (p. 4). This feminist-infused curriculum distinguishes this leadership program from other programs that may be housed in other departments such as business, ROTC, or political science. These other areas and disciplines often focus on traditional leaders in positions of power that have been historically male, often excluding or minimizing diverse women's contributions. Concurrently, there are established and burgeoning programs on leadership in the United States, yet disappointingly, many still focus on traditional, non-transformative, corporate, and management aspects of leadership, ultimately perpetuating the status-quo. Alternatively, feminist expressions of leadership learning seek ways to disrupt the status-quo and to widen the passageways for which minoritized communities and individuals have a seat at decision-making tables.

EXPLORING THE NARRATIVES

Building on these theoretical analyses of women's leadership, I turn to narratives of alumni of the leadership scholars certificate program. In this chapter, I utilize findings from five interviews conducted with graduates from the classes of 2007–2015 who are 1.5- or second-generation immigrant women. Implementing feminist narrative analysis (Bloom, 1998), I considered themes that arose in their narratives, including (a) feminist conceptualizations of leadership and social justice, (b) the recognition of diverse women and their nuanced experiences, and (c) the understanding that feminist leadership involves, first, being empowered as a leader, then, committing to social action. For these alumni, access to feminist leadership education and college has been a transformative experience in their leadership identity development and practice.

Lien: "We Can Make a Difference"

Lien, who came to the United States at the age of 6 from Vietnam, reflected on the challenges of her earlier education experiences in urban New Jersey and the contrast she experienced in her education at the IWL. In her interview, she discussed feeling left behind because of her lack of knowledge about women's experiences and their societal contributions during her public, primary education. She also noted IWL put into perspective that committing to action starts with being empowered and perceiving oneself as a leader. Lien states,

> I just felt more empowered by the fact that there were so many women in my cohort who had such an incredible background of knowledge and experiences. IWL put into perspective that action starts with being empowered, being in a community of women. And we don't just call ourselves women, but women leaders. And it's great to be able to talk about history. How women have changed and shaped and influenced society. And also, for us to be able to complete, or even propose, our own social action project. It was because of the social action project, I must say, that really made me believe that I could also be a leader. Before then, it was just all theory, until I put those things into action. To this day, I even talk about the IWL because of its impact on my own life. I know that leadership education is never ending because

> I continue to see women in the field of education where I work, and even men, how together people can make such a big difference for children, each other, because of how we talk, how we approach one another. Leadership definitely starts with us recognizing that we can make a difference.

During her time in the leadership scholars program, Lien stressed one of her big takeaways was the experience of being in a community of women. Similar to reflections in Chapter 10, Lien shares how this community empowered her own leadership by experiencing a close-knit learning environment for the first time. Lien found a voice in representing the IWL on campus and in her work after graduating college. She recognized the potency of being in a community of like-minded yet diverse women who helped her build a leadership identity.

Hadiya: "Utilize It and Assist Others"

Hadiya, a second-generation American, grew up in New York. Her parents fled from Afghanistan before the Soviet invasion and spent several years in other countries before obtaining refugee status and resettling in the United States. Hadiya reflects,

> I think leadership to me is never losing sight of where you come from, or who you're working with. Like I learned at the IWL, leadership is often perceived as this one person leading everybody, and I really don't see it that way. I think that it's such a community effort, especially in my work. I work as a paralegal case handler in housing law, and a big part of our work is community lawyering. It's more impactful to have a group of people organize and take action, and I think as a leader sometimes you can get very self-involved and only see your ambition, but not really listen to what is best for everybody. I think that being cognizant of the fact that you are not it, is a very important facet of leadership. I really do believe this idea of social justice and I believe that we can have some sort of impact. Even if it's just letting somebody know about the issue that means a lot to me. I started to link things together, to understand why my life went in the way that it did, and it gave me so much access to all of these great resources. I know that sounds kind of abstract, but it allowed me to understand why things played out the way that they did in my world and also outside of my world, or the intersection between [them]. I started to see things more clearly, especially when it came to social justice. I think coming from a background that's really been marginalized, I finally

> learned the terms for things. But it also made me aware that education is a huge privilege because I work with a client base that doesn't have access to these resources, or they don't—excuse my language—they don't give a shit about what that means. They don't care, and I'm not going to sit here and explain to them that the system is why they're facing this housing problem. I am extremely grateful for my education. I think that it's allowed me to see things with so much clarity. You have to be careful how you use your education as well and understand that not everybody has access to it. You have access to it, and the best thing that you can do is utilize it and assist others.

Hadiya talks about leadership as knowing oneself and not letting oneself get in the way. In the leadership scholars program, she began to reframe the meaning of leadership from a singular notion and positional, to a community effort. Now she enacts leadership through her organizing work. Hadiya shares how she deepened her understanding of the connection between the personal and political as it relates to identity as she started learning about structural dynamics of power and privilege. In addition to rebuilding a definition of leadership that aligns with her vision and values, she feels that her undergraduate education is a privilege that not everyone is afforded, and that having an education comes with certain responsibilities. Hadiya realized that once she was able to see her lived experiences with more clarity—and having gained a feminist consciousness—action must occur. She commits to using her education to assist others, but with the caveat that it comes from a place of equity and power-sharing. She reflects on the importance of staying humble, and to embody and relate to others, with the non-hierarchical power dynamics that we are seeking to create.

Sadia: "I Never Thought I Was Doing Leadership"

As an undocumented, 1.5 generation woman from Bangladesh, Sadia saw the leadership scholars certificate program as a means to financial independence. She had her eye on the future and a focus on being economically stable on her own, allowing for self-autonomy.

Sadia discusses,

> I never thought what I was doing at the time as leadership. I thought of it as more of survival. Of it just being choices we all have to learn to make, to navigate the world. I will say—in terms of how my education [was] impacted—being part of the IWL, I knew I couldn't just sit back and whine

> about it or talk about it, that I needed to act. An advantage I had over my peers in having these 2 years of doing the leadership scholars program was that I knew I needed to sit down with my LinkedIn and literally go through a list and see every person that was living in New York that could possibly help me and reach out to them. I knew I had to work on making sure my resume was up to date and my cover letters were professional, that I was prepping for my interviews. I kind of knew regardless of what it was that I had to always be in action.
>
> I chose that [the IWL]. I just wanted to be part of something that could teach me concrete skills in how to get wherever I needed to go. In college I had no idea what that was, I just knew I wanted to make a difference in the world. I had no idea what that meant in terms of how to get there and it seemed like the IWL would give me concrete steps of how to get there. Not that it had all the answers, but I think that that's what attracted me to it. I remember very clearly panicking the first semester in, being totally overwhelmed by all of these issues we were talking about in class that were all so important and in need of attention in the world. I was just wondering how what I was going to do after graduation was going to put me in a place to care about this stuff and to make a difference about this stuff. And I always had that in the back of my head that whatever I wanted to do with my life I wanted to feel like I was making a difference.

Sadia clearly identifies with making the decision, once in college, to pursue a certificate in women's leadership. This was not her family's decision or suggestion. Similar to Hadiya, Sadia knew that she had an advantage of going through a 2-year leadership program that set her apart from her other peers. She felt that whatever she did, she had to be in action, but she reflected and thought about her leadership approach. Sadia understood the privilege in having time dedicated to reflecting and learning, a privilege not afforded to everyone including her family members.

Sadia came to the IWL to be part of something that could help her achieve her goals, although it took a lot of courage and healthy risk to get there. Sadia shares that leadership education is about training scholars on communication, self-awareness, recognizing limitations, and acknowledging what you don't know so you can approach life with empathy and humility.

While undocumented students in higher education are not a monolith, many have noted personal accounts of the fear, drive, and survival threads that create a throughline in their experiences (Hernandez et al., 2010). Hernandez et al. (2010) underscore that the added layer of burden undocumented students carry with them—due to the precarity of their citizenship status—has often evoked qualities of persistence and admirable determination. Sadia embodies both of these traits. In hindsight, she shares that the program supported and bolstered a secondary need to make a difference, but not at the expense of being able to care for herself and provide the resources she needs to live an independent life.

Sadia considers leadership as relational and teaches us the importance of reaching out to others to build a network of support. In IWL, she learned to inspire others to do better and to take action. She notes in her narrative that she did not recognize prior to IWL her ways of approaching the world were ways of enacting leadership; rather, she simply thought of these skills as "survival." She highlights how IWL impacted this perception—by learning she had the leadership skills she needed to act, to make a difference in this world.

Laila: "She Is Going to Be Independent"

Laila was born in the southern United States (second-generation). Her parents and grandparents were highly transient throughout the Middle East due to political instability and the United States for educational opportunities. Laila's parents have Palestinian, Turkish, and Iraqi origins with residence in Libya. She arrived in New Jersey during her high school years, living in a three-generation household. Laila, like Saida and other narrators, felt a strong impact from the IWL model of education. Having participated in other leadership programs after her undergraduate education, she felt other programs were "more corporate" and "not as effective." Laila remembers,

> Starting the [IWL] program, my mother was very encouraging of it. When I told my dad I was minoring in women's and gender studies he was very taken aback. He was like, "You shouldn't call yourself a feminist." "Why [I asked]?" He was like, "Don't use that word." In his mind, to some degree, feminism has an adverse effect on household dynamics, and if you have a very traditional idea of what household dynamics should look like—I can see how feminism would break that. I don't necessarily agree with that, and it's kind of sad because some women think that, and a lot of men think that, or at least a lot of like Muslim Arab men who I've talked to—that feminism is a bad idea because they think it breaks up households, the women are too independent or something, but I think that's silly. If a woman is going to be independent, she is going to be independent whether you like it or not. You should talk about how you are going to navigate her career and your career. That is my model. But I think it took time to reach that, because sometimes, I still think in a very traditional way [about] relationships. Anyway, that is the piece about him being not so excited about the women's leadership thing. My mother encouraged women's and gender studies; my father warned of

> it. My grandma liked that I did my IWL social action project in the mosque. She likes it when we go to mosque. I think in general I was well encouraged.
>
> I think the IWL taught identity, and through identity you kind of understand your role as a leader and what you can do and what you can't do and your strengths and weaknesses. I think that was really critical because I remember the first class with Charlotte Bunch, and even the Women, Culture and Society [class] that I took helped me understand my experiences as a child in high school. And so, I started to see. I started to think about my dad and the things he'd done, and how that may have been like a silent patriarchy, or more of maybe a patriarchy of a marginalized man in America. And I saw my mother's experience as something like a feminist experience or a feminist outlook she had and that she gave to me. But it just became so much more explicit. And understanding what intersectionality meant and how that manifests in my life.
>
> Having the tools to describe my own experience as a person helped me realize that these experiences are not just unique to me. Charlotte Bunch's class helped us understand the universality of that. And then we had the Women in Work class and the Leadership Scholars, and so I felt like it transitioned very well and, so I think the identity piece is very critical, and I think building from that you start to see how your identity is part of a larger identity.

Similar to Hadiya and Sadia, Laila described how IWL gave her the tools to describe her own experiences and helped her connect the personal to the political, her individual experiences with the collective. She sees a powerful component of the program as "helping students with how to cope with challenges" and how to help build relationships through the independently designed social action projects. As discussed in Chapter 6, Laila's story affirms the integral way Women of Color weave together family and leadership development. As part of a diverse community of peers and women educators, she felt the program helped normalize the challenges she faced. She recognized many of her peers were also navigating roles within their families as first- and second-generation immigrant women. Through the program and the social action project, Laila found a way to honor her family's traditional values while still developing her own ideas about leadership for social change within her own community.

Acela: "Education Is Liberation"

Acela emigrated to the United States with her mother and a younger sibling at the age of 11 from Cuba. She sees education as a path to equality and the influence around her perspectives on education came from her grandparents and their history of fighting for justice. Acela says,

> Education I know was always a priority. Both of my grandparents on my mom's side were pretty big revolutionaries. They fought in the Revolution in 1959. They were both uneducated because of money, they came up very poor. And so, for me, [the message] was always, "You need to get educated because it is shameful not to be able to read or write" because of my grandparents' experiences. It was this idea that education is liberation, and if you ever want to be free you need to be educated.
>
> I think college was another really rough transition because I once again went from being in a place that I knew, to a place in the very beginning where I felt really isolated. I know my freshman year I called up my last teacher—my social justice teacher—often telling him I wanted to drop, I wanted to go home, I want to quit, I'm done. And I think a big part of it was just encountering discrimination in a way that I hadn't before, because I do come from a town where most of the people are like me, you know, an immigrant community. And in college I definitely faced, from peers, comments like, 'Oh, of course you're cleaning windows, 'cause that's what Latinas do." Things like that that I didn't know how to respond to because I hadn't experienced it before—that blatant ignorance. I struggled academically. I got my first F ever in college in one of my journalism classes. And I realized that I really needed to take ownership of my education.
>
> [Being in a women's leadership program] I knew what my purpose was, and I was surrounded by people who had a similar purpose. And at [IWL] I felt like I had a purpose, and I was surrounded by people who had a similar purpose and were pushing to that. I think that one thing that the [leadership scholars] program does is allowing me to feel really empowered. [Women's] leadership education—I think—is allowing people to feel like they can be leaders, which is sometimes really difficult, especially for women to identify themselves as leaders. Because we think of leadership, or we're told to think of leadership in this traditional way; leadership means you're in control, you're in power, and other people report to you, or you're the manager, all of that. But I think it's telling anyone that they could be leaders if they decide to. They have that ability to think. First, I think, it's allowing people to feel empowered.

When Acela arrived at Rutgers, she had a jarring experience encountering overt racism, which made her want to give up on her higher education aspirations. In her freshman year, she called up a former high school teacher who was a strong role model for her and said that she wanted to drop out. Instead, Acela found purpose in the IWL leadership scholars program. She shares positive feelings about being in a community of other women who shared passions for social justice. She emphasized the importance of being in a program that encourages women to see themselves as leaders. Like in Chapter 13, Acela and her peers were supported to "take up their leadership" and feel empowered through their participation in a feminist-oriented women and leadership experience.

WEAVING THE NARRATIVES

There are many ways that the narrative authors in this chapter help us expand our understanding of leadership. From these highlighted narratives, we learn the themes of empowerment—embracing a leadership orientation that commits to social justice-based action and pluralizing the concept of leadership. Our narrative authors stressed the importance of ensuring leadership encompasses those that have been historically excluded. Further, they charge us to disrupt notions of hierarchical leadership entrenched in inequitable power systems that leave out immigrant, Women of Color leaders.

Empowerment principles are an important pedagogical approach to any education and equity driven endeavor. A strong foundation of empowerment-focused pedagogy specific to the community needs is a key ingredient for transformation. Transformative leadership can be fostered within networks that may include individuals with recent generational migration experiences. Lien, Hadiya, Sadia, Leila, and Acela come from five countries of origin, yet they all came to the leadership scholars program with aspirations to make a difference in the world. Finding a cohort experience of women who are passionate about social justice issues transformed their undergraduate experience and continues to influence their lives years after. At the time of the interviews, 3 to 11 years after graduation, the narrative authors have reflected nostalgically on the strength of the program's effect on them and the lasting impact of feminist leadership education on their lives.

Years after graduating, narrative authors described their conceptualization of leadership in broad, inclusive, and transformative ways. We can benefit from a wider definition of leadership that includes those not often seen or considered to "be" leaders. Hartman (1999) affirms the value of teaching leadership from the parameters that include household, neighborhood, and community leadership roles that women have traditionally held. Narrative authors like Sadia, Lien, Hadiya, and Acela help us see the lasting impact of women and leadership development programs, such as IWL.

All of the narrative authors have gone on to graduate and attend professional schools. Some have become lawyers and educators. Another became an analyst and program manager, and a researcher and public health advocate. Regardless of which field or industry they entered, the graduates from IWL continue to find ways to enact their women and leadership training in service of societal transformation while simultaneously redefining relationships and families. They do so by developing roots in their communities and carving out support structures, creating leadership opportunities for others in their spheres of influence.

APPLYING THE NARRATIVES

Women's lived experiences and contributions as leaders are often rendered invisible. Exploring narratives and producing research through feminist narrative analysis and an intersectional lens creates possibilities for non-dominant perspectives to emerge. Learning about and from diverse women on a wide set of issues, telling their stories, and creating scholarship that counters the misogynist mainstream, has transformed the way we see leadership—in ourselves and in the world. Inspiring women, encouraging a younger generation to act based on feminist values of social justice, and helping them develop the skills to do so can place more women in positions to theorize and enact leadership.

Feminist values can provide important contributions to evolving the field of leadership education to address 21st century social and global issues. Transformative feminist models of leadership education can become the thread to weave the myriad of ways individuals and organizations enact social change. If dominant discourses fall back on conventional notions of leadership constructions of the late 20th century, we fall short in providing a usable framework for our current historical moment. As a hyperaggressive version of society plays out its assault on humanity and our life systems, it appears to me that we have come to a crossroads, one that requires a more nuanced understanding of gender, power, and leadership within the current ways of existing.

CONCLUSION

In this chapter, I sought to make visible the important perspectives and embodied transnational experiences of 1.5 and second-generation immigrant women who chose to complete a 2-year certificate program for women and leadership for social change as part of their undergraduate career at Rutgers University. As an alumna of the program, I came to this writing with both insider and outsider perspectives (Hesse-Biber & Leavy, 2007). I feel I have benefitted from this unique positioning in the narrative collecting and analysis process. I feel fortunate to be able to participate in this collaboration of scholars and educators across five universities that are committed to raising young women's voices and are dedicated to teaching and building women and leadership development programs in service of a more equitable and just world.

This book is a product of the interweaving of women's voices alongside leadership educators and theorists who have come together to make visible the complexities of women's leadership in action. It is my hope that we, as authors, reveal innovative and dynamic practices of transformative, rising women leaders to highlight and emphasize women's leadership education as a more widely accepted paradigm for leadership learning and a rich site for knowledge production in higher education. With critical 21st century challenges at hand, integrating women and leadership programs in our academic opportunities can influence and inform a shifting paradigm for leadership and subsequently leadership education—to co-create stronger, more equitable communities.

REFERENCES

Antrobus, P. (2000). Transformational leadership: Advancing the agenda for gender justice. *Gender & Development, 8*(3), 50–56. https://doi.org/10.1080/741923780

Antrobus, P. (2002). Feminism as transformational politics: Towards possibilities for another world. *Development, 45*(2), 46–52. https://doi.org/10.1057/palgrave.development.1110349

Batliwala, S. (2010). *Feminist leadership for social transformation: Clearing the conceptual cloud.* Creating Resources for Empowerment in Action. https://creaworld.org/wp-content/uploads/2020/11/feminist-leadership-clearing-conceptual-cloud-srilatha-batliwala.pdf

Bloom, L. (1998). *Under the sign of hope: Feminist methodology and narrative interpretation.* State University of New York Press.

Bunch, C. (1990). Women's rights as human rights: Toward a re-vision of human rights. *Human Rights Quarterly, 12*(4), 486–498. https://doi.org/10.2307/762496

Bunch, C., & Gray White, D. (2002). *Power for what?: Women's leadership, Why you should care?* Institute for Women's Leadership Consortium at Douglass College, Rutgers, the State University of New Jersey.

Hartman, M. (Ed.). (1999). *Talking leadership: Conversations with powerful women.* Rutgers University Press.

Hernandez, S., Hernandez, I., Jr., Gadson, R., Huftalin, D., Ortiz, A. M., White, M. C., & Yocum-Gaffney, D. (2010). Sharing their secrets: Undocumented students' personal stories of fear, drive, and survival. *New Directions for Student Services, 2010*(131), 67–84. https://doi.org/10.1002/ss.368

Hesse-Biber, S. N., & Leavy, P. L. (2007). *Feminist research practice.* SAGE.

hooks, B. (2014). *Teaching to transgress.* Routledge.

Institute for Women's Leadership. (n.d.). *Our mission.* http:/iwl.rutgers.edu/

Trigg, M. K. (Ed.). (2010). *Leading the way: Young women's activism for social change.* Rutgers University Press.

PART III

WEAVING AND APPLYING THE NARRATIVES

Art by Sam

While there will always be grief and loss, there is also love and life and the beginning of new friendships. Leadership, for me that night, became a commitment to healing. By remembering and honoring each other's truths, we were reclaiming ourselves and our identity. Through these acts of remembrance, healing becomes social change.

—Amna, Chapter 5, p. 88

CHAPTER 15

WE ARE THE SUN

Trisha Teig
Rebecca Shetty
Brittany Devies

Rain lashed against the wall of windows as chills went down my (Trisha's) arms. We sat in awe and appreciation of each other, of the process, and of the stories we were fortunate to read and share. In December 2022, almost 2 years to the day from when Julie encouraged me to start the book process, eight of the chapter authors met and presented about the book at the 2022 Leadership Educators Institute in New Orleans. We presented to a crowd of 30 other leadership educators and students. We began and ended with the stories—and recognized the power of our collective voices and experience. At the end of the presentation, a young African American woman came up to speak to us. "Thank you for this book," she said. She shared that she was an undergraduate student in leadership studies, but she had yet to encounter content in her courses that aligned with her experience, with her leadership story. Her graciousness and gratitude made our hearts swell with joy, as she is who we wrote the book for!

Often when writing an academic text, there is a formula:

1. Gather the "experts" and ask them to write.
2. Consider all former literature from other "experts."

> 3. Manage each chapter as editors, without connection or conversation across authors.
> 4. Editors review and submit final book.
> 5. Editors present on "their" book.
>
> Abandoning this recipe, we co-created a book at each stage of the process, and in this moment—presenting in a freezing conference room at the Hilton Hotel after a tornado warning in downtown New Orleans—we all owned every part of this book and yet we did not own it at all. For the very process of gathering and sharing stories about leadership from over 50 women means it is for and should be shared by all of us.

IT'S ABOUT THE PROCESS, NOT JUST THE PRODUCT

In Chapter 11, Imani wrote, "I want to be the sun." She wrote about a desire to "release a heat of healing and growth" and for her and her planets to build a great solar system together, one that is "able to reach beyond itself." It is the truest and most encompassing metaphor for the process of writing this book and the product of the book itself. For the authors whose voices fill this book, the process was filled with moments of healing and growth as we reflected on our own stories of leadership as women. Collectively, we built a system of support amongst one another during the process. In addition to this revelatory, healing journey, a beautiful outcome of this process is the creation of an actual product, this book, so other women in our solar systems can continue to come together on their own journeys of leadership healing and growth. We hope this book reaches far beyond itself. We are beyond thankful to Imani for her beautiful words that so encapsulate what this experience has meant to us all.

We learned from the joint nature of this process and from each of the narrative authors individually and in collective form. The outset of this project intended collaboration—and we believe we achieved it beyond expectations. We hoped to be disruptive, constructive, and inductive in our process of narrative analysis. Chapter author Adrian noted, "One of the things that I most appreciated about this book is the integrity of the process." She explained that when she was invited to the project, it was still in the early stages of development, but that Trisha promised: "However it [the project] unfolded, it would be a collaborative effort." Additionally, Adrian stated from a methodological perspective, the editors were, "clear that the book was first and foremost about the narratives of the women in the study and that as chapter authors, our charge was to highlight their narratives in their entirety while weaving in additional analysis and insights." This meant that all the narratives were presented intact; there were not any modifications of these women's stories beyond their initial first draft.

In reflecting on their experiences in writing their chapter, chapter authors Sharrell and Aoi stated:

> A key learning/take away from writing the chapter was a connection and confirmation of the current reality of how we experience daily life as Women of Color engaging in leadership. We often felt like what we were dealing with was unique and not representative of our colleagues. We were able to find a community, by reading other narratives, that were familiar with our own experiences. We felt seen, heard, and affirmed. Rather than having others critique or try to fix challenges we faced as leadership educators and in leadership positions, we felt that there was a space for us to be understood and accepted. Through narratives, a space was created in which we could communicate our truth and engage in activism by sharing our stories.

Our ideas of collaboration for producing positive change are influenced by Communities of Color and women's advocacy and organizing histories. We know viewing leadership from a collective lens is a well utilized tool from social movement organizers across the 19th, 20th, and 21st centuries (Nardini et al., 2021). This project was also informed by our grounding in critical feminist, engaged pedagogy (Freire, 2000; hooks, 1994) which centers relationships, collaboration, and power sharing in educational environments. In *Teaching Community: A Pedagogy of Hope*, hooks (2013) emphasized we must mobilize our shared capacities to effect liberatory practices in and outside of the classroom. These ideas influenced my (Trisha's) understanding of leadership learning and pedagogical practices, but also influenced how this research project was conceived and implemented. We worked to give full space (both literally and figuratively) for the narrative authors' stories. Further, we focused our efforts on ensuring the narratives were fully centered and highlighted within the book. Chapter authors—Sharrell and Aoi—noted they appreciated "the students' vulnerability to share their narratives and we received them as a gift that gave us insights to injustice they experience as Black, Indigenous, Women of Color." Further, they "saw growth from the students and us as authors and found possibility and hope for the future to reimagine leadership that accounted for and centered our identities in spite of the oppressive nature of leadership we experienced." The process itself was a series of intentional choices rooted in humility and a desire for social change. From creating our collective team to doing research that honors and centers women's narratives to collaboratively writing an edited book this unique and particular way, these were all choices that led to this greater whole of which we are so proud. As we practiced liberatory leadership at all levels, the process for us was just as important as the product.

LEARNING, CO-LEARNING, RE-LEARNING

Each step of the process in writing this book offered an opportunity for learning about leadership. We learned how to share with and learn from the narrative and chapter authors. We learned that the extra effort to collaborate across an "edited" book created a work that is profoundly integrated, considerate of each other's voices, and ultimately, a far more cohesive story. We also learned important lessons on women and leadership from our chapter and narrative authors. Below, we highlight some of these crucial takeaways related to the following themes: women as a mosaic, not a monolith; the role of family and mentors; resisting the system and oppression; leadership identity development; reconsidering resilience; and redefining expertise. Through our reflections below, we hope you see the power and profundity in the narratives and the knowledge they impart.

A Mosaic, Not a Monolith

In Chapter 8, Adrian reminded us we (specifically White women) often treat shared social identities—such as being women—as a broad, synonymous group. Women of Color feminists have articulated frustration and ongoing disappointment that this centering of middle to upper class, white women's experiences continues in feminist movements (Beck, 2021; hooks, 2015; Hurtado, 1996; Lorde, 1984; Orgeta, 2006; Roth, 2004; Schuller, 2021). To disrupt these assumptions, we set out to emphasize how each narrative is unique because of the experiences and social identities of each author. We can draw out themes and similarities, but there will always be distinctive elements to each person's story. This is why we wrote the book in this manner—to incorporate as many women's stories across a variety of locations, ideas, moments, and experiences as possible. Narrative author Ariana, from Chapter 5, gave us a beautiful analogy, that we are all pieces of a mosaic; each piece is distinct and matters both for its individual beauty and purpose as well as how it connects with other pieces to form an interesting and impactful work of art.

Support From Family and Role Models

Ignoring women's familial and role modeling contexts can lead to missed opportunities to better support women's leadership development. In Chapter 6, Lauren explored how family shapes leadership identity development for Women of Color. Lauren stated,

> Families within Communities of Color are rich with stories, experiences, and lessons of caretaking, survival, and coping that impact leadership identity development, and they should be acknowledged. Thus, those working with Women of Color should strive to understand their family influence and context and help Women of Color to make the connection between their family experiences and their leadership experiences.

As Lauren brilliantly noted, those essential lessons learned within the family environment around caretaking, survival, and coping are all deeply important in leadership development, especially in creating leaders orientated for positive social change. For so long, leadership has been viewed as hierarchical and position driven, but so much of early socialization around what leadership can and (sometimes) should look like happens first inside a home and/or familial context. In Chapter 9, Jessie described the socialization she experienced through her relationship with her mother; her mother had distinct views on femininity and how a woman should lead, views she passed on to Jessie. Jessie stated that later on in her life "my mother and I learned very important stances on feminism from each other. She taught me that I was capable of doing anything a man can do, and all the same I taught her how to embrace her femininity." In Chapter 14, Acela saw her revolutionary grandparents pave the way for her family and encourage her to embrace an education as a means of liberation; her education led her to courses that eventually shaped her leadership development. Like Jessie, Acela learned from her family context important lessons on leadership, how to approach leadership, and which values were most important.

While some familial influences—like those of Jesse and Acela—may be positive, some family relationships create barriers or challenges in leadership. At worst, family members may provide examples of leadership we don't want to emulate. In Chapter 9, Kat writes about feeling abandoned and rejected by her mother, ending her narrative to her mother as, "I need a hero, I'm waiting for a leader. Someone to guide me." In Chapter 10, Skye reflects on her mother's lack of vulnerability, an example of leadership that was strong but isolated. In Chapter 12, we see Jocelyn grow up in a household rooted in *machismo* and traditional ways of thinking about gender roles—an environment in which exploring leadership as a possibility was nearly impossible. Family members and parental figures are undoubtedly influential in women's leadership development; however, this influence may lead women to a thriving sense of self as a leader or may suffocate women in their desire to lead at all.

While families are a key factor in socialization, and often lay the foundation for leadership learning, we also give credence to the important position role models play in the lives of young leaders seeking to learn, grow, and flourish. In Chapter 7, chapter author Simone noted,

> When you truly feel like you belong, your contributions and sense of self-worth take on a fierceness that comes across as commanding, confident, and caring. By learning from role models, you begin to see your true self in the mirror.

The mirror is a wonderful metaphor for role models, as they often serve as a guide on your own reflective path to self-discovery. This can come in a multitude of ways, as we see evidenced in Chapter 7 and throughout the book. Simone also clarifies in Chapter 7 that "role models are not only those in 'positions of power' but rather those that touch and feed the most inner part of our identity development."

Additionally in Chapter 7, Simone describes, "In a full circle moment, where my aspirations have now become inspirations, I give a similar love and support to the next generation of women leaders." This concept aligns with many grounding ideas from this book, including Harro's (2013) cycle of socialization explored throughout the book and the fifth stage (generativity) of the leadership identity development model that focuses on how leaders pour into and cultivate the next generation of leaders (Komives et al., 2006; Komives et al., 2005). Positive influence and generativity are beautiful sentiments for role modeling relationships. However, they should be considered with thought and intention.

Often, we discuss mentoring and role modeling as a process of "empowering" others to lead. In Chapter 5 we were asked by Trisha to consider, "Does the very framing of 'giving' others 'access' to leadership through the act of 'empowerment' perpetuate the system it claims to dismantle?" We acknowledge the critical role mentoring (through family, professional connections, organizations, etc.) plays in women's leadership development. At the same time, we offer an alternative perspective for alluding to this work as *empowering*. Simone (Chapter 7) highlights the crucial element of a mutually beneficial relationship between role model and role aspirant. If we seek to co-learn about leadership across identities and experiences, we must be thoughtful of our language and purpose. Mentors do significant work to connect, inspire, and encourage their mentees in leadership development, but this should be through shared power and in a recursive relationship. Using the terminology of "empowerment" actually takes away power from the mentee/role aspirant. We are not "empowering" women when they join critical, feminist leadership programs, we are providing support and connection for them to identify and grow their own power; we must shift our framing to see the work of leadership learning as a we-powering (co-sharing power) instead of em-powering (giving/allowing power) effort for collective change.

Resisting the System and Its Expectations

The omnipresence of systemic oppression and violence directly informs how women navigate the world. Without scrutinizing this context, we cannot also consider how or why women lead. Chapter 4 opened with a quote from Pam, comparing her experiences navigating systemic oppression to paddling relentlessly through "choppy waves." Sadia in Chapter 14 reflected, "I never thought what I was doing at the time as leadership. I thought of it as more of survival." Connecting across ideas, Ariana and Prasamsha from Chapter 5 identify how these truths can also impact how we show up, in our minds and in our bodies as leaders. In Chapter 11, Sam describes the danger of a bigoted society that will sweep your identities under the rug to avoid addressing difference, hiding behind colorblindness, heteronormativity, and passive aggression. Sam acknowledges how this type of culture can wreck a person's psyche,

> When you purposely suppress your identities, it is easy to ignore how much influence they hold over you. It's a fairly serious trade-off you commit to as a kid: unrestricted access to the model suburban lifestyle for the low, low price of your entire identity.

In this world of harm, Ariana reminds us, "We carry our scars"; they inform our leadership. We must consider how our stories of pain and building resilience, in community and in solidarity, can bring us together into new possibilities.

In Chapter 9, we were introduced by Brittany to considering leadership capacity and efficacy through either a fixed or growth mindset. This framing requires consideration of a systemic context. When women are socialized within a system not to see worth in their identities or abilities, or alternatively only to see people with privileged identities (White, cisgender, straight, able-bodied, men) in leadership roles, it is possible (and perhaps likely) to develop a fixed mindset about who can do the work of leadership. Further complicating this issue, even when women have developed a growth mindset about their leadership capacity and efficacy, the external expectations of how or when a woman should lead influences her abilities to lead authentically in many spaces.

Through a societal lens, often women's intersecting identities and leadership are in diametric opposition. When women feel they are not valued or seen as leaders, this can lead to self-doubt. In Chapter 8, Adrian discusses imposter syndrome and the attention given to this phenomenon; she writes about the importance of acknowledging imposter syndrome as a means of creating support and solidarity for those who experience it (not only women experience imposter syndrome). However, she complicates this framing by asking, "In focusing on imposter syndrome as an individual deficit and building interventions and leadership development programs that address it, are we creating a self-fulfilling prophecy where women might internalize temporary feelings of discomfort and nervousness as imposter syndrome?" Women may need to process all manner of feelings on their leadership journey, and we must be ready to facilitate what is needed rather than anticipating women will experience imposter syndrome in the same way or at all.

Just as imposter syndrome arose as a theme for the women's stories in leadership, we also see evidence of *hustle culture* embedded within the narratives in this book. We see women working hard, twice as hard, or swimming against the tide in an attempt to be seen as a credible leader. In Chapter 13 we see narrative author Cathy resist the systems that reward women for overworking, overperforming, and burning out as a means of obtaining success or achievement. Cathy wrote,

> I'm never fully present in my work or home life. (Don't worry—I have a therapist!). But these realities are not just about me; I'm realizing now that despite any success that may come from it, my perpetuation of this culture of overwork is the opposite of leadership. Being able to act as an effective leader means being able to identify what leadership means to us as women in spite of what society says, a society that only validates women when they work and beat themselves to death for the sake of looking like a "good leader."

A question posed by chapter author Paige leaves us considering how we support and encourage women knowing there may be challenges and trauma behind their projected image of leadership. Paige asked, "How do we provide space for individuals to process the challenges and systems they may be navigating as they take up their leadership (as often we only see the actions of others and not the struggle behind the actions)?" This question connected to understanding the invisible challenges women are likely facing to lead "authentically."

In Chapter 11, Julie and Lauren highlighted the complicated maze queer people and Women of Color must navigate to authentically step into their leadership. They note: "Due to stereotypes and discrimination, leaders with marginalized identities make decisions about how much of themselves to reveal." Our narrative authors' stories affirm this assertion and previous scholarship highlights the messiness of "authentic leadership" for anyone who identifies as a woman, Person of Color, queer, trans or gendering non-conforming, or neurodiverse (Eagly, 2005; Jones, 2016; Jones et al., 2012; Jourian, 2014; Liu et al., 2015; Miller & Vaccaro, 2016; Ngunjiri & Hernandez, 2017). We center these narratives to emphasize the complex links between imposter syndrome, oppressive systems, and the access or ability to lead "authentically" and develop a growth mindset for leadership efficacy and capacity. Much like Pam described uncertain waters, the book centers narratives of women discerning the complicated effort of taking up their leadership while swimming in dark, shark-infested depths of systemic oppression. This complexity is a key learning element of the work—the narrative and chapter authors not only emphasize the intricacies of these challenges but also articulate powerful ways to resist dominant systems and find power in their personal claiming of leadership.

Leadership Identity Development

Understanding how leadership identity fits into our existing psyche and integrates with our existing identities has been a significant consideration, particularly for young adults and college students (Bitton & Jones, 2021; Guthrie et al., 2021; Komives et al., 2005). The leadership identity development (LID) model (Komives et al., 2005) has proven foundational for the field of leadership education by allowing us to consider how students come to see themselves as leaders. Through the narratives in this book, we can both challenge and add insight into leadership identity development as we see women grappling with questions around their social identities and redefining leadership in resistance to dominant and oppressive conceptualizations.

In her reflections on the writing of this book, Adrian provided powerful insight on leadership identity development as seen through the narratives in this book. She noted:

> We acknowledge that context, socialization, and social identities are critical aspects of leadership identity development, but perhaps the "big shift" in development is not entirely encapsulated in moving from Stage 3 to Stage 4 (independent/dependent to interdependent in the LID model). The narratives throughout this book highlight that part of the big shift is in developing a deep and personal understanding of leadership that may or may not align with our socialization or dominant narratives of leadership through a lens of critical consciousness.

How an individual then uses their newfound conceptualizations of leadership to root, guide, and transform their leadership is perhaps an even truer, more powerful mark of leadership identity development and growth. In Chapter 7, Mia wrote:

> I am not perfect, I do not have to be
> But yet I'm expected to be perfect and smile and to shhhhh…
> Which makes me just want to be WORSE
> But it isn't really worse,
> It's better, it's more powerful.

Here we see Mia recognizing both her own limitations and the unfair expectations of who society wants her to be. In whatever way she defines "worse," she reclaims who she wants to be as a leader, and whoever that person is—she is powerful, and she is better than the expectations with which society would have her comply.

We would be remiss if we didn't acknowledge how power, context, privilege, and socialization play in leadership identity development and its many stages. Leadership identity development is influenced by so many factors, particularly the patriarchy systems that perpetuate perspectives of leadership that center Whiteness, heteronormativity, wealth, and other privileges. When women face oppression, discrimination, imposter syndrome, and harm as described in this book, understanding oneself as a leader becomes an even more complex process.

In Chapter 11, Julie and Lauren remind us "that we cannot limit how students make meaning and define leadership, each student will develop their own understanding and by doing so, will likely embody and recognize the characteristics of leaders within themselves." The identity exploration and self-awareness demonstrated by our narrative authors shows they continue to develop new ways of thinking about leadership and this creation of knowledge is an ongoing, lifelong process. The development journey is captured in Jocelyn's narrative in Chapter 12; she wrote: "I may not be the best leader, and my leadership skills are still developing as time goes on. However, I'm still more of a leader than I give myself credit for."

Ramifications of Resilience

Next, we turn to the idea of resiliency and question its place in the work of critical leadership and liberation practices. In her member checking response, narrative author, Amna, pushed back against the reoccurring exaltation of "resiliency" for Communities of Color. We should not singly center this storyline—particularly for Women of Color, queer folx, and survivors of gender-based and/or racialized microaggressions and violence. We must "reimagine leadership, community, and healing past resilience" (Amna). We should not idolize a woman's strength because of how well she navigated the sexist, racist, and violent world around her. We should not be raising women and girls to expect trauma and therefore integrate a requisite need for healing through "resilience" as the only outcome or outlook. Rather, we should envision and co-create a world where these traumas are not the gauntlets required for women to run to achieve their leadership dreams.

Redefining "Expertise"

In a critical inquiry conversation, Irwin et al. (2023) troubled the notion of "expertise" in leadership scholarship. Their critique brought to light the perpetuating cycles of academic expectations that contain power within the ivory tower, including limited access to writing and reading literature; antiquated publishing guidelines crafted to keep ideas in or out; the practice of uplifting certain voices over others; and lauding "perfection" in grammar, mechanics, and writing from a western/White/global northern framework. Aoi's narrative in Chapter 4 captures the frustrations of these pillars of expertise as a Japanese immigrant and non-native English speaker, academic scholar. We amplify her lived experience and question expertise as a standard for leadership development.

In Chapter 13, we explore the notion of "taking up one's leadership." This is particularly powerful as we think about women conceptualizing leadership, developing confidence, and seeing their identities as strengths, not barriers. As we've discussed, society, the system, and oppressors are the barriers; women with their intelligence, ambition, work ethic, and passion are the sun. Women have the power to gift their spheres of influence (their planets) their wisdom, insight, and expertise. In Chapter 10, Becka notes the narrative authors' descriptions of leadership are "everything from poetic to messy to concise to more stream-of-consciousness." In many ways, the nature of these conceptualizations is much like leadership itself; leadership can be beautiful to experience and witness, messy when we get it wrong, effective and productive, and sometimes a winding path as we learn and grow. Throughout this book, we see women literally creating new definitions of leadership for themselves influenced by peers, mentors, teachers, family, but also through their own sheer brilliance. Bitton and Jones (2021; also quoted in Chapter 4) wrote: "Just as the dominant narrative of leadership exerts pressure on the individual, individuals also have agency to resist contextual forces to advance more socially just societies, whereby leadership experiences and conversations take on new meaning" (p. 171). We see this quote in action throughout this book as both our chapter and narrative authors reexamine life experiences through liberated lenses that allow them to be bold, brave, and proud of who they are as leaders.

Within these contexts, we find it imperative to critically explore the role of expertise in leadership learning. We agree with Bitton and Jones (2021) that, "Leadership learning requires a redistribution of power by validating multiple ways of knowing" (p. 64). As the authors in our book have shown, they are adroitly able to define what attitudes, beliefs, behaviors, and philosophies of leadership they find useful, and which they do not. In Chapter 10, Becka reminds us:

> By recognizing what leadership is not, these women were freed from the constraints and burdens of societal expectations and allowed to think and dream without hindrance. In their reflection, thinking, dreaming, and conceptualizing, they were able to weave together a new narrative of leadership for themselves.

In light of the knowledge generated by our authors in the creation of this book, we ask ourselves: "What makes an expert?" We are all experts of our own lives. Only we can know the innermost workings of our own minds, intentions, and capabilities. Only we know our experiences with discrimination, microaggressions, and oppressive barriers. Only we know what has worked best and what has worked poorly regarding our own leadership practice. With reflection, we are all capable of recognizing which leadership frameworks and approaches make us feel most authentic, centered, and effective when also considering our intersecting identities.

We are the experts. The women in this book are the experts; and the women not in this book are the experts. They shed light on current issues for women in leadership, and they are creating new definitions, new solutions, and new ways of thinking, being, and doing related to leadership. Let us not be arrogant enough to think expertise only lies behind the marble walls of academia; in the CEO's 80th floor corner office; or with straight, cisgender, wealthy, White men. Let us be humble enough to see the wisdom in the youth of new generations. Let us recognize there are as many ways to approach leadership as there are people in the world, and each way has its own pieces of expertise and merit. Stephanie is an example of a young woman taking up her leadership and becoming the expert of her own leadership knowledge. In Chapter 8, Stephanie described her resistance to cultural norms and her newfound sense of self. She reflected:

> I started sticking up for myself and for my own beliefs. I started questioning everything I was taught... I started asking, "Why am I doing this and who am I doing it for?" If the answer wasn't for myself then I would tell myself that I couldn't expect that of myself because they weren't my own expectations.

Stephanie's words remind us all that our personal expectations, integrity, and curiosity guide who we are as people and as leaders. In addition, our learning and growth moments are not only for our own benefit but also serve towards the creation of new knowledge for others to absorb and from which to learn. This book demonstrates that knowledge is created and co-created by a myriad of different types of people, voices, and perspectives, all worthy of acknowledgment.

Tying It All Together

Access to feminist leadership education provides significant impact to learning in higher education and beyond. The reflections of the narrative authors in Chapter 14 and across the book highlight the profound impact of feminist leadership education. As Laila stated in Chapter 14, "Having the tools to describe my own experience as a person helped me realize that these experiences are not just unique to me." Expanding upon these women's experiences, we recommend leadership training and education programs should focus strategic effort to champion and integrate critical feminist leadership education. This requires intentional reformulation of curriculum and content to include individual, organizational, and systemic change. In Chapter 12, Julie and Adrian stated, "Feminist leadership learning requires going beyond individual learning to also interrogate and disrupt organizational, institutional, and systemic dynamics (Owen et al., 2017)." To implement critical, feminist leadership learning, we offer below important questions and thoughts:

- We must learn to notice, understand, deconstruct, and dismantle systemic oppression as a consistent practice of leadership.
- Power can be a positive tool or a violent detriment; empowering others does not always mean we are supporting or "creating space" for women as leaders. How do we we-power and model co-sharing power and encouraging women's recognition of power in themselves?
- How do we foster and embrace drive and persistence in women? Alternatively, how do we challenge the systems in place that often demand such drive and persistence for women in regard to leadership?
- How do we make space for and honor the role of family in the leadership journey?
- How do we help women (and specifically queer/gender non-conforming and/or BIWOC) navigate and prepare for "being the first" or "being one of the only" (and what supports do we have in place and need in place for this to happen)?
- By designing programs that specifically center imposter syndrome, are we being counter-productive and perpetuating the notion that women will or should experience imposter syndrome? Are we asking women to overcome the system that makes imposter syndrome possible to begin with rather than funneling our efforts towards creating more equitable spaces that remove barriers and allow the most people to thrive?
- "How can we reimagine leadership, community, and healing past resilience?" (Amna)

- How do we embrace BIWOC and White women as active contributors to and experts in the creation of new knowledge related to leadership and leadership learning?

Every one of these questions stems from the insights offered by the authors of this book and a desire to leave the world a better place than we found it. This work is necessary. As Trisha noted in Chapter 5, "There is violence against women, always present, always lingering as a dark shadow over the hopeful flight each woman dreams to take." We do not take this lightly; and this work is a direct response to the harm women have faced in life and in their leadership journeys.

SHE IS THE SUN

We wrap up this text by returning to narrative authors Acela's, Imani's, and Amna's words and by geeking out with a bit of theory. Many gender and queer theory students/scholars are familiar with Judith Butler's troubling of finite, firm notions of gender. Butler (2004, 2006) described gender as performative, an act perpetuated by our socially constructed expectations across cultural landscapes which is reified by our very normalized and cyclical requisite participation in doing gender. Butler deconstructs universal assumptions of womanhood and reconsiders how we act out our genders as affirmation of our places in society. Leadership scholar Leigh Fine (2016) considered how Butler's concepts of gender performativity related to leadership. Fine (2016) noted we must explore how we think a leader is "intelligible" in relationship to gender performativity (and we argue, other subject identities):

> Intelligibility in Butler's work generally refers to the ability to be seen, heard, or otherwise interpreted as a valid social subject (Butler, 2005). Because performativity can be fragile, individuals have the potential to contest the boundaries of what is intelligible through misperformances. (p. 72)

In considering the narratives and insights across this book, we seek to identify a response to Fine's (2016) questions about who and how a leader/leadership is recognized. Specifically, she questioned:

> Who is intelligible as a leader? Whose leadership is intelligible and can be interpreted as leadership by others? Whose leadership might be concealed, overlooked, or ignored if viewed through the framework of dominant discourse? (p. 74)

Fine posed these questions within the discourse of a dominant narrative of leadership. Critical leadership scholars have denounced the connection between the intelligibility of leadership with traditional masculinity, body-type, charisma, and White, male, hetero-cisgender normalizations (Knights, 2022; Ospina & Foldy, 2009; Sinclair, 2005). Acela, in Chapter 14, reflected on her understanding of leadership and pushed back against this traditional framing:

> [Women's] leadership education, I think, is allowing people to feel like they can be leaders, which is sometimes really difficult, especially for women to identify themselves as leaders. Because we think of leadership, or we're told to think of leadership in this traditional way; leadership means you're in control, you're in power, and other people report to you, or you're the manager, all of that. But I think it's telling anyone that they could be leaders if they decide to. They have that ability to think.

Fine (2016) might argue Acela's words and the other narratives in this book represent "misperformance" to this dominant discourse of leadership. She noted, "All leaders also have the ability to, potential to, and even experience of using misperformance to contest the leadership status quo" (p. 74).

In disruption of this framing of dominant discourse, we contend the knowing of leadership must be a multiplistic, intersectional, and pluralistic understanding, as well as a collective process. It is not useful to assume we can all know the same Truths about leadership, nor whose bodies or lives intelligibly produce it; as we argued before, we are all experts of our own lived experiences and the knowledge produced by them. Our project affirmed the numerous, unique, and interesting ways women across multitudes of identities articulated their understanding and application of leadership concepts in relationship to their intersecting identities of gender, race, class, religion, and ability.

With this foundation, we question: "When do consistent unique narratives become more than 'misperformance' in relation to a 'dominant narrative'"? Often, we identify conceptualizations of women's voices, stories, experiences of leadership as "alternative to" and connect this as a championed example of other/counter/different in response to the "dominant" discourse. But what does *dominant* discourse mean? In a common thesaurus, synonyms to dominant include "leading, main, prevailing, foremost, and transcendent" (Thesaurus.com, 2023, p. 1). In her introduction to the first edition of her preeminent feminist work, *Feminist Theory: From Margins to Center*, bell hooks (2015) offered insightful language to understand movement in space across "margins" and "center" from her experiences as a lower class, Black girl growing up in the segregated south:

> Living as we did—on the edge—we developed a particular way of seeing reality. We looked both from the outside in and the inside out. *We focused our attention on the center as well as on the margin. We understood both.* This mode of seeing reminded us of the existence of a whole universe, a main body made up of both margin and center. Our survival depended upon an ongoing public awareness of the separation between margin and center and an ongoing private acknowledgement that we were a necessary, vital part of that whole. (p. xvii; emphasis added)

We are tired of years, decades, generations of Women of Color, LBGTQ+ folx, and neurodiverse and differently abled women sequestered as an "alternative" rather than acknowledging the simplistic notion of a "dominant narrative" of leadership as an untruth in and of itself. If, as we have offered in this text (and many have shared, extolled, and harangued before us), the best understanding of leadership is as nuanced, dynamic, and multiplistic, can we also disabuse ourselves of the notion that these stories are inherently only marginal and instead believe they represent, as Imani imagines, being the sun, "releasing a heat of healing and growth" within an "existence of a whole universe"? We offer this perspective not to disbelieve the reality of systems of power, privilege, and oppression in our society where women's lives are decidedly not centered; rather, we see these narratives authors claiming the space of both experiences: the awareness and truth-telling of being within the margins and the claiming of their being as the *sun*, the *center*. We did not capture anything that has not already been alive and well in women's day to day lives. *These* are the "dominant" (leading, main, prevailing, foremost, transcendent) narratives of leadership—co-creation, love, messiness, creativity, possibility, uncertainty, pain, disruption, purpose, socio-emotional learning, growth, and harnessing of reflective, collective capacities of learning from our past for the prosperity of our present and futures.

Amanda Sinclair (2008) offered an alternative and expansive leadership definition:

> A more meaningful way to think about leadership is as a form of being (with ourselves and others): a way of thinking and acting that awakens and mobilises people to find new, freer and more meaningful ways of seeing, working and living. (p. 66)

The authors in this book have identified and shared ways of being in leadership, of taking up our leadership, and of claiming leadership for ourselves and future women. Through this book; in its words; the process of co-creating it; and in the significant stories, moments, and persons who live within its pages, she/they/ella are the sun, the planets, and the constellations that make up the complex possibilities of women and leadership. Further, just as the creation of this book allowed a process of healing for its participants, we hope it grounds those who read and engage with its stories as a healing act for social change. As Imani stated her celestial intention, being the sun that releases heat for healing and growth, she connected with her fellow narrative author, Amna. Amna described a transcendent moment of understanding, "Leadership, for me that night, became a commitment to healing. By remembering and honoring each other's truths, we were reclaiming ourselves and our identity. Through these acts of remembrance, healing becomes social change."

REFERENCES

Beck, K. (2021). *White feminism: From the suffragettes to influencers and who they leave behind.* ATRIA.

Bitton, A. L., & Jones, S. R. (2021). Connecting social class and leadership learning through intersectionality. *New Directions for Student Leadership, 2021*(169), 61–68. https://doi.org/10.1002/yd.20421

Butler, J. (2004). *Undoing gender.* Routledge.

Butler, J. (2005). *Giving an account of oneself.* Fordham University Press.

Butler, J. (2006). *Gender trouble: Feminism and the subversion of identity.* Routledge.

Eagly, A. H. (2005). Achieving relational authenticity in leadership: Does gender matter? *The Leadership Quarterly, 16*(3), 459–474. https://doi.org/10.1016/j.leaqua.2005.03.007

Fine, L. E. (2016). Judith Butler and leadership: Reimagining intelligibility, social change, and leadership discourse. *Journal of Leadership Studies, 10*(2), 69–81. https://doi.org/10.1002/jls.21466

Freire, P. (2000). *Pedagogy of the oppressed: 30th anniversary edition.* Continuum.

Guthrie, K. L., Beatty, C. C., & Wiborg, E. R. (2021). *Engaging in the leadership process: Identity, capacity, and efficacy for college students.* Information Age Publishing.

Harro, B. (2013). The cycle of socialization. In M. Adams, W. J. Blumenfeld, R. Castaneda, H. W. Hackman, M. L. Peters, & X. Zuniga (Eds.), *Readings for diversity of social justice* (3rd ed.; pp. 45–52). Routledge.

hooks, b. (1994). *Teaching to transgress.* Routledge.

hooks, b. (2013). *Teaching community: A pedagogy of hope.* Routledge.

hooks, b. (2015). *Feminist theory: From the margins to the center* (2nd ed.). Routledge.

Hurtado, A. (1996). *The color of privilege: Three blasphemies on race and feminism.* University of Michigan Press.

Irwin, L. N., Reynolds, D. J., Bitton, A. L., Hassell-Goodman, S., Teig, T., & Tapia-Fuselier, N. (2023). Insights from a critical inquiry in leadership scholarship. In S. R. Komives & J. E. Owen (Eds.), *A research agenda for leadership learning and development through higher education* (pp. 255–272). Edward Elgar Publishing.

Jones, S. R. (2016). Authenticity in leadership: Intersectionality of identities. *New Directions for Student Leadership, 2016*(152), 23–34. https://doi.org/10.1002/yd.20206

Jones, S. R., Kim, Y. C., & Skendall, K. C. (2012). (Re-)framing authenticity: Considering multiple social identities using autoethnographic and intersectional approaches. *The Journal of Higher Education, 83*(5), 698–724. https://doi.org/10.1353/jhe.2012.0029

Jourian, T. J. (2014). Trans*forming authentic leadership: A conceptual framework. *Journal of Critical Thought and Praxis, 2*(2), 113–125. https://doi.org/10.31274/jctp-180810-78

Knights, D. (2022). Disrupting masculinities within leadership: Problems of embodiment, ethics, identity and power. *Leadership, 18*(2), 266–276. https://doi.org/10.1177/17427150211004053

Komives, S. R., Longerbeam, S. D., Owen, J. E., Mainella, F. C., & Osteen, L. (2006). A leadership identity development model: Applications from a grounded theory. *Journal of College Student Development, 47*(4), 401–418. https://doi.org/10.1353/csd.2006.0048

Komives, S. R., Owen, J. E., Longerbeam, S. D., Mainella, F. C., & Osteen, L. (2005). Developing a leadership identity: A grounded theory. *Journal of College Student Development, 46*(6), 593–611. https://doi.org/10.1353/csd.2005.0061

Liu, H., Cutcher, L., & Grant, D. (2015). Doing authenticity: The gendered construction of authentic leadership. *Gender, Work and Organization, 22*(3), 237–255. https://doi.org/10.1111/gwao.12073

Lorde, A. (1984). *Sister, outsider*. Crossing Press.

Miller, R. A., & Vaccaro, A. (2016). Queer student leaders of color: Leadership as authentic, collaborative, culturally competent. *Journal of Student Affairs Research and Practice, 53*(1), 39–50. https://doi.org/10.1080/19496591.2016.1087858

Nardini, G., Rank-Christman, T., Bublitz, M. G., Cross, S. N., & Peracchio, L. A. (2021). Together we rise: How social movements succeed. *Journal of Consumer Psychology, 31*(1), 112–145. https://doi.org/10.1002/jcpy.1201

Ngunjiri, F. W., & Hernandez, K.-A. C. (2017). Problematizing authentic leadership: A collaborative autoethnography of immigrant women of color leaders in higher education. *Advances in Developing Human Resources, 19*(4), 393–406. https://doi.org/10.1177/1523422317728735

Opsina, S., & Foldy, E. (2009). A critical review of race and ethnicity in the leadership literature: Surfacing context, power and the collective dimensions of leadership. *The Leadership Quarterly, 20*(6), 876–896. https://doi.org/10.1016/j.leaqua.2009.09.005

Ortega, M. (2006). Being lovingly, knowingly ignorant: White feminism and women of color. *Hypatia, 21*(3), 56–74. https://doi.org/10.1111/j.1527-2001.2006.tb01113.x

Owen, J. E., Hassell-Goodman, S., & Yamanaka, A. (2017). Culturally relevant leadership learning: Identity, capacity, and efficacy. *Journal of Leadership Studies, 11*(3), 48–54. https://doi.org/10.1002/jls.21545

Roth, B. (2004). *Separate roads to feminism: Black, Chicana, and White feminist movements in America's second wave*. Cambridge University Press.

Schuller, K. (2021). *The trouble with white women: A counterhistory of feminism*. Bold Type Books.

Sinclair, A. (2005). *Doing leadership differently: Gender, power, and sexuality in a changing business culture*. Melbourne University Press.

Sinclair, A. (2008). *Leadership for the disillusioned: Moving beyond myths and heroes to leadership that liberates.* Allen & Unwin.

Theasarus.com. (2023). *Dominant.* Retrieved from https://www.thesaurus.com/browse/dominant

ABOUT THE EDITORS

Trisha Teig (she/her) is a teaching assistant professor in leadership studies at the University of Denver. She is the faculty director for the Colorado Women's College Leadership Scholars program—a legacy program of the Colorado Women's College which focuses on leadership development and college support for first generation college students, Women of Color, and/or LBGTQ+ undergraduates. In this role she serves as (co)instructor, (co)facilitator, and (co)mentor for and with the program coordinator and the amazing CWC scholars. She also teaches in the PLP leadership program at DU. Her research interests include gender and leadership, social justice/inclusive leadership, and leadership development for college students. Prior to her faculty journey, Trisha worked as a student-affairs professional across a multitude of areas and still has a big heart for the work of college student development in and out of the classroom! She is also a lover of cats and doggies (especially her own pets, Sophie, Sampson, and Dale), a runner with a firm commitment to consistently practice yoga, a traveler ("Where can we go next?!?!"), and a person deeply committed to working towards the best world we can co-create together. She is also addicted to learning and is always interested in more podcasts and books! She earned her PhD at Florida State University in higher education, her MA in counseling and guidance from Texas State University, and her BA in communication studies and theater from McMurry University.

Brittany Devies (she/her) serves as the program manager for Leadership Studies and Development at the University of Maryland, College Park, focusing on academic and co-curricular leadership education initiatives. She cares deeply about creating accessible and equitable leadership learning environments for all students. She also serves as an adjunct faculty member at Florida State University, teaching in their undergraduate leadership studies certificate and serves as a research associate with the Office of the Vice President for Student Affairs at Florida State University. Her research interests include the intersections of gender and leader identity, capacity, and efficacy development, culturally relevant leadership learning, and the experiences of women in higher education. Her dissertation work specifically examined the phenomenon of undergraduate women's leadership capacity and efficacy development. She has authored and coauthored 14 book chapters and a dozen journal articles on leadership education and learning. She is co-authoring a forthcoming book, *Foundations of Leadership: Principles, Practice, and Progress*. She has received several honors and awards, including the NASPA NOW Inquiry Award, NASPA Student Leadership Programs Outstanding Emerging Professional Award, and ACPA's Annuit Coeptis Emerging Professional Award. She was inducted into the American Association of Colleges and Universities' Future Leaders Society and named a 33 Under 33 Featured Alumni for Delta Delta Delta national fraternity. She received her PhD in higher education from Florida State University, her MS in higher education from Florida State University, and her BSEd in early and middle childhood studies with a minor in leadership studies from The Ohio State University.

Rebecca "Becka" Shetty (she/her) is the director of the Follett Student Leadership Center at the University of Texas Arlington. In this role she supervises a team that offers centralized leadership education for the university community through student organizations, programs, workshops, and retreats. Her career spans a decade in student affairs focused on leadership education and leadership learning in student activities and organizations, orientation, and leadership departments. In a former role, she established the leadership education functional area at the university. Through this process, Becka led a collaborative, cross-departmental team to develop an institutional leadership framework for her campus. Her research interests include leader/leadership identity development, women and leadership, and the intersection of justice and leadership. Her dissertation resulted in the development of a leader identity development model for Black women in college. Becka is a devout reader and loves fiction novels and fantasy. She is a proud wife and mother of three. She earned her PhD at the University of Georgia in counseling and student personnel services (counseling education and supervision), her MS from Florida State University in higher education, and her BA from Baylor University in English.

ABOUT THE CONTRIBUTORS

Adrian L. Bitton (she/her) is a PhD candidate at The Ohio State University in the higher education and student affairs program. Prior to pursuing her doctorate, Adrian worked as a leadership educator at multiple universities. She has taught classes within three undergraduate leadership programs related to diversity and social justice in leadership, service-learning and leadership, team and organizational leadership, and introductory leadership theories and development. Her research interests include socially just leadership education, leadership learning and pedagogy, critical leadership studies, and leadership educator preparation. Adrian's identities as a White, first-generation, Jewish, cisgender woman who holds dual citizenship, have deeply influenced her experience in the academy and the world and guide her commitments to equity and justice.

Lauren R. Contreras (she/they) is an assistant professor in educational leadership at Northern Arizona University. Previously, Lauren was the program coordinator of the CWC leadership scholars program at the University of Denver, where she also completed her PhD in higher education. Lauren's research utilizes critical frameworks to center the experiences of historically marginalized student populations, particularly Women of Color, and first-generation college students, with the goal of making higher education more equitable and just.

Brittany Devies (she/her) serves as the program manager for Leadership Studies and Development at the University of Maryland, College Park, focusing on academic and co-curricular leadership education initiatives. She cares deeply about creating accessible and equitable leadership learning environments for all students. She also serves as an adjunct faculty member at Florida State University, teaching in their undergraduate leadership studies certificate and serves as a research associate with the Office of the Vice President for Student Affairs at Florida State University. Her research interests include the intersections of gender and leader identity, capacity, and efficacy development, culturally relevant leadership learning, and the experiences of women in higher education.

Shenhaye Ferguson is an adjunct professor at the University of Denver, Colorado. Dr. Ferguson's research critically examines the experiences of first-generation university students from marginalized and volatile communities, utilizing (post)colonial, decolonizing, and Caribbean research methodologies. As a passionate educator, Dr. Ferguson engages graduate students in courses related to power, privilege, oppression, and leadership and supervision skills. She has over 10 years of experience in higher education administration and obtained an MA in higher educational management and a BA in history from the University of the West Indies, Mona, Jamaica.

Simone Gause (she/her) is currently an assistant professor in the Department of Education Sciences and Organizations and director of the quality enhancement plan at Coastal Carolina University. She earned her PhD in educational administration in 2016 from the University of South Carolina. Her scholarly interest primarily focuses on issues of privilege and power and how they impact gender equity, racial equity, and leadership diversity in educational settings. Specifically, her research examines the continued disproportionality and intersectionality of race and gender in educational leadership through historical and contemporary contexts, the experiences of marginalized students and faculty in higher education, faculty diversity, and mentorship.

Valeria Gomez's (she/her) family is from Mexico and she is a first-generation Latina student in her last year at the University of Denver completing a Bachelor of Science in business finance with minors in leadership and business ethics and legal studies. She worked with Dr. Trisha Teig since the beginning of her college career and feels grateful to have been a part of this book.

Paige Haber-Curran (she/her) is professor and program coordinator for the student affairs in higher education master's program at Texas State University. Paige served as a Fulbright Scholar in 2018 in Salzburg, Austria. Her research focuses on student leadership development, gender and leadership, emotionally intelligent leadership, and teaching pedagogy.

Sharrell Hassell-Goodman (she/her) PhD, is a recent graduate of the George Mason University Higher Education program with a concentration in women and gender studies and social justice and a certificate in qualitative research. Her dissertation research was with the First-Generation Women of the African Diaspora collective in which they went on a journey to find fullness through (re)membering, an endarkened feminist participatory action research project. Sharrell is a part of a research collective interested in shifting research practices to be more inclusive, less oppressive, and explicitly anti-racist and decolonial. Her research interests are Black women in higher education; diversity, equity, and inclusion (DEI) pedagogy; social justice advocates in higher education; identity and leadership; and critical participatory action research.

Julie Henriquez Aldana (she/her/ella) serves as director of student leadership and engagement at the Newcomb Institute of Tulane University. As a Latina and emerging human resource development and leadership scholar, Julie's research interests focus on the intersection of identity and leadership, cultural competence, and organizational culture in the workplace. She teaches the senior research seminar in the Newcomb Scholars program, a cohort-based feminist leadership program, and a gender and leadership seminar for first-year students.

Neda Kikhia (she/her) is a Colorado local with a passion for community engagement and its potential to initiate sustainable community change. Trained in community organizing, Neda looks for opportunities, events, and programming that focus on elevating the voices and stories of people that move folks to action. She has a master's in communication studies with a focus on social movements from the University of Denver, is an avid podcast listener, travel enthusiast, and spoken word fanatic.

Julie E. Owen (she/her) is an associate professor of leadership studies in the School of Integrative Studies at George Mason University. She is the author of *We Are the Leaders We've Been Waiting For: Women and Leadership Development in College* (Stylus, 2020). Her research explores the intersections of leadership identity and women's adult development, as well as the scholarship of liberatory leadership teaching and learning.

Kristen Pender is very passionate about Black and Brown liberation and psychological wellness. Her interests grew through lived experience as being Black and queer navigating predominantly White and heteronormative spaces. Her passion and inquisitiveness led her to earn a doctoral degree in social and community psychology from North Carolina State University as a new mom in 2020. She also has a master's degree in community and social change (University of Miami) and a Bachelor of Science in psychology

(University of Central Florida). Dr. Pender's expertise is in identity development, counter-storytelling, and qualitative research methods.

Rebecca "Becka" Shetty (she/her) is the director of the Follett Student Leadership Center at the University of Texas Arlington. In this role she supervises a team that offers centralized leadership education for the university community through student organizations, programs, workshops, and retreats. Her career spans a decade in student affairs in roles focused on leadership education and leadership learning. Her research interests include leader/leadership identity development, women and leadership, and the intersection of justice and leadership.

Sasha Taner (she/her) is the program director and research coordinator at the Rutgers' Institute for Women's Leadership. Sasha recently completed her PhD candidate in global affairs at the Division of Global Affairs at Rutgers-Newark. Her expertise includes women's leadership education and intergenerational mentoring, first-generation and immigrant narratives, and feminist multimedia knowledge production. Sasha has works in the field of education and her contributions to the community include aiding resettlement processes of refugees and serving women and children survivors of domestic violence.

Trisha Teig (she/her) is a teaching assistant professor in leadership studies at the University of Denver. She is the faculty director for the Colorado Women's College Leadership Scholars program—a legacy program of the Colorado Women's College which focuses on leadership development and college support for first generation college students, Women of Color, and/or LBGTQ+ undergraduates. She also teaches in the PLP leadership program at the University of Denver. Her research interests include gender and leadership, social justice/inclusive leadership, and leadership development for college students.

Maritza Torres (she/her/ella) is a leadership and talent development partner with AdventHealth (AH), where she creates and facilitates leadership learning programs for clinical and nonclinical staff. Prior to her current role at AH she worked in higher education for over 10 years as an administrator and adjunct faculty member. Throughout her career she has taught, advised, developed curriculum, facilitated, and published articles and books on leadership learning and scholarship in higher education.

Michele Tyson (she/her) is a clinical assistant professor of higher education at the Morgridge College of Education at the University of Denver. Her scholarship broadly reflects her interest in understanding higher education as a system that has impact on and is impacted by other social systems.

She understands institutions of postsecondary learning to be the organizations in which students make humanizing decisions about engagement with identity and becoming. She teaches courses in leadership, access, and retention and organization and governance.

Aoi Yamanaka (she/her) is an assistant professor and associate director of academic services in the School of Integrative Studies, George Mason University. Grounded in her experiences as a clinical and international faculty member as well as an associate director of academic services, her current scholarship focuses on social justice issues in higher education, cultural leadership, socially just and inclusive learning and pedagogy, administrators' acculturation strategies to meet the needs of special populations in higher education, advocate archetypes, and campus community activism. She also designs and teaches online and face-to-face courses on social justice and leadership courses.